Considering Alan Ball

ALSO EDITED BY THOMAS FAHY

*Considering Aaron Sorkin: Essays on the Politics,
Poetics and Sleight of Hand in the
Films and Television Series*
(McFarland, 2005)

Considering Alan Ball

*Essays on Sexuality,
Death and America in the
Television and Film Writings*

EDITED BY THOMAS FAHY

McFarland & Company, Inc., Publishers
Jefferson, North Carolina, and London

LIBRARY OF CONGRESS CATALOGUING-IN-PUBLICATION DATA

Considering Alan Ball : essays on sexuality, death and America in
   the television and film writings / edited by Thomas Fahy.
         p.   cm.
   Includes bibliographical references and index.

   ISBN 0-7864-2592-X (softcover : 50# alkaline paper)

      1. Ball, Alan, 1957– — Criticism and interpretation.   2. Ball,
Alan, 1957– American beauty.   3. Ball, Alan, 1957–   Six feet
under.   4. Ball, Alan, 1957–   Five women wearing the same dress.
5. Sex in literature.   6. Death in literature.   7. Popular culture —
United States.   I. Fahy, Thomas Richard.
   PS3552.A4543Z63   2006
   812'.54 — dc22   2006008341

British Library cataloguing data are available

©2006 Thomas Fahy. All rights reserved

Cover image ©2006 Stockbyte Photos

Manufactured in the United States of America

McFarland & Company, Inc., Publishers
   Box 611, Jefferson, North Carolina 28640
      www.mcfarlandpub.com

Contents

Contents

Sexuality, Death, and the American Dream in the Works of Alan Ball: An Introduction

Thomas Fahy

The theater always enchanted Alan Ball. As a child, he dreamed of being an actor. He wrote his first play at the age of six, and he spent countless afternoons directing other neighborhood kids in small productions. By the time he entered Florida State University in Tallahassee, he had decided to major in theater. Ball graduated in 1980, and a few years later he moved to New York, where his focus shifted primarily to writing — to creating characters and building worlds through dialogue.

After working as an art director for the trade publications *Adweek* and *Inside PR,* Ball started a theater company with three friends from college — Alarm Dog Repertory. As he recalls, "I was a starving playwright trying to make my way in the world of New York theater, and I ended up living in a brownstone in Brooklyn with three other guys and a dog named Mom" (Ellis 1). This small company produced several of Ball's early plays, including *Power Lunch* (1989), *Your Mother's Butt* (1990), and *Bachelor Holiday* (1991), which later became the inspiration for his short-lived sitcom *Oh Grow Up* (1999).

At the same time, some of his other plays were starting to reach a wider audience, including *The M Word,* which premiered at the Lucille Ball Festival of New Comedy in 1991, and *Made for a Woman* (1993). But it was the Manhattan Class Company's successful production of *Five Women Wearing the Same Dress* (1993) that caught the attention of Hollywood. A television talent scout saw the play, and soon Marcy Carsey and Tom Werner offered Ball a job as a script editor and staff writer for *Grace Under Fire.* "I had never even written a television spec script," Ball explained in a recent interview. "It's not that I wasn't interested. It just never occurred to me" (Ellis 1). It may not have occurred to him to write for television, but in 1994 he moved to Los Angeles to give it a chance.

Alan Ball has repeatedly — and colorfully — described his experiences as a staff writer and producer for *Grace Under Fire* (1994–1995) and *Cybill* (1995–1998): "It was really frustrating. It was infuriating. [...] It was like being a member of the court of some mad monarch who was completely insane and power hungry and crazy and doing completely destructive things to the country, but nobody could say anything" (Champagne). In large part, Ball's resentment came from the fact that so much of the final product was shaped by personal politics and commercial demands: "You just really couldn't be too invested in it because everything got changed daily based on the whims of certain people. If you were invested in it, it was just too painful" (Chumo 26). So Ball spent these years doing formulaic writing, or "factory work" as he has called it, and feeling disconnected from his art.

After three seasons on *Cybill,* Ball began to pursue a career in feature films. He didn't want to be pigeonholed as a comedy television writer, and he longed to write something that he could feel passionate about, something meaningful. With the support of his new agent, Ball returned to a project that he had started in the early 1990s — a project inspired in part by the media frenzy surrounding the Joey Buttafuoco trial. "Underneath this thing [the trial] that we were all looking at — that we were sort of repulsed by and entertained by [...] was this really terrible tragedy that had ruined lives. [...] I tried writing it as a play but that didn't work. I got about thirty pages out and set it aside and forgot about it" (Ellis 2). It wasn't until 1998 — after years of disillusioning work for television — that Ball was ready to tell the story of Lester Burnham's midlife crisis as a film. In his original conception, Lester — a character inspired by Buttafuoco—"was a man who was shut down. Who had given up. Who doesn't really have any passion for his own life. [...] That's been something that's been happening to me, both artistically and in life in general" (Waxman). This was the genesis of *American Beauty.*

American Beauty won five Academy Awards in 1999, including Best Picture, Best Original Screenplay (Alan Ball), Best Actor (Kevin Spacey), and Best Director (Sam Mendes). Ball has joked that winning this award changed his status in Hollywood because people started listening to him. Winning this award also changed the television industry's attitude about what Ball was capable of as a writer. Soon after the success of *American Beauty,* Carolyn Strauss (former senior vice president for original programming and current president of Home Box Office Entertainment) proposed an idea for a television show about a family-run funeral home and America's relationship with death. Ball hesitated at first, but after his sitcom *Oh Grow Up* was cancelled, he wrote the pilot for *Six Feet Under* (2001–2005).

For Ball, writing *Six Feet Under* has been a cathartic experience. "The show has forced me to face death on a daily basis," he told Sharon Waxman in an interview for the *Washington Post.* "The show is about the loss I've felt in my life. [...] The grief I've felt over loss, the people I've lost. [...] It's about moving on. About greeting grief and being able to move past it." Much of the anguish that Ball has worked through in the process of writing *Six Feet Under* comes from the traumatic loss of his sister. On her twenty-second birthday, Mary Ann Ball was driving Alan to his piano lesson. She pulled out into a blind intersection and hit an oncoming car. The accident broke her neck, killing her instantly. As Ball recounts in the book *Six Feet Under: Better Living Through Death,* her death "[sliced his] life in two: everything before the accident, and everything after" (79). He was thirteen years old at the time.

Ball wasn't able to write about this loss—or that of his father, who died of lung cancer several years later — until *Six Feet Under.* In the opening moments of the pilot episode, a man called Nathaniel Fisher dies suddenly in a car accident, and his presence throughout the rest of the series (along with the other "clients" of the funeral home who appear to the Fisher family) serve as a reminder of the ways in which the dead are still with us. It is a testament to the ways in which Alan Ball's sister is still with him. This show gave Ball the opportunity both to transform his own experiences with grief into art and to confront the culture of avoidance that surrounds death in America. "I actually spent many years holding the grief back. [...] But ... we live in a culture that goes out of its way to deny mortality" (Chumo 34). Ball further explains in the DVD commentary about the pilot, "One of the reasons I wanted to set the show in LA is because LA is the world capital of the denial of death." Perhaps young Nate Fisher best summarizes Ball's point and the importance of this issue for *Six Feet Under* at his father's funeral: "No! I refuse to sanitize this anymore.... [Death] is a goddamn part of life, and you can't really accept it without getting your hands dirty."

Week after week, the series got our hands dirty. It depicted the sudden, ugly, heartbreaking, and painful reality of death. It delved into the psychological and emotional hardship of loss. And it did so through characters that struggled, suffered, failed, and tried again in their quest for healing.

A Violent Wake-Up Call: The Early Plays

With the founding of Alarm Dog Repertory, Alan Ball began writing, acting, and directing plays in New York. These early works employ strategies and wrestle with themes that would become the hallmarks of his style. In this way, they provide a useful introduction for this collection and for understanding Ball's art more broadly. From the dangerous impact of consumerism to conservative ideologies that promote repression instead of self-awareness, Ball has always examined the forces in American culture that stifle individual identity and expression. As he explained in an interview about *American Beauty*,

> I find the very image-conscious culture that we live in to be incredibly oppressive. I think I was writing about that, about how it's becoming harder and harder to live an authentic life when we live in a world that seems to focus on appearance. It fascinates me, especially now in this media-driven age, that we're encouraged to purchase per-packaged experience rather than have the experience ourselves. [...] We continue to have less and less community with each other; we continue to have more and more distance between ourselves and nature and the natural world [Chumo 32].

For Ball, consumer culture has not only corrupted the American Dream — as it does in F. Scott Fitzgerald's *The Great Gatsby* and Arthur Miller's *The Death of a Salesman* — but it also prevents people from living an authentic life. Carolyn Burnham, for example, is enraptured by Buddy Kane's philosophy in *American Beauty*: "In order to be successful, one must present an image of success, at all times." For both of these characters, appearance is more important than a real understanding of the self, and this belief has tragic consequences in the world of Ball's fiction.

Throughout his career, Ball has tried to send viewers a wake-up call about the dangers of embracing an artificial existence. His writings suggest that we have become too complacent, too accepting of the value placed on material success in America. One tool that Ball uses to break through this haze is violence. Not the kind often associated with Hollywood — the kind that "doesn't have consequences" and "is sort of cartoonish" (Chumo 34) — but the kind situated in realism. Ball consistently depicts moments of sudden, disturbing violence (whether literal or imagined) to shock his audience into awareness — to challenge them to reject some of the more oppressive aspects of American culture (such as materialism, sexism, racism, homophobia, and conservative Christian ideology) and to live more authentic lives.

His play *Made for a Woman* (1993), for example, satirizes consumer culture through its portrait of a young couple's dangerous obsession with appearance and commercial goods. Carly spends most of her time on the phone with 1–800 operators, asking questions about products and talking in advertising jingles. "My boyfriend just bought me the Mega Lifestyle size of your Spring Morning Dew scented antiperspirant for Baby Fresh Extra Sensitive Skin. Well, the box is really big, but the actual antiperspirant, the product itself, is quite small. So I just wondered, how can you sell something so small and insignificant in a box that makes it look like there's something really big and important inside?" (15). This question, along with her absurd feelings of betrayal at the thought of being misled by the advertising industry, reinforces Ball's view on commercialism here. Its promises are illusory. It manipulates desire, promising a "Mega Lifestyle" or a "healthy zest for living" (12), but it can't deliver. Ultimately, material things don't bring this couple (or arguably any of us) happiness. They only offer artificial substitutes. Lester Burnham echoes a similar sentiment when he says to his wife in *American Beauty:* "This isn't life. This is just stuff! (*He gestures toward the things in their living room.*) And it's become more important to you than living."

The violent denouement of *Made for a Woman,* however, transforms this story of a materialistic, self-involved couple into something far more disturbing:

> Look at those idiots down there. Stupid vacuous people with boring insipid lives. I bet not one of them is a person who acts. [...] Trent, I want

to show you something. I got this the other day. I meant to show it to you, but I forgot. Look! Isn't that sweet? It's a Lady Smith & Wesson. Specifically designed for the delicate contours of the feminine hand. Little pearl handle. I love this gun. I *love* it! *(She watches the people below for a moment, then casually fires a shot in their direction. Smiling, she looks back at Trent to see if he's paying attention; he isn't, of course. She fires another shot; a scream is heard from below. She is getting giddy. She fires a third shot. Excited.)* Trent! I hit one [17]!

On one hand, the idea that guns can be marketed in ways similar to antiperspirant underlines Ball's critique of the advertising industry's manipulative power — its ability to package gender, to literally define what it means to be a man or a woman.[1] On the other hand, this scene suggests that being invested in such a superficial culture creates an explosive, violent resentment for others. Spending time trying to look good and following the trends promoted on television doesn't help Carly and Trent achieve the American Dream. In fact, it cuts them off from each other and fuels an aggression that requires some kind of outlet. For Trent, it is working out obsessively (at the gym and on his rowing machine). For Carly, the outlet is shooting people. (Lester shares a similar passion for working out in *American Beauty*, and Carolyn finds release through shooting a gun at a firing range: "I love shooting this gun!")

In fact something explosive lurks beneath the surface for most of Ball's characters, and he often shows them at the breaking point to demonstrate the destructive power of repression and the inauthentic. Realestate agent Carolyn Burnham, for example, bursts into tears and slaps herself violently after a failed open house; Meredith Marlowe suddenly flashes her breasts at her sister's wedding party and yells obscenities at her mother in *Five Women Wearing the Same Dress*; in the pilot episode of *Six Feet Under*, Ruth Fisher falls to her knees with a primal scream at her husband's grave. Whether it's the unhappiness and frustration that erupt from Carolyn, the conflicted feelings that Meredith carries around as a victim of sexual abuse, or the sorrow and guilt that torment Ruth, Ball's characters struggle with the forces and emotions that, at times, make them want to explode.

In *Civilization and Its Discontents*, Sigmund Freud examines the role of aggression in culture and the individual psyche, arguing that

men are not gentle creatures who want to be loved [...] they are, on the contrary, creatures among whose instinctual endowments is to be reckoned

> a powerful share of aggressiveness. As a result, their neighbour is for them not only a potential helper or sexual object, but also someone who tempts them to satisfy their aggressiveness on him, to exploit his capacity for work without compensation, to use him sexually without his consent, to seize his possessions, to humiliate him, to cause him pain, to torture and to kill him [68–9].

Freud goes onto explain that this aggressive response doesn't require provocation. In many cases, it just happens spontaneously, "[revealing] man as a savage beast" (69). But the violence that Freud sees in the world — on a global scale — concerns him less than the impact of repression on the individual. "My intention to represent the sense of guilt as the most important problem in the development of civilization and to show that the price we pay for our advance in civilization is a loss of happiness through the heightening of the sense of guilt" (97). For Freud, guilt holds civilization together. It prevents men from destroying each other completely, from breaking apart the social order. But guilt also compromises our individual happiness. It makes us turn our aggression inward (84).

In many ways, Alan Ball depicts characters that demonstrate Freud's thesis. Guilt and repression have robbed them of happiness. After internalizing their problems and feelings for years (because society places such a high premium on propriety), these characters finally reach a point where they lash out through violent action or fantasy. These moments reveal what these characters need and long for. These moments reveal what forces have been holding them back. And this is what Ball wants us to see. In "The Room" (1:6) from *Six Feet Under,* Nate envisions his father shooting a rifle through a second-floor window at the crowds below. Nate is trying to understand why his father would keep a secret room from his family, and this violent vision (along with those of card games and prostitutes and rock music) suggests that his father's duties to his business and his family had forced him to compromise part of his identity — to repress the part that other people knew as funny and wild, the part that Nate will never have access to. Ruth Fisher, Nate's mother, is a character so consumed with guilt that she seems virtually incapable of happiness. Instead, she continually erupts in tears, breaks into sobs, and yells suddenly. When explaining to her lover why she told her sons about their affair ("The Will," 1:2), Ruth blurts, "It was guilt!" Unlike Freud, Ball doesn't see these moments as a threat to civilization. Instead, they often — over time — bring a certain degree of enlightenment and freedom to the individual. They are essential before one can start living an authentic life.

In other words, violence — or imagining violent action — provides many of Ball's characters with an important psychological release from repression. In *Bachelor Holiday* (1991), a short play about three friends living in a New York apartment, Ford wonders whether he should interview for a job. "Well, what if I get all dressed up and go into the city and then this guy doesn't want to hire me? What if I just lose control and kill him? It's already happened once today" (45). Here, Ford uses this violent fantasy — and his guilt over killing a mouse — as an excuse to stay home and drink. Ford is not simply being lazy; nor is he on the verge of becoming a spree killer. He is struggling to define himself against the grain. He wants to be more than a typical American worker and consumer. Yet he jokingly admits: "I'm a Taurus, right, and I have this psychic need for material comfort" (28). Later in the play, Norris chastises him: "You're just as shallow and greedy and materialistic as any other American. You can meditate, chant, and burn incense all you want, you can pay some asshole to jab needles into your face and another one to analyze every single little thing that ever happened in your life, but when is the last time you gave your lunch to somebody who was starving?" (44). Both Ford's violent fantasy and Norris's unprovoked outrage are moments of painful realization. Both men recognize — if only for a short time — the oppressiveness of consumer culture in America. They recognize that greed has replaced compassion and humanity. Materialism has made both of them selfish and, in many ways, cut off from the needs of others.

Despite fleeting moments of awareness, the danger for these characters — and arguably most of us — is that they still want these things. As the concluding lines of the play suggest, commercial culture creates an insatiable desire in consumers for more things:

> **Hunter:** If we had cable, before you know it we'd have a cleaning person, and then we'd have to get real furniture for them to keep clean, and then somebody would have to get a fax machine, then we'd all have to get real jobs, go to networking parties, get ulcers, high blood pressure, have to stop eating salt, date women who are smarter than we are, invest in socially irresponsible profit-making schemes, get married, get fat, lose our hair, and explode. It's not worth it.
>
> **Norris:** I still want it [48].

Even though Norris recognizes these as self-destructive clichés, which ultimately make one want to "explode," he can't fight it. Ball presents Norris's resignation, then, as a challenge for us to recognize and resist the ways that our desires have been programmed by social norms and the marketing industry.

All of these examples wrestle with themes and ideas that continue to fascinate Alan Ball. Whether we're watching Carly's shooting spree in *Made for a Woman*, learning about Meredith's sexual assault in *Five Women Wearing the Same Dress*, witnessing Lester's murder at the end of *American Beauty*, or cringing at the abrupt deaths at the beginning of each episode of *Six Feet Under*, violence seems to be an essential tool for Ball's artistic vision. In a media-saturated culture that often glamorizes and sanitizes violence, Ball's use of realism has the potential to make audiences more aware of the real consequences of repression. Just as his characters desperately need to change — to recognize their own complacency in the face of the social forces that restrict them — we too need to examine society more closely. As Claire Fisher laments to her high school therapist in "Brotherhood" (1:7), "Is that the only option? Go to college. Get a job so you can be a good consumer until you drop dead of exhaustion? I don't want that!" Ball demands that we ask the same question: Is being a good consumer the only option?

His writing suggests that we need to consider the ways that materialism and consumer culture have shaped our desires and our interactions with others. We should address the topics that we avoid talking about, such as death, sexuality, race, and class. And ultimately, his writing challenges us to reject the prejudices and fears that promote intolerance and repression.

Perhaps Trisha's outburst toward Frances in *Five Women Wearing the Same Dress* best encapsulates this message.

> **Frances:** I will *not* tolerate you making fun of the Bible. [...] My religion happens to be very important to me, and I don't want to listen to you criticize it. [...]
>
> **Trisha:** Then leave. [...] Go someplace where people don't have ideas. Where everybody is willing to trade their God-given intelligence for any old blind set of rules just because they don't want the responsibility of making their own decisions. I'm sure you won't have to go very far (41].

Ball wants to open up the discussion. He wants people to take responsibility and to stop accepting things without question.

9

Overview

This collection offers numerous perspectives on these and other issues in Alan Ball's work. The first perspective is that of Ball himself, provided in a 2005 interview. Next, scholars Ann C. Hall, Susanna Lee, Susann Cokal, and Kirstin Ringelberg discuss his award-winning film, *American Beauty,* which opened the door for *Six Feet Under* and brought *Five Women Wearing the Same Dress* to national attention. Their essays consider the intersections between life and death, self and other, and art and beauty in Ball's screenplay.

In "Good Mourning, America: Alan Ball's *American Beauty,*" Ann C. Hall reads *American Beauty* in terms of a medieval morality play. She argues that the voice-over in the film not only makes the audience identify with Lester Burnham more than any other character but it also gives him an Everyman quality. In the tradition of medieval art, Lester's life and death — as well as the words used to shape the meaning of both — act as a *memento mori;* they tell a story that attempts to prepare the audience for death. As Hall explains, Lester only understands the meaning of life through his death, and he shares this lesson with the audience at the end of the film. "Further, he is able to amend Ricky's original statement, reminding us that we can experience beauty not by American determination but by letting go." Hall sees this as one of the central morals of the film — a moral that Ricky Fitts communicates as well. From the beginning, Ricky is the visionary character, the artist whose strength comes, in part, from the fact that he doesn't fear death. He finds beauty in ordinary, everyday things, even in death: "Unlike many of the characters in the film, Ricky does not run from death, and what the film makes clear is that that this courage enables Ricky not only to live but to share his life with another person, in this case, Jane. His art is borne out of some understanding regarding the close relationship between life and death, the living and the dead, the physical and the spiritual." It is this moral that both Ricky and Lester try to impart to the audience. It is the message that Alan Ball uses to challenge people to live life more fully.

Susanna Lee's "The Space Between Us: The Psychology of Houses in *American Beauty*" argues that this film is about the ways in which individuals come to terms with themselves in life and that this process of self-discovery occurs "both within houses and in the interaction and movement between houses." The setting of suburban America, in other words, captures the importance of both private and communal spaces in the quest for self-awareness and understanding. As Lee explains, the characters in *American Beauty* "develop, or redevelop, desires and, through interaction with or mere observation of others, either reject or gain consciousness of parts of themselves. To go to another person's house is a form of reaching out." This act of reaching out — occupying one's own home as well as the homes of others — is essential in the development of the self. Thus, the relationship between neighbors and houses in this film enables characters to become who they really are. Domestic spaces, Lee concludes, offer an opportunity for characters to engage in the complicated interactions between self and other — the kind of interactions that help one build an authentic self.

In "A Heart Caves In: The Dangerous Aesthetics of *American Beauty*," Susann Cokal questions the aesthetics of beauty in Alan Ball's artistic vision, arguing that there is an unresolved tension between the film's message and the failure of its main character "to break convention and revel in beauty to the fullest extent." On the surface, the film presents beauty as a transformative experience — one that makes the viewer responsible for recognizing beauty in the ordinary, the unexamined. In order to appreciate the unexpected beauty of life, the film suggests that we need to reject culturally constructed notions of the beautiful. But, as Cokal explains, "the danger is that conventional beauty will lead [Lester] to break social convention — just as, in a similar way, the *challenge* to the viewer is to look closer and break down conventional ideas of the beautiful." In other words, Lester's unwillingness to completely break with convention — to cross certain taboos such as having sex with an underage girl or with another man — shows that the film is only able to go so far; it does not validate desire that can be seen as destructive and immoral. Cokal examines this duality in the film through both the erotic power of physical beauty and the metaphoric power of artistic beauty (as represented in the images of the paper bag and the red rose). Even though these images reveal Ball's critique of the American Dream as artifice, they don't resolve the problematic tension between passive appreciation and active desire. Nor do they communicate the experience of beauty that the film promises. Ultimately, the aesthetic philosophy of beauty in *American Beauty* asks the audience only to appreciate the beautiful from a passive standpoint. Since true beauty can only be appreciated in death, we must continue to wait. As Cokal concludes, "*American Beauty* is an empty bag that points the way to beauty but is not beauty itself. If we feel comforted after watching, it's more because of the promise of beauty than the actual experience of it."

Kirstin Ringelberg's essay, "'You Have to Develop an Eye for It': Anti-Aesthetic Art in Alan Ball's Vision," however, reads the function of art and beauty in his works as demanding action on the part of the viewer. Looking at the prominent role of artist figures in both *American Beauty* and *Six Feet Under*, Ringelberg argues that Alan Ball's anti-aesthetic stance resonates with the kalliphobia of postmodern art. This element of kalliphobia — "fearing or hating traditional notions of beauty as the goal of art making and experiencing" — reinforces Ball's critique of the ways in which American culture often validates and celebrates beauty over substance. As Ringelberg explains, "Ball uses our expectations for pleasure in the superficial to point out their emptiness. Look at the plastic bag, not the roses; the blood, not the family photo; Jane, not Angela. Look at what you normally ignore; don't allow yourself to be swayed into mindless catharsis by well-crafted surface." Ultimately, Ball is challenging his audience to be socially engaged. Through the struggles and vision of characters like Ricky Fitts and Claire Fisher, Ball reminds us that seeing beneath the surface is essential for becoming socially and politically active. It is essential for recognizing the problems around us and doing something about them.

With Ringelberg's discussion of *Six Feet Under*, the collection begins to consider Alan Ball's work for television. The serial nature of any television show allows its writers to develop characters and themes over a long period. In the case of *Six Feet Under*, the audience is not only faced with a new death in the first few moments of every episode (which links its thematic content with that of *American Beauty*), but other recurring elements, such as therapy and sexuality, are hallmarks of the series. Robert F. Gross, Lorena Russell, and Craig N. Owens explore these ongoing issues, particularly in terms of desire — the desire for self-help and therapy, for kinship and love, and lastly for living fully.

In "Meet the Chenowiths: The Therapeutic Drama of *Six Feet Under*," Robert F. Gross analyzes the therapeutic marketplace in *Six Feet Under*, arguing that "the frequent appearance of therapy is not merely the result of the series's attempt to realistically depict American middle-class life, but is more importantly a reflection of the therapeutic ethos that pervades the series." Whether it is through self-help books, seminars, therapy, medication, and even hospitalization, Ball's characters demonstrate a continual investment in the tools of therapy as a means for personal growth. But as good consumers, they do so cautiously — viewing therapeutic culture as a commodity like any other purchase. As Gross explains, "the high modernist notion of the psychoanalyst as guru has deteriorated, as clients have learned to be shrewd consumers." This pragmatic approach to therapy also reflects some of the ambivalences, and arguably the dangers, surrounding therapy in American culture. *Six Feet Under* captures this, in large part, through the Chenowith family, who embody some of the worst excesses of psychotherapy — manipulation, exploitation, co-dependency, and ethical (as well as psychological) violations. As Brenda, Billy, and the Fishers attempt to balance the fear of therapeutic violation with their need for help, the show invites us to consider our own conflicted relationship to therapeutic culture. "*Six Feet Under* repeatedly dramatizes," Gross argues, "both the need for therapy and its concomitant dangers, a variation of the series's broader theme of the need for intimacy and its dangers."

Lorena Russell's "Strangers in Blood: The Queer Intimacies of *Six Feet Under*" continues with the broader theme of intimacy in her discussion of kinship. The complexities of intimacy "invite viewers to suspend narrow judgments about proper relationships, and to imagine instead a broadening array of identities, sympathy, attachment, pleasure and love." Russell calls this process "queering" and argues that the use of death in *Six Feet Under* challenges the audience to exercise a "queer imagination"— one that considers alternative, or nontraditional, forms of kinship. As Russell explains, this notion of queering extends beyond the presence of gay characters in the show; it creates a space for reconsidering — and resisting — social norms. The imaginative possibilities of queering come, in part, from the ways in which Ball asks viewers to see death (particularly the images associated with it) in aesthetic terms— in terms of beauty. This portrait of death not only enables us to suspend our repulsion and discomfort with the morbid, but it also demands that we "reconsider our (often reactionary) relationship to those symbols and what they represent." In doing so, Ball explores broader social issues, such as homophobia, and raises philosophical questions about life and death, love and disgust, and the complex nature of human sexuality.

Craig N. Owens situates Ball's work in two literary traditions that reflect on death — the Oedipal and the Absurdist. Through these traditions, Owens's essay, "When We Living Awaken," examines the ways in which death and desire shape the narrative of *Six Feet Under*. Ball often presents characters caught somewhere between stasis and action. Unlike the Oedipal narrative, which tends to unify narrative and character death (privileging closure), *Six Feet Under* disrupts unity and closure; like Absurdist drama, it embraces in-between spaces. This middle ground, Owens contends, enables Ball to scrutinize American culture and to portray life "as a kind of death, as a kind of automatic, routinized, and directionless wandering that demands disorientation, pain, and effort as the price of living." In *Six Feet Under,* this call to action is often signaled by the haunting presence of the not-quite dead. These figures "reveal to the characters and the audience the degree to which they and we are also not quite alive." In other words, death operates as a wake up call for Ball's characters and his audience. It challenges all of us to awaken and live with desire.

Finally, this collection concludes with discussions of Alan Ball's breakthrough work for the theater, *Five Women Wearing the Same Dress.* Both Johanna Frank and Mardia Bishop examine the play's depiction of women and its problematic gender politics. Johanna Frank's "Bridesmaids, Bosoms, and Booze: Visibility and the Veiling of Conservatism" specifically explores the duality between the visible and invisible in Ball's play. Using *Five Women* as an example of the problems with visibility politics in contemporary theater and feminist art more broadly, Frank argues that art needs to move beyond the visible. In the case of *Five Women,* the trope of visibility, which promises a kind of political and social empowerment for women, "reinforces the very binaries and conservative social institutions it aims to disrupt." Though the characters in this play learn to see beyond their surface-level impressions of each other, reinforcing the theme that "nothing is what it seems," the play fails to apply its critique of the social norms restricting women to the outside world. The message here, Frank points out, remains interior, private, and closeted, raising questions about the effectiveness of visibility. The essay concludes by examining the role of visibility in the Feminist Art movement, interrogating the ways in "which contemporary plays rearticulate an essential identity of Woman under the banner of radical performance politics and/or uphold consciousness-raising as an end." For Frank, visibility was an important first step in promoting the radical politics of feminism, but it is not an effective goal. "While there are several stakes in such work—disrupting notions of the body as an original, authentic site of experience; of the materiality of the body as a site of feminist politics; of a politics based on the legitimating narrative of consciousness-raising as self liberating—the potential benefits outweigh the risks."

In "Always a Bridesmaid, Never a Bride: The American Dream in *Five Women Wearing the Same Dress*," Mardia Bishop focuses on the ways in which Ball critiques and reinforces the myth of the American wedding. For many women, marriage embodies the American Dream, promising women an elevated social status, financial security, and personal happiness. But as Ball's play demonstrates, the pursuit of this promise can be personally and psychologically damaging. "This continual belief in the American Wedding leads to the most significant problem with having women's success tied to marriage in that it forces them to engage in unhealthy behaviors, primarily pursuing men and pursuing beauty." As Ball reveals the individuals underneath these matching dresses, however, he reminds us that appearances are deceiving. The heartbreak, pain, and frustration of these women not only highlight the artificiality of the American Wedding/Dream, but they also provide a damning critique of the social and cultural imperatives that wedding rituals reinforce—a diminished sense of self-worth for many women. At the same time, Bishop reminds us that *Five Women*—despite its attempt to deconstruct the myths surrounding the American wedding— also reinforces these same myths. "Although the play suggests that alternative relationships to the traditional marriage may be better, the basic premise of women needing to be rescued is maintained." In the end, even as the play suggests that women don't need a wedding, the appearance of Tripp suggests that women still need to be rescued by men.

Whether it involves our culturally constructed notions of marriage, beauty, death, or sexuality, Alan Ball challenges us to see beyond the surface of things—to see underneath the matching bridesmaids dresses and beyond the white picket fences. He wants us to recognize the deadening impact of consumerist culture. As Lester Burnham, Ricky Fitts, and the Fisher family eventually show us, living fully requires one to break away from social norms that are stifling and repressive. And as all of the essays in this collection demonstrate, Ball's artistic vision is about getting people to see the world differently—to look at death, love, and even plastic bags with more open, critical eyes.

Notes

1. Ball makes a similar criticism through the parodic commercials in the pilot episode of *Six Feet Under*. Here, he wants to confront both the problematic tendency in American culture to sanitize death and, as he explains in the DVD commentary, "the prevalence of marketing at all points, [including] the way that sex is used to sell anything — even embalming fluid."

Works Cited

Ball, Alan. *Six Feet Under: Better Living Through Death* New York: Pocket, 2003.
_____. *Five One-Act Plays: Made for a Woman, Bachelor Holiday, Power Lunch, The M Word, and Your Mother's Butt.* New York: Dramatists Play Service, Inc., 1994.
_____. *Five Women Wearing the Same Dress.* New York: Dramatists Play Service, Inc., 1993.
Champagne, Christine. "Gaywatch: Alan Ball Goes 'Six Feet Under.'" Planetout.com. June 29, 2001. http://www.planetout.com/entertainment/news/?sernum=363.
Chumo, Peter N. *"American Beauty:* An Interview with Alan Ball." *Creative Screenwriting* 71 (Jan–Feb 2000): 26–35.
Ellis, Hazel. "On the Ball: A Talk with the Screenwriter of *American Beauty.*" Reel.com (Hollywood Management Company). 2000? http://www.reel.com/reel.asp?node=features/interviews/ball.
Freud, Sigmund. *Civilization and Its Discontents.* Trans. and ed. by James Strachey. New York: W. W. Norton and Company, 1989.
Waxman, Sharon. "Alan Ball's Life After Death." *Washington Post.* Sunday May 26, 2002. G01.

An Interview with Alan Ball

Thomas Fahy

JULY 29, 2005

Fahy: I want to begin by asking a few questions about your early work in the theater. In 1984, you started a theater company in New York, Alarm Dog Repertory. How did that come about and what were some of artistic goals of Alarm Dog?

Ball: Well, I didn't start it myself. I started it with a lot of people I had known in college and in Florida where I lived prior to moving to New York. We basically were a group of actors, writers, and directors who loved to work. We had had similar companies in Florida, and also I had worked with a lot of these people in college. We just sort of found this vibe of working together, and it gave us something to do—rather than sitting around, going to auditions, and asking for permission to work. I've never been a big believer that you have to get other people to give you permission to work. I've always been a self-motivator, and even though I do have formal training, the majority of what I've learned has come from experience. From doing it yourself. So we didn't really have any formal goals, but we basically wanted to do new work that was either written by or developed by the company.

Fahy: How do you feel those experiences as a playwright and actor shaped your writing?

Ball: I think having some experience being on stage as an actor has made me very conscious of how I'm writing for actors. I think about what I myself

Alan Ball directing the pilot episode of *Six Feet Under.*

might have a hard time saying, for example. It has also made me aware about what is stageable and what is possible. I did acting and writing and production stuff and publicity. All sorts of things. So I learned about what goes into making and producing a play. I also learned that it's important to get a sense for what the people who are working for you are doing and to respect it.

I love actors. I feel like my work really needs good actors because in the wrong hands it can be very ... flat. It walks a line. And I really have a lot of respect for actors and the process.

Fahy: I'm also curious as to which playwrights and writers have influenced your work?

Ball: One person who has a lot of influence on me — just because I was exposed to his work at a very early age — is Tennessee Williams. Also being from the south myself and being gay myself, I think it spoke to me in many ways. I love the theatricality of it. I love the strong female characters. I feel there is an inherent sexism in most mainstream entertainment — in the movies more than anything else where women characters are basically just props or things to win or things to suffer and die horribly so that the hero will be motivated to seek vengeance. I also think the gay sensibility and the poetic outsiderness of Tennessee Williams's work was very influential.

I greatly admire the films of Robert Altman and Woody Allen as well.

Fahy: Woody Allen has such an amazing sense of place. He makes you feel like you're walking along the streets of New York in every scene.

Ball: Exactly. I also enjoy the playfulness of his films. When I first saw *Annie Hall* in college, I just loved the bittersweet sadness that ran through all of the comedy. I also admire his playfulness with form. All of those theatrical techniques that he uses — jumping into animation and having her get out of her body and watch him while she is having sex with him. All of those things influenced me, and I thought they were very creative.

Fahy: Looking back on some of your early plays, like *Made for a Woman, Five Women Wearing the Same Dress,* and *Bachelor Holiday,* what do you consider to be some of the most important themes and issues driving those works?

Ball: Well, I don't tend to think of my work that way. My process is much more mysterious to me, and I kind of like it that way because then it becomes a journey of discovery as opposed to having an outline and writing a term paper. But having been interviewed a lot about my work now, I sort of feel like the overriding theme that interests me is the difficulty that people have trying to live an authentic life in this country.

Fahy: Your characters in *American Beauty* and *Six Feet Under* certainly struggle with this.

Ball: Yes. And with the saturation of the media and the unbelievable levels of denial on all fronts that we live with in America — denial of the truth, denial of death, denial of aging, and denial of what our culture really is (which is basically a corporatocracy and a welfare state for the rich) — I think it is increasingly difficult to live an authentic life. The levels of denial are so pervasive and so entrenched that I feel like the human spirit yearns to be authentic. But it's so hard. We don't want to see these problems. We don't want to talk about them.

Fahy: Do you think the medium of television is particularly effective for addressing these problems?

Ball: Well, I think the medium of television can be very powerful when it is used effectively, but I also think we get a very skewed perspective from it. The television media is often very self-serving for the ruling class. It's sad. People know they're being lied to. They either can't deal with it and they have this knee-jerk Jesus patriotism, or they just become cynical. If you really sit down and look at what's happening in the world, it's so painful. We're destroying our planet. Our high standard of living is being paid for by people all across the globe. It is really painful to realize that. And we don't want to talk about it at all. It's a big house of cards, and if you really acknowledge the truth about what's going on, our entire system collapses. We're basically thugs and rapists and exploiters.

At the same time, who wants to drop out of life? There is a real tension that is created by living in the society that we live in and having human independence. We are so often defined by what we do and not by who we are in America.

Fahy: How have you addressed this tension in your writing?

Ball: A lot of my early work in the theater was a satire of corporations. And it was theatrical and funny and sketchy, but ultimately I don't think it was about actual characters, actually recognizable people. Also at that time, I was working in a corporation, so I had a tremendous amount of anger about that. Technically, I believe I'm still working for a corporation — one of the more insidious ones. But I'm pretty much left alone, and I get to do work that I find meaningful. So I don't have that same kind of frustration.

Fahy: I also want to ask about the role of art in your work. Both Ricky Fitts and Claire Fisher seem to be most comfortable in the world when they're taking pictures of it. Could you talk a little bit about artist figures in your writing? Why they are so important? How they contribute to some of the larger themes in your writing?

Ball: Again, that's not a conscious choice. I think I consider myself an artist, and I aspire for the work that I do to be art. I don't really know what that word means. My work for me is the closest thing I have to a religion. It is a discipline that is very meaningful, and it allows me to process what it means to be alive and what it means to be human. So I guess it is no mistake that I like characters who are exploring life through art.

I've veered away from characters who are writers because I find them to be really tedious. But I definitely have always had a creative bent. Even as a small child, I was doing and creating things.

Fahy: You have a lot of fun with psychiatry in your play *Your Mother's Butt*. Of course, we see a much broader portrait of psychiatry and the therapy industry in *Six Feet Under*. From self-help books to The Plan, therapy is ... unpredictable at best. How would you characterize the role of therapy in *Six Feet Under?*

Ball: I have conflicted feelings about the therapeutic process. On the one hand, I've been in therapy on and off for at least half of my life, and it has been very beneficial. On the other hand, it encourages a kind of narcissistic navel-gazing, a self-involvement that is one of the biggest afflictions in our culture. A lot of us have lost the ability to just be instinctive, to live spontaneously. At the same time, had I not gone to therapy, I probably would have descended into some self-destructive behavior or become some sort of an addict. I was really in a lot of pain, and I didn't understand it. I needed help figuring it out.

Again, I don't make a conscious choice for characters to be in therapy or to be therapists. In my life, I have known people who are therapists. I have known a lot of people in therapy. I have been in therapy myself. I know people right now who are going to school to become therapists. So that stuff becomes part of my writing. I basically write about the world that I know. Things that find their way into the show come from some place in my life.

The controversial episode of *Six Feet Under* where David was kidnapped ... that happened to my brother's girlfriend. The AVM condition that Nate Fisher had ... my cousin had that. I know a lot of people who have died. A lot of people in my family have died. And that's just where it comes from. This is the world that I know. These are the things that the people I know have to deal with.

Certainly, if one of my themes is about the struggle to live authentically, therapy for a lot of people is a real step along the way, but at the same time, it can be its own trap. It's like everything. It works, and it doesn't work. There is good, and there is bad. It always comes down to balance.

Fahy: So what's next for you? Do you see yourself returning to television?

Ball: I actually do have an idea for a series that I wouldn't mind developing and creating. I don't want to run a show any time soon just because it is really grueling and exhausting. And I'm interested in pursuing things on the feature side for a while.

I definitely think TV is a great medium because you get to spend a really long time with characters. You can see them grow and change over time in a way that is realistic. You don't have to cram everything into two hours. It is probably the closest I'll ever come to writing a novel. Even though saying that, I didn't write all of *Six Feet Under*. I had several writers that I worked with. I never could have done it myself. They had perspectives and experiences that I never could have brought to the table.

Also, I recently wrote my first play in ten years. That was a really great experience. It felt so relaxing to be able to lay back and luxuriate in language. Because I'm an avid reader — I read much more than I watch TV and go to the movies — it is so nice just to write a scene that lasts for twelve pages. To have a character start talking and talk for a really long time because what they're trying to express is complicated and they have all kinds of different feelings about it. So I really enjoyed that. I miss the theater. My playwriting career was just really starting to get off the ground when I got the offer to come out here and work in television.

I would love to be able to continue to work in all three mediums. I even have a dream of maybe one day actually writing a novel. I have a much easier time with dialogue than I do with prose, so I don't know if that is going to happen or not. It's a dream.

Good Mourning, America: Alan Ball's *American Beauty*

Ann C. Hall

Alan Ball has established his reputation in the death business through the darkly comic *Six Feet Under*. Documenting the life, loves, and losses of a family in the funeral parlor business, the series takes up where Ball left off in *American Beauty* This is not a shocking revelation, since death makes its appearance early in the film through comments by two of the screenplay's major characters, a daughter and her father. Though very different from the great Bergman film *The Seventh Seal* (1957) in which death and life are personified and represented through a knight and death playing a chess game, Alan Ball's representation of death is not only just as powerful but in some cases downright medieval in its morality—a morality that is often elided by the reviewers of the film. As many have noted, the film is about the "meaning of life," gender identification, and the hollow existence of the American suburbs, but few mention the close relationship between life and loss, eternity and morality, life and death.[1] As any good medieval knight or modern Freudian can tell you, the relationship between Eros and Thanatos is a close one. Alan Ball's contemporary Willy Loman, for example, is not necessarily worth more dead than alive, but he is, in the end, more alive in death than he was in life. The film reminds us that life and death are two sides of the Moebius strip. Specifically, life is not always what it seems, and we are closer to death than we think, a moral that will encourage us all to save our own lives from the hollow suburban hell represented in *American Beauty*.

The film opens highlighting speculation and spectacle. A young girl is being videotaped by someone — a man, as we learn through his voice-over. The young girl is frustrated with her father's poor behavior, concluding, "Somebody should really put him out of his misery" (1). The male voice-over volunteers to do the job, and she agrees. In the next scene, we hear the voice of the film's main character, Lester Burnham, who admits that he will be dead in a year. He says, however, he is unaware of this fact at this point in the narrative. We also learn that the young girl, Jane, who wanted to kill her father in the opening scene is, in fact, Lester's daughter. In this way, the film misleads us from the very beginning. It appears that the daughter, Jane, is the final cause of Lester's death, which we later learn is not the case. By offering the audience an explanation for Lester's death, albeit an incorrect one at this point in the film, the screenplay frees the audience from the need to look at the action of the film in terms of a mystery; instead, the audience is now free to view the film and its philosophical issues, admittedly under a false pretense.

The use of the voice-over also causes us to identify with Lester Burnham more than any other character. Unlike the early voice-over in which the physical body and the male voice were separated — the traditional structure of the voice-over — we experience Lester's voice and body vacillating between unification and separation throughout the film. Such alternation does not make Lester omnipotent, and as a matter of fact, there are times that we know more about the plot than Lester, but these structures makes us empathize with this character. We feel for him when he discovers, for example, that his wife is sleeping with the real estate king. The voice-over technique protects Lester from being a non-entity, something that happens to him through the course of the narrative. As he tells Buddy, the real estate king, "I wouldn't remember me either" (44).

In her recent work grounded in terrorism and American politics, *Precarious Life: The Powers of Mourning and Violence*, Judith Butler examines the propensity of the American press to report only American casualties, not Palestinian or Iraqi casualties:

> Violence against those who are already not quite living, that is living in a state of suspension between life and death, leaves a mark that is no mark. There will be no public act of grieving (said Creon in *Antigone*). If there is a "discourse," it is a silent and melancholic one in which there have been

no lives, and no losses; there has been no common bodily condition, no vulnerability that serves as the basis for an apprehension of our common-ality; there has been no sundering of that commonality [36].

This argument clearly emphasizes the current political climate, as well as the important role of the voice-over in this film. Lester's status as a non-entity, combined with the fact that we see most of the film through his perspective, actually makes him more sympathetic. He becomes the American Everyman who is "in a way ... already dead" (2). This is cru-cial to the film's thematic purpose, because if we do not relate to Lester or we dismiss his angst, we would not be moved by his death. Thanks to the voice-over, Lester not only interests us, but the technique affords the screenplay the opportunity to have Lester comment on the action of the film even after his death in a non-intrusive way. We are, after all, accustomed to hearing Lester's disembodied comments.

Moreover, if we conclude, as Lester does, that his life is already over, the rest of film offers us not only philosophical prompts regard-ing the meaning of life but also the meaning of death. Like many of us and the other characters in the film, Lester responds to his mortal rev-elation by looking for a "quick fix" to the loss by choosing Eros through his obsession with Jane's young friend, the beautiful Angela Hayes. In crude Freudian terms, death is the ultimate castration, so fantasizing about a young woman confirms Lester's potency. Again, Butler notes:

> When grieving is something to be feared, our fears can give rise to the impulse to resolve it quickly, to banish it in the name of an action invested with the power to restore the loss or return the world to a former order, or to reinvigorate a fantasy that the world formerly was orderly [29–30].

In addition to Angela, Lester idealizes a summer in his youth when he did nothing more than work, smoke pot, and get laid — his version of his world's "former order."

Lester's death and grief may be solitary, but he is not alone when it comes to avoiding grief. His wife, Carolyn, who, as we learn from Lester, "used to be happy," tries to control and overpower not only her grief but everything in her life. As Lester tells us when we first see her, "That's my wife, Carolyn. See the way the handle on those pruning shears matches her gardening clogs? That's not an accident" (3). She embod-ies not only the Puritan work ethic, but the New Age spin on the Amer-ican dream. Using affirmations, tapes, and self-help jargon, she hopes to contort her life into her vision of success, affluence, and a perfect family. When she begins to sell a house, for example, she fills herself with positive affirmation while scrubbing the house clean. Despite her best efforts, however, the house does not sell. In a wonderful image for the typical American working woman, Carolyn begins to cry with disappointment, but she slaps and berates herself for being so emotional, "the" mortal sin in twentieth-century American, corporate culture. If she had only believed in herself more, if she had only done more, if she had only been able to delude her clients more, if she had only been more like a man, embodied by the character Buddy, the real estate "king," she would have sold the house. Rather than examining her needs, desires, and losses, she takes up the entire burden; she is completely responsible for this outcome.

And while some have argued that the only really normal people in the film are the gay men who live next door, their affinity with Carolyn, their brief dealings with their dog, and their welcome-wagon mentality suggest that they, too, are buying into an American dream that is hollow (Portman). They, too, may be trying to control their worlds as closely as Carolyn.

The new neighbors, who have replaced the old neighbors, aptly named the Lomans, are led by a military father, Colonel Fitts, who not only tries to control his domain, as Carolyn and the gay couple do, but also represents American individualism at its cruelest. His family is literally kept under lock and key, and when the gay couple makes an attempt to welcome him to the neighborhood, he is abusive. His wife is a broken woman who sits staring off into space in her immaculately clean house. When a doorbell does ring, all in the house tense and it is easy to see the Colonel scanning the perimeter of his personal space in the moments it takes to open the door.

His dealings with his son, Ricky, are perhaps the most despicable. As Ricky tells Jane:

> When I was fifteen, my dad caught me smoking dope. He totally freaked and decided to send me to military school. ... Well, of course, I got kicked out. Dad and I had this huge fight, and he hit me ... and then the next day at school, some kid made a crack about my haircut, and I ... just snapped. I wanted to kill him. And I would have. Killed him. If they hadn't pulled me off. ... That's when my dad put me in the hospital. Then they drugged me up and left me in there for two years [104].

Given a superficial reading of Ricky, it would be easy to dismiss him as another damaged, drug-dealing teenager who merely lies to his parents and feeds his own greed for hi-tech toys and drugs. The film, however, goes to great lengths to show us that he is the visionary of the piece, perhaps even its spiritual and mystical center, a modern-day shaman. For many sensitive people, Ricky's experiences with his father would have destroyed him and his life. Somehow, he finds his way, and up until the very end of the film does not even hate his father for the things that he has done. Ricky's method of coping is through artifice. Early in the film when his father expresses his disgust for gay men, Ricky tries to defend them, saying that they do not see their sexuality in a negative light. Ricky immediately realizes that this was too honest a response for his homophobic father and tries to hide his true tolerance for diverse peoples and situations. His father says, "Don't placate me like I'm your mother, boy." Sexist undertones aside, Ricky is now forced to take his disgust to another level, and he eventually placates his father by expressing a bigoted sentiment he does not believe. Ironically, Ricky's revision is so extreme and presented in such a way that his father believes him and is, finally, placated by an even more outlandish lie. Ricky says, "Forgive me, sir, for speaking so bluntly, but those fags make me want to puke my fucking guts out" (37). As he tells Lester later when he explains that his father thinks that he pays for his video equipment through catering jobs, "never underestimate the power of denial" (70).

Ricky's use of artifice is not only protective; it is creative. He is an artist, a videographer of the beautiful in ordinary things. He videos students, birds, bags, his mother, Jane, and many other seemingly ordinary subjects, and it is through these scenes that we, too, begin to see the beauty in the ordinary. More important, he also videos death. In a wonderful juxtaposition of Eros and Thanatos, the film shows Jane and Ricky walking home together, a very significant walk, since Jane has left her friend Angela for Ricky and it is the beginning of their romance. As they are walking, a funeral procession cuts the screen in half, and Ricky asks, "Have you ever known anybody who died?" He then proceeds to tell Jane about the time he videoed a homeless woman who had died. Jane asks, "Why would you film that?" He replies, "Because it was amazing. ... When you see something like that, it's like God is looking right at you, just for a second. And if you're careful, you can look right back" (84). Jane asks, "And what do you see?" "Beauty," he responds (85).

Unlike many of the characters in the film, Ricky does not run from death, and what the film makes clear is that that this courage enables Ricky not only to live but to share his life with another person — in this case, Jane. His art is borne out of some understanding regarding the close relationship between life and death, the living and the dead, the physical and the spiritual. This understanding gives him courage, a confidence that attracts Jane and her father, Lester, which ultimately leads them to leave their dead lives and live new ones. As he says when he shows Jane the most beautiful subject he has ever videoed:

> That's the day I realized that there was this entire life behind things, and this incredibly benevolent force that wanted me to know that there was no reason to be afraid. Ever. ... Sometimes, there's so much beauty in the world I feel like I can't take it ... and my heart is going to cave in [88–89].

Given the fact that the scene that prompted this episode was nothing more than a plastic bag dancing in the air, which the film makes as beautiful as this speech, it is no wonder that Ricky becomes the spiritual center of the movie.

As Ricky and Jane begin their relationship, the screenplay juxtaposes the cartoonish relationship between Carolyn and Buddy, the real estate king, perhaps as an emblem for the real connection possible between two people and the artificial connection encouraged by the American Dream the two Realtors pursue. To underscore the falsity of the relationship, the film reveals that Buddy's secret to success is shooting a gun at a range: "Nothing makes you feel more powerful.... Well, almost nothing" (83). The film makes it clear that Buddy and later Carolyn, who also takes up the sport, paradoxically use death to avoid death. The gun gives them a sense of control, but in the end, its promise of power is empty. The confidence that Carolyn experiences after her trips to the range are short lived and not life fulfilling. When she meets Lester after shooting a few rounds, he senses her confidence, but as he tries to seduce her, she will not let go long enough to rekindle their relationship and she continues the affair. It is only at the end of the film, when Lester is killed, that she is able to experience her true feelings for Lester. Symbolically, she throws the gun away, and embraces Lester's shirts in a moving image of grief.

Like Carolyn, the Colonel is also deluded by his perceptions and his weaponry. When he sees his son and Lester together through a window in the house, he assumes that Lester and his son are having oral sex. Truthfully, the camera confirms this interpretation, and if we did not know what in fact was happening, we might conclude the same. In this way, the film calls even itself into question; things, even when the camera is on, are not always what they seem.

When Ricky's father confronts him, Ricky realizes that he will never receive unconditional love from his father, so he once again fulfills his father's fantasy by admitting that he is a male prostitute, in this case not to placate but to offend. To complicate matters further, when the Colonel goes to the Burnham house to confront Lester, our own fantasies or stereotypes about this character are challenged. The Colonel does not go to confront Lester about his relationship with his son; instead, he goes to Lester for comfort and kisses him during their short meeting. Surprised as we are by this turn of events, Lester makes it clear to the Colonel that he has misread the situation. Clearly, the Colonel's homophobic responses earlier were designed to cover his own homosexual desires. In addition, the Colonel's behavior, while surprising, is pathetically consistent with the behavior of all the other characters in the film. Everyone is searching for some type of connection to another person. The Colonel seeks a comrade in arms. Carolyn looks to Buddy to solve her problems in real estate and her marriage. Lester seeks solace in Angela Hayes. According to Charlton D. McIlwain, this death and this desire for contact is also part of our society's obsession with death:

> The longing to know death is, to some degree, an expression of our will to conquer it. But beyond this, it is an expression, a longing, a crying out for and seeking connection and community — what one needs to make the isolation of life, and the individuality of death, more bearable ... in order to create community, we must reinvigorate a different conception of (life)-(time) — our connection between birth and eventual death — such that death is allowed to play a prominent role in moderating our public values, discourses, and politics [14].

Death can create community. For the Colonel, his own desires are so abhorrent to him that he must kill the object of his affection rather than experience self-examination. In this way, he does not embrace life through an experience of death. He kills another and symbolically that part of himself he cannot accept.

The character of Lester, however, manages to face his death-in-life and open himself up to the possibility of change this loss creates. According to Judith Butler:

> perhaps mourning has to do with agreeing to undergo a transformation (perhaps one should say *submitting* to a transformation) the full result of which one cannot know in advance. There is losing, as we know, but there is also the transformative effect of loss, and this latter cannot be charted or planned. One can try to choose it, but it may be that this experience of transformation deconstitutes choice at some level. I do not think, for instance, that one can invoke the Protestant ethic when it comes to loss. One cannot say, "Oh, I'll go through loss this way, and that will be the result, and I'll apply myself to the task, and I'll endeavour to achieve the resolution of grief that is before me." ... Something is larger than one's own deliberate plan, one's own project, one's own knowing and choosing [21].

Consequently, when Lester is confronted by the reality that underlies his fantasy of Angela Hayes, he is able to love rather than kill in response. In the final scenes of the film, for example, Lester and Angela seem destined to a liaison. This is Lester's fantasy come true, and given Angela's comments about Lester throughout the film, it appears as if she is ready, willing and able to participate. The film and Lester have led us to believe that she is the perfect nymphet. What, in fact, happens, is very similar to the experience that the Colonel has with Lester — disillusionment. Angela is not a nymphomaniac; she is a virginal teen whose sexual experience has just been a cover for her inexperience. Unlike the Colonel who cannot adjust to the disillusionment, however, the moment of his lost fantasy transforms Lester. He sees the fantasy for what it is, and with that fantasy removed, he acknowledges his deep love for his family:

> Something at the edge of the counter catches his eye, and he reaches for ... the photo we saw earlier of him, Carolyn, and Jane, taken several years ago at an amusement park. It's startling how happy they look. Lester crosses to the kitchen table, where he sits and studies the photo. He suddenly seems older, more mature ... and then he smiles: the deep, satisfied smile of a man who just now understands the punch line of a joke he heard long ago [142].

In the film, of course, this information is communicated non-verbally, and not only is it a testimony to the cast and crew of this film, but the fact that the realization is communicated in the film without words underscores its importance. No longer does Lester translate for us. We see it happening before our eyes, and this technique makes a very strong impression. It is one of those moments of tragic awareness. And like all great tragedies, this realization comes too late. Just as Lester makes this connection with his family, the Colonel shoots him.

Ricky peers into Lester's face, and we see what he previously described seeing in the homeless woman: the face of God in Lester's smile. This event does not interrupt Ricky's plans to leave for New York with Jane. In many ways, these two are the only characters who begin to understand the important issues developed in the film. They realize how important their relationship is; they realize that there is more to life than meets the eye; and they realize the close relationships among life, death, and beauty. In effect, they are the film's new Adam and Eve, a couple who has a chance to fulfill their own dreams, not the futile and hollow American Dream presented in the film.

Lester's final voice-over, too, offers hope not in life but in death. He prepares us for death, in fact, much the same way that medievalists created *memento mori* art. He tells us that contrary to the cliché, his life did not pass before his eyes in the moments before his death. Instead, it is much more expansive; time "stretches on forever, like and ocean" (144). And the film concludes with Lester echoing the words of the artist and visionary Ricky. Death is not a waste, and he is not angry:

> but it's hard to stay mad, when there's so much beauty in the world. Some-times I feel like I'm seeing it all at once, and it's too much, my heart fills up like a balloon that's about to burst ... and then I remember to relax, and stop trying to hold on to it, and then it flows through me like rain and I can't feel anything but gratitude for every single moment of my stupid little life. ... You have no idea what I'm talking about, I'm sure. But don't worry. ... You will someday [148–149].

Through his death, Lester has come to understand the meaning of his life, particularly how the two are so intertwined. Further, he is able to amend Ricky's original statement, reminding us that we can experience beauty not by American determination but by letting go. In this way, we will be able to experience the force that underlies the life we lead, a force that only a few people — the artists and the visionaries— people like Alan Ball, are able to see while they are alive.

Notes

1. As Sam Mendes notes, the film is about redemption and "the breakdown of the family unit and relationships between husband and wife" (quoted in James). Roger Ebert comments

that the film is about Lester's "rebellion," as well as the "yearning after youth, respect, and, of course, beauty." Jay Carr says the film "is a bracing and biting comedy of American emptiness that's both sad and corrosively funny and has about it an air of a millennial classic ... What makes it special, what informs the screenful of richly layered acting, is its recognition of the bleak isolation into which its lonely and loveless family members are locked." And in one of the more unusual readings of the film Roger Kaufmann argues that the film is a "thinly veiled 'coming-out story' transferred onto a straight character" and that the film is cloaking its "gay sensibility in heterosexual context while also stereotyping the few characters who are openly gay" (quoted in Portman).

Works Cited

Ball, Alan. *American Beauty.* New York: Macmillan, 2000.

Butler, Judith. *Precarious Life: The Powers of Mourning and Violence.* New York: Verso, 2004.

Carr, Jay. "*Beauty* Is a Biting Look at America." *Boston Globe.* 17 September 1999. C4.

Ebert, Roger. "*Beauty* Is More Than Skin-Deep: Middle-Age Rebel's Tale Hits Universal Truths." *Chicago Sun-Times.* 24 September 1999.

James, Stan. "Golden Beauty for Mendes." *The Advertiser.* 27 January 2000. 44.

McIlwain, Charlton. *When Death Goes Pop: Death, Media, and Remaking of Community.* New York: Peter Lang, 2005.

Portman, Jamie. "The Outing of *American Beauty*: Psychologist's Claim That the Movie's a Thinly Veiled Gay Manifesto Feeds Lively Debate." *The Gazette* (Montreal). 2 April 2000. C7.

The Space Between Us:
The Psychology of Houses
in *American Beauty*

Susanna Lee

Much is made in *American Beauty* of houses—their insides and outsides, the semi-obscured garage, the fences that enclose and deter, the liminal yards and landscapes, empty pools, the moving vans that bring families from one space to another, and the windows and doors that constitute houses' ultimate permeability. Within individual houses, we see divisions between rooms, movement from one room to another, listening at doors, copying keys, and invading closed spaces. In many ways, these domestic spaces and the movements between them reflect the interaction between self and other in this film — in particular the development of the self through identification with and differentiation from the other.

Freud's definition of the self as a coherent, desiring entity has been debated by critics and analysts for many years. In *The Freudian Subject*, for instance, Mikkel Borch–Jacobsen questions this representation of the self:

> The chronology Freud most frequently indicates has to be inverted. Desire (the desiring subject) does not come first, to be followed by an identification that would allow the desire to be fulfilled. What comes first is a tendency toward identification, a primordial tendency which then gives rise to a desire; and this desire is, from the outset, a (mimetic, rival-rous) desire to oust the incommodious other from the place the pseudo-subject already occupies in fantasy. If desire is satisfied in and through

identification, it is not in the sense in which a desire somehow precedes its "gratification," since no desiring subject (no "I," no ego) precedes the mimetic identification: identification brings the desiring subject into being, and not the other way around [47].

While Freud sees the self as an entity whose existence predates and enables its interaction with others, Borch-Jacobsen, with Ruth Leys and others, sees that interaction as an organic building component of that self's very existence (Leyes). *American Beauty* provides us a *mise-en-scène* of Borch's proposed process of identification — the process of a coming into being of a desiring subject through identification with another. In its spatial relations, in other words, instead of a classically Freudian model of an identity that precedes desire, decision, and action, *American Beauty* chronicles a building of the self through a series of mimeses and differentiations, invasions and rejections, a progressive trafficking between inside and outside.

The question of when, if ever, a self can claim a solidity or immutability — indeed, an ownership of itself — is fundamental to *American Beauty*. Lester's opening voice-over ("I'm forty-two years old. In less than a year, I'll be dead" [1]) tells us that we are going to see a chronicle of a life, a two-hour journey from start, or middle, to end. But the addendum, "And in a way, I'm dead already" (2) announces that this narrative also describes an evolution or tension between a story already formed and finished and a story not yet begun. With these opening lines, and with the movie's subsequent unfurling, we see privileged the idea of the self as mutable, as a site of possibilities. And yet, though permeable, that self is nonetheless stable enough, contained enough in its corporeal envelope, to have a story and to interact with others. The journey of self-discovery is subsequently played out through domestic spaces — both within houses and in the interaction and movement between houses.

American Beauty is a chronicle of American suburbia, and suburbia is a theater of private property. One house stands beside another house, which in turn stands beside another house. In the city, public or at least unresidential space (a store, a dry cleaners, a restaurant, a vacant lot) can intervene in any given block. In the suburbs, though, a block is most commonly composed of houses alone, and where one ends, another starts. Furthermore, the suburban scene emphasizes neighborly interaction through yards and across fences, through liminal but nonetheless restricted points at which one house becomes open to another. Not surprisingly, the yard, this site of simultaneous connection and contrast, where separation opens to the possibility of union and absorption, is the scene of many a television commercial. The green of the neighbor's lawn! The sleek lines of the neighbor's new car! These commercials rest on the simple truth that one can become more (or other) than what one is through association with another, be it an association of imitation or repulsion.

In this movie, domestic space is used to chronicle self-development. To occupy a house is to live in one's own self. To live in the world, in the company of other humans, is to live near other houses. The importance of the suburban setting lies precisely in this relation, this sense that what lies beyond the property lines of a particular person is not some abstract public space, but rather another individual, another immediate private party. By moving within and outside their own houses and others' houses, the characters in this film find and, to use Borch-Jacobsen's paradigm, become themselves. They develop, or redevelop, desires and, through interaction with or mere observation of others, either reject or gain consciousness of parts of themselves. To go to another person's house is a form of reaching out. But as Borch-Jacobsen wrote, as cited above, it can also be an aggressive action: "What comes first is a tendency toward identification, a primordial tendency which then gives rise to a desire; and this desire is, from the outset, a (mimetic, rivalrous) desire to oust the incommodious other from the place the pseudo-subject already occupies in fantasy" (47). Identification, then, implies a sort of rivalry; in order to stand in the symbolic space occupied by another, that other must vacate. And yet, once vacated, that catalyst of identification and thus of self-definition no longer functions as the essential placeholder that it was. This dynamic becomes quite complicated, evidently, when the identification in question is a source of pain or loathing, as in the case of the Colonel who sees homosexuality looming in and from the neighbors' houses.

First, let us consider how the characters are associated with houses and with other private and semi-private spaces. Second, let us consider the interactions among the three houses that form the nucleus of the narrative: the Burnham house, the Jims' house, and the Fitts house. While *American Beauty* is on one hand the story of a marriage, it is also a story of individuals coming to terms with themselves and, important, coming to terms with themselves through others. Indeed, that this is about a man's relationship to himself is immediately underscored when we see the "high point of his day"—Lester in the shower, in sexual communion with himself. In the film's opening sequence, Lester is shown in a series of rectangular frames: his bed, his shower, his window. And, encompassing these frames, his house. Where he goes within and from the house will govern his development.

Throughout this movie, the people who can claim a space of their own are the ones who are the most substantial, the most able to grow, for the house is symbolic of the ground or the foundation; Ricky is also shown in his house, as is Jane, as is the Colonel. Those who do not have houses, or who are not associated on screen with houses, are presented as fragmented or unrooted. In one sense, the limited visual association of characters with houses is part of the economy of the movie—one cannot trace every movement of every character, so it is not surprising, for instance, that Angela is seen only in the Burnham house, in cars, and at school, rather than in her own space. But a more striking counterpoint to Lester's, Jane's, and even Ricky's association with home is Carolyn, whose relationship to domestic space, like her relationship to personal development, her own and others, is actively unenthusiastic and destructive.

Carolyn is, we assume, co-owner of the Burnham house, but her first appearance on screen is in the yard. And her first act on screen is to cut one of her garden flowers off at the stem, an act that exemplifies fragmentation, a tearing off from the roots. Indeed, it is some time before we see Carolyn in the house, inhabiting the space that is hers. The spaces with which she is associated are the car, the house she wants to sell, the real estate convention banquet hall, and the motel.

Carolyn is the character who is most uncomfortable with hearth and home; she is sometimes pictured outside, in the yard, looking into the garage from the outside. It is she who returns to the problematic physicality of home ("Lester. You're going to spill beer on the couch" [69]), which thus deprives it—for her—of emotional or symbolic significance. In a similar vein, and most important to Carolyn's place in the film, is her role as real estate agent. In this capacity, rather than occupying a home of her own, she attempts to "show" and then "sell" other houses—empty houses whose ownership is in limbo and in which Carolyn, ironically, seems to spend more time than anyone else. Hours spent in these houses are emblematic of Carolyn's disengagement from the idea of home and self. It is in one of these houses for sale, for instance, that we see Carolyn in a lace slip, vacuuming. Sexuality and domesticity, united in an almost cartoonish manner, are thus deployed in this least domestic of domiciles—whereas they are not, we learn, in her own home.

Indeed, it is in this early house-selling scene that we see an implied relationship between house and self. All the prospective buyers are couples, unnamed, visual representations of the family unit. All are silent, observing the space, noticing its spatial and atmospheric insufficiency. The only prospective buyers who articulate a reaction to the house are the women who respond to the pool: "The ad said this pool was 'lagoon-like.' There's nothing 'lagoon-like' about it. Except for maybe the bugs" (13). To which the second woman adds: "There's not even any plants out here.... I mean, I think 'lagoon,' I think waterfall, I think tropical. This is a cement hole" (14). The reference to a cement hole, an emptiness where presence should be, goes to the symbolic heart of Carolyn's own emptiness. These are two "fortyish" women (13), the closest in demographic to Carolyn of any of the prospective buyers. When these women point out that the pool is but a "cement hole," an emptiness rather than a presence, that there are no plants, and that the house is (for this and other reasons) unacceptable as a home, they place themselves on the side of home and nature, in sharp contrast with Carolyn's vacuousness.

The substance of home versus the emptiness of what is not a home emerges also in the motel scene. We see two parked cars outside the motel. The immobility of these cars in this scene contrasts with the freedom of Lester, who cruises down the street listening to music in the following scene. The motel room is an ersatz home, where one goes when one has no home in the area or has chosen not to be there. The merging of Buddy and Carolyn in the motel is physical and literal, but not emotional; the shot of them having sex shows his torso and her legs, and neither of their heads, resulting in a strangely depersonalized composite being. Her (repeated) presence in that motel, in that depersonalized space, becomes part and parcel of her disengagement.

Another curiously anti-domestic space associated with Carolyn is that of the real estate convention. The banquet hall is impersonal and devoted to business functions. Though the business at hand is that of domestic spaces, the conversation between Buddy and Carolyn within that banquet hall is the foundation of their subsequent infidelity, a wandering from home. Similarly, standing in an alley outside a real estate convention is in one sense emblematic of a striking exclusion from the very notion of home, but it can also be seen as an exclusion from the cold notion of home as commodity. It is in this outside space that Lester forms a friendship with Ricky, for instance, and is introduced to the idea of quitting his job and pursuing freedom.

A word can be said about the role of the car in this movie. It is in the car, for instance, that we see the three Burnhams together for the first time. On the one hand, this vehicle represents a life in motion — evolving from one point or stage to another. On the other hand, the cars in this movie usually follow a fairly predictable route — to and from the office, to and from the drive-through. This is not a road movie, but rather a house movie; development is plotted not through the linear motion of travel from one place to another, but through a subtle interaction among structures and entities.

Association with a house, a house of one's own, functions as an indication of full personhood. And yet, to return to Borch-Jacobsen's point that what we consider the self is in fact a (perhaps unwittingly) collaborative product, even as we point to the house as representative of the self, we must also see it as a permeable structure whose very nearness and openness to other structures implies a mutable model of home and interiority. There is an important symbiosis between the house and its neighbor, as between the self and its others. Within the first few scenes, for instance, we learn about the situation of the Burnham house with respect to other houses, and thus about the connections — random or fortuitous — that will drive the movie. From the first scene, we see that the Jims live next door on the one side and soon, we see a moving van coming, bringing new adjacent selves with whom Lester can connect on the other side. The arrival of the moving van occasions a conversation about neighbors — new neighbors and old neighbors — during which we learn that tension had arisen when Carolyn had cut down her neighbors' sycamore. As Carolyn puts it in a rather striking phrase, when Lester points out that the cutting-down might have contributed to the neighbors' decision not to use Carolyn as their real estate agent, "I wouldn't have the heart to just cut down something if it wasn't partially mine, which of course it was" (8). The idea in the movie is that in cutting down another, one is cutting down a part of oneself — the property metaphor is quite apt here. As is the tree metaphor: "A substantial portion of the root structure was on our property!" (8) This movie is about trying to resuscitate some sort of root structure, as well as about the idea that root structure is always in some sense shared.

On the one hand, we know that this movie is to be substantially about Lester. The house is emblematic of the self, and the structure of the house, of the "root structure" of the human being. And yet, on the other hand, when we learn that root structure, both in the yard and in the soul, is necessarily communal, we see the movie's paradox of individualism and connection. In one sense, then, this movie celebrates the individual as a coherent unit with a core self.[1] But in another, it emphasizes that that building takes place through connection to others. And that connection, means to get to it, and obstacles to it, are represented in the neighborhood.

If the house represents the self, then interaction through spaces represents the characters' process of human development through contact with another person. One person learns from others by meeting them in their space. We can think of the scenes of intimacy that take place within the houses (Jane and Ricky watching the plastic bag video, Lester and Angela talking, Lester and the Colonel in the garage, etc.). These scenes of connection contrast starkly with the scenes of intimacy in, for instance, the motel or the restaurant or the real estate convention. As the film makes clear, sex and intimacy are not one and the same. As Annalee Newitz remarks about Lester and Angela, "what *American Beauty* believes is the point of erotic desire [is] to end up having an honest conversation about their lives" (167).

Much as visual association with a house reads as a visual clue to the substance or nature of a character, an important measure of richness of character is willingness to go to another's house. We can think of Ricky's catatonic mother, who, though associated with her own home, remains on her own first floor throughout the film. She is perhaps the film's most stagnant character, her refusal to go out emblematic of a closed manner of being.

Let us consider the interaction among houses that drives the film. The connection among houses and people, on the visual plane, is a horizontal arrangement: one house beside another. Lester's house is in the center, between the Jims' house and the Fitts house, and this linear house-to-house connection is crucial to the process of Lester's evolution. His desire to please Angela leads him to want to exercise, which sends him out to jog down the street, which in turn connects him with the Jims, who do the same. The three of them run down the street, stopping directly in front of Ricky's house. The Jims thus act as an instrument for Lester to connect with Ricky, leading Lester down the street to the Fitts house. Once there, he enters that house, in search of an altered consciousness, but also, it could be said, in search of a consciousness more similar to that of Ricky. To enter the house, he pretends, interestingly, to be looking for the movie, *Re-Animator* (45), for indeed, Lester's re-animation is enabled in part through Ricky.

Ricky's own evolution also happens through a (primarily visual) penetration of the Burnham house. He watches the house through much of the movie, seeing across the fence and into the kitchen or onto the porch. But at the end of the movie, when he is prepared to leave for New York, he does so through the turnstile of the Burnham house, crossing into their space and lying next to Jane, where he rests at the moment of Lester's murder.

The horizontal disposition of the houses, particularly the idea of three houses lined up with Lester as a middle term, is replicated in various scenes of connection throughout the film. In the episode when Ricky shows Jane his videotape of the plastic bag, for instance, the television and its viewers are shown from the back, the plastic bag between their heads; that bag becomes the middle term that joins them. In the very next scene, in the Burnham house for dinner, Jane is between Carolyn and Lester: the child who has kept them together.

Contrasting with this horizontal juxtaposition and demonstrating divisions rather than affinities, there is a visual metaphor of vertical formation running through the film. During the initial flyover shot, we see not houses but streets, lined up one next to another in a way that suggests more methodical placement than community and camaraderie. When Lester is seated in his cubicle, a vertical partition separating him from the others, the numbers on his screen are set up in vertical lines; boredom and routine business are embodied in this formation. When the Fitts are watching television, an old military comedy, we see soldiers doing exercises on the screen in vertical formation, lined up like the streets and the numbers on the screen. Finally, when Carolyn is shooting at the range, we see the range in profile; the shooting booths are separated from one another so that we see vertical lines, with hands with guns in between. These vertical lines, in each case symbols of rigidity or separation, contradict the horizontal connection that is formed from person to person, house to house.

Evolution through movement from one house to another is best demonstrated, though, not by the example of Lester but by the example of the Colonel. In the first scene of the Fitts at home, we see the Jims come to the door. In terms both of the structure of the story and the arrangement of the neighborhood, the Jims cross Lester's house to come to the Colonel. (Later, it will be through Lester that the colonel arrives at an identification with the Jims). The Jims come to offer "Just a little something from our garden." Reminiscent of the commonality of root structure, that "something" will become, as the narrative continues, the commonality of the Jims and the Colonel.

The Jims are not just the couple with whom the Colonel identifies, the couple with whom he has homosexuality in common; they also embody identification by being of the same sex and even having the same name. In this sense, they serve a symbolic function similar to that of the female couple in the house-selling scene. When the women in that scene point out the absence of plants, we are once more reminded of the "root structure" and the cut-down sycamore, and the sense of connection that Carolyn lacks. When the Jims come to the Colonel's house, bringing something "from their garden," they thus bring the Colonel face to face with connection, and with himself.

The Jims' visit to the Colonel provides an open door, a narrative precedent for the Colonel's visit to Lester's house. When he comes to this house, it is to connect with him, with the "root structure" or secret desire that they share, or that he imagines they share. With this act, or with this desire, he also connects with the neighbors on the other side, who had brought him something from "their garden."

At the end of the movie, there is some apparent ambiguity as to who shot Lester. Carolyn is the one with the gun, the one with the most visible rage against Lester. We see her gun just before and after the shooting. The Colonel, on the other hand, is shown with blood on his shirt and gloves on his hands, pacing in front of a gun case from which one gun is missing. This short shot of the Colonel is the one indication that it is in fact he who has murdered Lester. But his shooting makes sense in the psychological economy of the movie, reminiscent as it is of Carolyn's words at the start: "I wouldn't have the heart to just cut down something if it wasn't partially mine, which of course it was." What he is cutting down, of course, is like that sycamore: a living manifestation of a root structure that in fact lies on his own property, in his own self. With these unfoldings, interestingly, *American Beauty* treads between the Freudian model of an immutable and preexisting self and the Borch-Jacobsen model of a desiring subject born of a tendency toward identification.

What appeals in this movie is the organic connections among the characters—the sense that Lester (and the Colonel) are not so much discovering something new but rather becoming, with a sense of homecoming, themselves. Or rather, doing both at the same time. For to merely permeate the home of another is not enough, and to remain within the confines of one's own home is also not enough—we see examples and consequences of both these limitations in the various secondary characters. Instead, we need a combination of the two, to convey both openness and authenticity.

As Alan Ball said during an interview, "We continue to have less and less community with each other; we continue to have more and more distance between ourselves and nature and the natural world. I guess I didn't realize it when I sat down to write this, but these ideas are important to me" (Chumo, 32). Through domestic spaces, and through movement among them, we see an interconnectedness that is psychological rather than spiritual. Ricky's words to Jane ("That's the day I realized that there was this entire life behind things, and this incredibly benevolent force that wanted me to know there was no reason to be afraid. Ever," [60]) is often read to indicate an "aesthetic perspective [grounded] in a concerted theism" (Spiegel, 1). This film, I would propose, does not simply give a sense of the characters being held together by some higher force—rather, it provides a humanist vision of an inner, terrestrial connection. David Smith writes, "Paradox arises because the world of *American Beauty* is a closed, culturally deterministic system. Its characters are perfect creatures of their social locations. They may hope for something 'more,' but their very conception of this 'more' derives from the culture that confines and defines their desires. Their stories are correspondingly bleak and self-defeating" (1). The sense of possibility that Ricky understands in terms of a benevolent force can be cast in terms of a humanism that, perhaps, can transcend the cultural limitations of "more."

American Beauty's representation of domestic space as emblematic of the self and of self-development resonates in another of the film's principal concerns—that of videotaping. The first shot of the film is Jane on screen, looking at the camera in a moment of *mise en abîme*. This shot is a personal space, a frame filled with Jane; and yet, is this her image in the true sense of possession? Does it belong to Ricky, the holder of the camera? That image, what we as spectators see, is a shared or collaborative product, though not necessarily consciously so; a combined outcome of the one who sees and the one who is seen. This dynamic, present in filming—especially here, when the act of filming is itself filmed—raises questions of space and its ownership. One critic, for instance, points out the empowering nature of the filming: "With the help of a video camera ... Jane learns to see herself through her lover's eyes" (Hentzi, 28). This dynamic accords a fundamental importance to being an object—to being available, consciously or not, to the alternate subjective vision of another. There is no doubt that Jane gains from Ricky's camera attention. But while being seen by another is fundamental—thus the redeeming power of film—the act of seeing is also granted considerable value in this film. Early shots of Ricky are preceded by a shot of Jane in his video frame, so that we see her, and then, second, we see the person who is seeing her. By showing Jane first, we get the sense that it is seeing—seeing and absorbing this other person—that brings Ricky into being. His corporeality, his presence on screen, his presence to us, is preceded by, made possible by, his act of seeing, much as the Colonel's tragic coming into his own homosexuality is made possible in part by his visual excursions next door.[2]

On the one hand, the frame created by the camera raises the question of ownership of an image and, by extension, of the person or thing represented. We have read what seeing does for the one who sees—the depiction of the camera as an instrument of empowerment rather than of exploitation. But in considering the theme of domestic space, I have meant to concentrate on the frame of the shot, on the space occupied by the person represented and the borders and permeability of that space. In the videotaping process, the space that contains Jane both enriches and is enriched by its permeation by another. This notion of enrichment or development through interaction and permeation is reminiscent of the same psychoanalytic questions of self-building, the same complex interactions between self and other that are mapped and explored through the representation of domestic spaces.

Notes

1. On various metaphoric levels, the movie privileges that which seems to lie at the root, the base layer. Gary Hentzi, for instance, remarked that "American Beauty has a tendency to invest teenagers with an aura of grace" (48). I would propose that "idealization" of adolescence is about an idealization of the foundational layer-of youth, or primal desire.

2. See also Ruth Leys' discussion of spectatorship in the relationship between self and other: "For [Morton] Prince no less than for Freud, although in different terms, mimesis is continually relegated to a secondary position: the hypnotized person is conceived not as imitating the "other" in a scene of unconscious, nonspecular identification unavailable to subsequent recall, but as occupying the vantage point of a spectator who, being distanced from the scene, can see herself in the scene, can represent herself to herself as other, and hence can distinguish herself from the model" (172).

Works Cited

Ball, Alan. *American Beauty: The Shooting Script*. New York: Newmarket Press. 1999.

Borch-Jacobsen, Mikkel. *The Freudian Subject*. Trans. Catherine Porter. Stanford: Stanford University Press, 1988.

Chumo, Peter. "American Beauty: An Interview with Alan Ball." *Creative Screenwriting* 71 (Jan-Feb 2000): 26–35.

Hentzi, Gary. "American Beauty." *Film Quarterly* 54:2 (Winter 2000–2001): 46–50.

Leys, Ruth. "The Real Miss Beauchamp: Gender and the Subject of Imitation." *Feminists Theorize the Political*. Eds. Judith Butler and Joan W. Scott. New York: Routledge, 1992. 167–215.

Newitz, Annalee. "Underground America 1999." *Underground U.S.A. Filmmaking beyond the Hollywood Canon*. Eds. Xavier Mendik and Steven Jay Schneider. London: Wallflower Press, 2002.

Smith, David. "Beautiful Necessities": American Beauty and the Idea of Freedom. *Journal of Religion and Film* 6:2 (October 2002).

Spiegel, James. "The Theological Aesthetic of American Beauty." *Journal of Religion and Popular Culture* 4 (Summer 2003).

A Heart Caves In:
The Dangerous Aesthetics
of *American Beauty*

Susann Cokal

"A Stupid Little Life": The Imperative to Look Closer

When Lester is shot to death at the end of *American Beauty*, he reflects, "It's hard to stay mad, when there's so much beauty in the world" (100)—a perhaps surprising pronouncement from someone who has spent nearly the entire film feeling frustrated, humiliated, and disappointed, happy only when pursuing exaggeratedly adolescent fantasies. The beauty of which he speaks is found in ordinary things, chiefly his memories of happy times with his now-alienated family but also summed up for the viewer with the image of an empty plastic bag blowing in front of a brick wall. It is tempting, then, to conclude that in this film, beauty is always available, located in direct sensory and emotional experiences that arise organically as we move through life; but in the end this aesthetic will prove false. If we do as the ad line says and "Look closer," we see that even that concluding transcendent sense of beauty is presented (perhaps inadvertently) as a hollow, artificial construct.

When Lester slumps over the kitchen counter into a pool of his own bright red blood, his voice-over — the film's consistent narrative voice — offers his final celebration of beauty.

> I guess I could be pretty pissed off about what happened to me ... but it's
> hard to stay mad, when there's so much beauty in the world. Sometimes I

45

feel like I'm seeing it all at once, and it's too much, my heart fills up like a balloon that's about to burst ... [...] and then I remember to relax, and stop trying to hold on to it, and then it flows through me like rain and I can't feel anything but gratitude for every single moment of my stupid little life ...
(amused)
You have no idea what I'm talking about, I'm sure. But don't worry ...
FADE TO BLACK.
You will someday. (100; unbracketed ellipses in original)

We can all, he is saying, expect find beauty in our lives; and it is to be presumed that the film is teaching, or has taught, us to appreciate it.

To train that appreciation, the original viewers of *American Beauty* were twice invited to "Look closer": first by the movie's poster, then — if they looked closely — by a motto posted in Lester's office cubicle. One of the film's messages seems to be that by looking closer we'll discover that beauty is not merely something to behold: It is an experience. It transforms the viewer. As Lester says, "It's hard to stay mad." Beauty soothes; it pacifies; it exalts. In short, beauty is not merely a good thing in and of itself; it is valuable because it performs a kind of work: It makes us feel, and it inspires joy.

In this sense, the film's concept of beauty echoes much twentieth-century art theory. Aesthetic theories usually assume that the beautiful object is an artifact, something made by an artist (a movie, for example), but these theories still apply to the more "natural" beauty this film locates in flowers, certain people, and the blowing white bag. As we shall see, whether the characters are aware of it or not, the beautiful objects and people of *American Beauty* tend to be themselves artifacts, carefully shaped, painted, or otherwise processed to suit a dominant and easily accessible aesthetic. Characters respond predictably to those cultural artifacts. Even Lester's epiphany at the end, when he finds an ineffable beauty in "every moment of my stupid little life," is presented as a culturally conditioned reaction to coordinated stimuli. Thus it is appropriate to point out that in *Art and Answerability*, M. M. Bakhtin writes, "A work of art, understood as *organized material*, as a thing, can have significance only as a physical stimulus of physiological and psychological states or it must assume some utilitarian, practical function" (264). He is referring primarily to verbal art forms, but what he says applies also to more visual media: Art (and *art* is usually defined as something that is beautiful in some way), should affect its audience physically and psychologically. Usually the effect is positive: Hans-Georg Gadamer writes in *The Relevance of the Beautiful*, "If we really have had a genuine experience of art, then the world has become both brighter and less burdensome" (26)—almost exactly the experience Lester describes in his final voice-over. *American Beauty* complicates this dynamic, however—perhaps unintentionally. Although Lester does respond to beauty, his appreciation of it doesn't transcend those culturally constructed norms. He responds physiologically and psychologically to Angela's beauty, which has no alternative utilitarian or practical function, but we might say he doesn't respond *enough*: He isn't completely transformed until the very end, and we will see that at that last moment it appears to be his death, rather than the beauty itself, that brings about his transcendence of ordinary things.

The key to *American Beauty*'s departure from the aesthetic philosophies it appears to support (and thus to its partial failure as a film) lies in the role of the viewer, the person transformed by beauty. Lester's speech advocates relaxing and letting the world's beauty wash through like rain, but most contemporary theorists agree that true art requires some effort from the viewer: "We must make an active contribution of our own and make an effort to synthesize [....] Every work leaves the person who responds to it a certain leeway, a space to be filled in by himself" (Gadamer 8, 26). All that "Look closer" asks us to do is to pay attention; true beauty will make the connections for us. This is also the aesthetic we'll see propounded by Ricky; he is the first to say that keeping open to beauty and seeking it in unexamined places—empty plastic bags, dead bodies—is the viewer's (almost sole) responsibility. In the end, his aesthetic, too, will be questioned.

In its relationship with the ticket-buying audience to whom Lester addresses in his voice-overs, too, the film seems to support that all-but-passive role for the viewer. As many reviewers pointed out, *American Beauty* is loaded (often deliberately) with clichés, images and situations about which we know immediately how to feel—whether they are beautiful (young Angela dancing in her cheerleader's uniform) or tiresome (Carolyn smiling with elaborate false cheer). A passive acceptance of beauty or the cultural clichés in the movie may prove momentarily transformative; we might feel uplifted by Lester's final epiphany. But, if we look closer, we'll be disappointed by its reliance on artistic techniques that emphasize the manufactured nature of even this "authentic" version of happiness. In a film that explicitly resists the passive acceptance of culturally prescribed ambitions and aesthetics, that ultimate championing of passivity becomes problematic. We must reject these received ideas—but we must do so in a passive way.

These two messages are, at the core, contradictory, and together they undercut Ball's critique of consumerist culture. The alternative to this passivity is desire—the drive to seek out beauty. And desire, particularly erotic desire, is violent; at the very least it can lead to the rupture of social mores that the film seems to want to break and to uphold at the same time. Because of this potential for violence, there is a contradiction and a tension between the way the film presents physical beauty's erotic power and the artistic power of metaphor, as located in the somewhat aggressive use of American Beauty roses and a dancing plastic bag as figures for consumerism and beauty. As Lester and a few other characters learn (or think they learn) to appreciate the unexpected beauty in their lives, we watch them explore some of its more obviously transformative powers and the authenticity of those powers. By the time we hear Ricky's alternative aesthetic, we are hyperaware of artifice, and if we do look actively closer, we have to question even his concept of beauty. So, in the end, the viewer has to ask, yet again, what is the "true" nature of the true, the good, and the beautiful? And how can this movie of mixed messages contribute to the sense of beauty in the viewer's life?

"The Most Beautiful Thing I Have Ever Seen": Beauty, Eroticism, and Death

One of our first glimpses of Lester comes as a silhouette against a steamy shower door; his voice-over instructs us to "Look at me, jerking off in the shower" (2). Though the script calls his tone "amused," the moment very tellingly connects the need to look with the impulse toward the sexual. That we already know Lester is dead at the time of his narration adds pathos to the moment; he uses the businesslike act as evidence that "in a way, I'm dead already" (2). When his desire becomes more than sexual—when it becomes erotic,[1] involving fantasies about beauty—he will come alive ... and the way his rebirth manifests itself will, in turn, lead to his physical death. Ultimately, death and beauty are engaged in a dialogic back-and-forth through the medium of erotic desire. The relationship between human physical beauty and the erotic is obvious; but that between beauty, the erotic, and death may require some unpacking. Beauty, like art, transforms the viewer; and the clearest form of transformation is the erotic desire awakened upon viewing a beautiful person.

Lester's awakening from suburban sedation and convention comes through just such an attraction, for sexuality is the great escape of contemporary culture. The opposition of convention and eroticism is widely established: In a discussion of mannerist painting, French philosopher Georges Bataille notes that "hatred of convention [...] alone made them love the heat of eroticism" (*Tears* 161). On their own, suburban life and a cubicle job could make Lester turn to the erotic as a way of breaking free; he does so in a small way when he masturbates in that early shower scene, but soon he will embark on something greater, what director Sam Mendes's DVD commentary calls "a mythical quest."

Lester further breaks convention — but in what we might say is a conventional way — by falling in lust with high school cheerleader Angela. This attraction to an underage girl has interested a number of critics, many of whom compared the storyline to Vladimir Nabokov's *Lolita*[2] — but the inappropriateness of his desire's object contributes to the erotic pull that allows him to break free of the expectations that have kept him "sedated" (5) and passive. As Bataille explains, "the prohibition determines the value — a dangerous value in principle — of that which it denies" (*Tears* 70). And Angela is valuable indeed. The shooting script describes her in her cheerleading uniform as "strikingly beautiful; with perfect even features, blonde hair and a nubile young body, she's the archetypal American dream girl" (15). Lester himself will later call her "the most beautiful thing I have ever seen" (96). Meeting her first puts him into a trance — he fantasizes that she's dancing exclusively for him, the two of them alone in a darkened gym — and then alerts him: In another fantasy sequence, he sees Angela floating naked and says, "I feel like I've been in a coma for about twenty years, and I'm just now waking up" (19). For the rest of the film, he vacillates between fantasy (denial of real life almost unto a deathlike trance, not unlike his pre–Angela sedation and coma) and life (his erotic drive, which makes him feel awake for the first time in years).

Angela is attractive to Lester not just because of her obvious, easily recognizable beauty but also by virtue of her American-ness: She is the archetypal *American* dream girl. She attends Rockwell High, presumably named for Norman Rockwell's cloyingly dear paintings of typically American situations. Her national identity is embodied in her uniform as much as in her blonde hair, as cheerleading is a uniquely American phenomenon, and as this dream girl, Angela represents, quite obviously, the American Dream. Originally a declaration that by coming to the United States and working hard, anyone from any background could achieve financial independence and prosperity, in the twentieth century the phrase has come to denote a fantasy of financial, physical, and emotional security. It is now commonly summed up with a wife, two kids, a dog, a job and a picket fence (which the Burnhams do have). That version of the Dream has proven unsatisfactory to Lester — the marriage and the child are hostile, the job in jeopardy, the suburbs stifling — so he turns to a more universal erotic dream about a girl who happens to possess typically American looks. The archetype (or cliché) jolts him out of the Dream.

Of course, Lester can't really be blamed for admiring an archetype; such types are how we define and recognize beauty. As Gadamer writes, "the beautiful is convincingly defined as something that enjoys universal recognition and assent. Thus it belongs to our natural sense of the beautiful that we cannot ask why it pleases us" (14). Though he might not be able to explain how, Lester has been trained to find Angela beautiful and erotically compelling; so have we all. The danger is that conventional beauty will lead him to break other social conventions that have kept him safe — just as, in a similar way, the *challenge* to the viewer appears to be to break down conventional ideas of the beautiful by giving them that closer look.

Conventions help construct Lester's desire in other ways. The American cultural taboo against sexual contact with an underage girl — a girl who could be her seducer's daughter — also enhances Angela's appeal. David L. Smith characterizes the relationship between this taboo and our culture in general by referring to Vladimir Nabokov's most famous novel: "As in *Lolita*, the hyper-romanticism of a tabooed attraction becomes a symbol of the culture that nurtures it — a culture of yearning, for which real life is always elsewhere" (3). Only at the end of the film, when Angela tells him she's a virgin, does Lester manage to control his lust and actually turn down her advances: There is one convention, one boundary, he is not willing to break, and he can no more mate with

Angela than he can with a real angel. His erotic drive just isn't that strong, and he falls back into another culturally prescribed, and more culturally acceptable, role: In a moment presented as moral redemption, he becomes fatherly toward Angela. He affirms her status as object of desire — this is when he calls her the most beautiful thing he's ever seen — even as he restores the taboo against her. Several writers have reported that in the original conception of the film, Lester was to have consummated the seduction anyway; the filmmakers changed their minds so as to retain sympathy for him. Director Mendes places this moral decision at the heart of the film when he calls *American Beauty* the story of a man who becomes "a father again" when he refuses to sleep with Angela (DVD commentary).

The end of the erotic arc is what Bataille might have predicted: Directly after turning paternal, Lester is murdered. He now sleeps with the angels. So breaking the stifling social conventions of an orientation toward certain consumer goods is one thing, but sex with an underage girl is another. Though we might applaud Lester's decision, through his unwillingness to break this taboo the film fails to validate desires/behaviors that can be seen as destructive and immoral. Thus it hobbles its own ability to celebrate its "new" aesthetic fully. It would have been a grittier film, and one Bataille might have approved of, if Lester had managed to make that final break.

Lester's trajectory takes him from sedation through erotic attraction and broken convention to, ultimately, death. Eroticism and death, often considered polar opposites,[3] are (perhaps because of that opposition) inextricably intertwined in our culture. In films, particularly, one leads to the other — James Bond pauses in a killing spree to have sex with the leading lady, or a cop investigating a murder falls into bed with a suspect; a woman loves her man so passionately she'll kill to keep him. Bataille explains the relationship between death and eroticism in Western culture: "Eroticism, it may be said, is assenting to life up to the point of death" (*Erotism* 11). His argument is that in an erotic union, two separate individuals become — for a moment — one continuous being, and in death the individual joins a collective of departed souls: "The final sense of eroticism is death" (*Erotism* 144). Then, too, the individual might be willing to accept even death if it comes with a moment of erotic release.

It is a pleasure to look at beautiful things and beautiful people, but the pleasure may not be so simple. Bataille would suggest that to desire a girl such as Angela (who is greatly objectified, even by herself) means to desire to ruin her: "If beauty so far removed from the animal is passionately desired, it is because to possess is to sully, to reduce to the animal level. Beauty is desired in order that it may be befouled; not for its own sake, but for the joy brought by the certainty of profaning it" (*Erotism* 144). By this reasoning, Lester wants not to celebrate Angela's beauty or to participate in it but to destroy it — to bring her down to his less-than-perfect level. But when he learns that she's actually a virgin, thus as yet undesecrated, untainted by animal contact, he thrusts her out of his erotic thoughts and makes her simply a beautiful object to be admired. He returns to the Dream of the picket fence, not the girl. Thus the connection between beauty and eros is ultimately destructive; shot by Colonel Fitts, who breaks another taboo (largely self-imposed) by desiring Lester's newly muscular body, Lester dies from the chain of events he begins by pursuing his American dream girl ... but he dies in a state of what the filmmakers would term *redemption*.

"The Punch Line of a Joke He Heard Long Ago": The Limits of the Beautiful

So, for Lester, redemption and happiness are short lived; in the film's emotional economy, it might even seem that his death results from the refusal to break convention and revel in beauty to the fullest extent. And yet that moment of moral redemption is still important — expressing the central message of the film, according to Mendes. When he refuses to deflower Angela, Lester becomes a father figure not just to her but, through her, to his own daughter, Jane.[4] After reassuring Angela that she is desirable — "You are the most beautiful thing I have ever seen" (96) — he makes her a sandwich, lends her a shirt, and asks how Jane is doing. He is delighted to hear she's in love. Angela then asks how Lester is, and he says appreciatively, "God, it's been a long time since anybody asked me that. [*Thinks about it*] I'm great" (96). If we are to believe that the "mythic quest" is to make him a father, we might conclude that he feels great because of Janie — though the script describes him "wondering why he should suddenly feel so content" (96). This is when he returns to the photograph of Carolyn, Jane, and himself enjoying themselves at an amusement park and "smiles: the deep, satisfied smile of a man who

just now understands the punch line of a joke he heard long ago ..."
(96) — just before the gun that will kill him slides into view.

The reason for his smile — the joke — is what the film presents as a
revolutionary vision of beauty, as articulated by Ricky. A carefully blank,
almost catatonic young man, Ricky films what is usually overlooked,
and some of his favorite subjects are dead. The first example we see,
filmed through Ricky's Digicam, is a dead bird on the high school campus; it "lays [sic] on the ground, decomposing" (52). When Angela asks
Ricky what he's doing, he says — in an off-camera voice-over that
reminds us of Lester's own narration:

> Ricky (O.C.): I was filming this dead bird.
>
> Angela: Why?
>
> Ricky (O.C.): Because it's beautiful.

Ricky then turns to Jane, filming her, and she asks him not to do it anymore. But something in the conversation has worked magic on her, and
she walks home with him rather than riding with Angela. It is the beginning of the love that is her partial redemption.

This notion of beauty is indeed magical, or at least inexpressible;
for the moment, there's no explanation as to why the dead bird is beautiful. Ricky's aesthetic philosophy must wait until the walk home, when
he describes filming "this homeless woman who froze to death once. Just
laying there on the sidewalk. She looked really sad."

> Jane: Why would you film that?
>
> Ricky: Because it was amazing.[5]
>
> Jane: What was amazing about it?
>
> (*A beat.*)
>
> Ricky: When you see something like that, it's like God is looking right at
> you, just for a second. And if you're careful, you can look right back.
>
> Jane: And what do you see?
>
> Ricky: Beauty [57].

God is beauty, but the exact nature of this beauty is still a little obscure.
Ricky seems to have a romantic association with death, decay, and mortality, but we will have to look even closer — at a humble plastic bag —
to get the complete meaning.

That bag is the film's most striking and memorable image; it whirls above a pile of brown leaves, in front of a brick wall in an empty parking lot. (A similar bag blowing outside the World Trade Center was the visual impetus for the original script, as Alan Ball says in his afterword [113].) In the script, "the wind carries it in a circle around us, sometimes whipping it about violently, or, without warning, sending it soaring skyward, then letting it float gracefully down to the ground" (60). With the word "gracefully," it becomes clear that any articulation of an aesthetic here will be not Ricky's quirk but the filmmakers' firm conviction. The DVD commentary reinforces this point explicitly, and when Alan Ball asks Mendes how he managed to get the bag to float as it does, Mendes refuses to tell; he seems to want to retain a sort of magic for the image. Ricky compares that empty, "dancing" bag to "a little kid begging me to play with it"; rather than play, however, he comes to a grave realization. "That's the day," he says, "I realized that there was this entire life behind things, and this incredibly benevolent force that wanted me to know there was no reason to be afraid. Ever. [...] Sometimes there's so much beauty in the world I feel like I can't take it ... and my heart is going to cave in" (60).

So Ricky finds God in an empty plastic bag, the eyes of a dead homeless woman, presumably in a dead bird, eventually in Lester's own blankly staring dead eyes (which make Ricky exclaim — insofar as someone so devoid of affect can be said to exclaim — "Wow" [97]). That transcendent religious experience is what David L. Smith calls Emersonian "beautiful necessity" (1); it is an unexpected appreciation for the beauty of an inevitable, generally unpleasant fate. Ricky's philosophy seems to be that trash is beautiful, and beauty is trash; given what he said earlier, when we look at trash, we look at both beauty and God. And again, an evocation of beauty has an erotic effect: soon Jane is sharing his feelings and his bed.[6]

It might be too easy to point out that Ricky's apparently radical aesthetic is really rather typical and predictable itself. A celebration of discards is common to adolescent rebellion, particularly among young people who want to be artists. In the 1970s, for example, punk rockers dressed out of trash barrels and decorated their clothes with safety pins in order to express defiance of convention and a new, personalized aesthetic; budding artists of all sorts (perhaps particularly those who attend conventional universities) get their bodies pierced and tattooed. The rejection, even the violent rejection, of clichés becomes itself a cliché, and Ricky's notion of beauty is part of the cultural trend. It might have been easier to recognize for what it is if it weren't coming from a boy with a crisp haircut and a white sports shirt.

As Lester slumps dead over the kitchen counter, his voice-over borrows some of Ricky's language to offer a final celebration of beauty: "Sometimes I feel like I'm seeing it all at once, and it's too much, my heart fills up like a balloon that's about to burst" (100). Shot in the head, Lester is experiencing what Ricky earlier described as a heart caving in, but it has been transformed into a positive image of the heart filling up like a balloon, bursting and turning outward rather than collapsing — turning outward in what may be a joyful explosion but is an explosion, a destruction, nonetheless. Either way, the world's beauty is all but unbearable, and it is necessary to let go of the world in order to enjoy it. Lester's use of present tense indicates that this experience of beauty continues, perhaps even intensifies, after death. The terms he uses ("flows through me like rain and I can't feel anything but gratitude" (100)) could be interpreted spiritually, as achievement of nirvana[7]; they might also be compared to a description of eruptive erotic release. It is important to note that the act of looking here produces an appreciation of beauty, not a desire for it: Appreciation is passive and peaceful, desire violent and desecrating. When Lester learns to passively appreciate Angela (and the rest of his "stupid little life") rather than actively desire her (or desire to change himself or his life), he is redeemed. And at that moment, he dies. Thus we might say that the film oscillates between the experience of beauty, which represents a life truly lived, and the end of experience, which takes the form of Lester's suburban sedation or, finally, his death. Ultimately, it favors passivity.

Ball's afterword to the shooting script reinforces the expressed moral to his tale:

> We live in such a manufactured culture, one that thrives on simplifying and packaging experience quickly so it can be sold. But as Ricky knows — and Lester learns — things are infinitely deeper and richer than they appear on the surface. And although the puritanical would have us believe otherwise, there is room for beauty in every facet of existence [114].

Ricky's transformative appreciation of small and neglected things could be a worthy aesthetic; it is after all part of Lester's epiphany at the end, and it is certainly an alternative to the expensive, stylized, and sterile aesthetic we get from Carolyn and other characters. By now, however, we may suspect the validity or the efficacy of this moral.

Although Lester echoes Ricky's language, he is not the one who listens to Ricky's aesthetic articulation. That person is Jane. We can read Lester's aesthetic, like Ricky's, as part of the adolescent rebellion Lester undergoes in the culturally prescribed ways (the cheerleader, the Firebird car, the rock-and-roll). By the time Lester dies and expresses the same feelings as Ricky has, however, his echoes can serve as a kind of shorthand for the aesthetic philosophy the film is upholding, and we expect to find this passive appreciation of beauty in overlooked things. It is significant, however, that Lester dies while still appreciating Angela — desexualized but still beautiful, though Ricky has rejected her as ugly, boring, and "totally ordinary" (88). Some critics might say this more expansive aesthetic is a mark of Lester's actual maturity, that he sees the beauty beneath the surface that a resentful misfit might overlook — or we might say he has just learned to accept all types of surface beauty, whether discards or cultural archetypes. The final image of beauty, a reprise of the plastic bag blowing in front of the brick wall, seems to indicate as much: All beauty lies in the surface, and beneath the surface is empty air.

It is ironic that Lester achieves the ultimate, peaceful experience of beauty as he dies; he asks us to look closer so that we might experience it in life — but the very act of looking, which could lead to desiring, might kill us if we let it go too far. Death is the one phenomenon every one of the film's viewers will surely experience one day, and Lester's final speech could be the ultimate reassurance for the audience: We will all experience beauty — even if it is a beauty contingent upon death. The message here is also passive. If Lester's revelation about beauty only comes in death, we as viewers are free of responsibility: We, too, can remain passive — not only wait for beauty to wash over us, but also wait for death to truly appreciate the beauty of life. And death is the ultimate passive state.

Egg Shells and Miracle-Gro: Raising a Metaphor

A further complication with Ball's message is the way in which it is presented: through a metaphor conflating sterility and sexuality, and through clichés that the film interrogates but doesn't entirely dismiss.

Since Lester's awareness in death is a passive act — like Ricky's message that appreciating beauty is a passive act — the film creates a space in which we can still embrace and accept clichés. We are not being challenged to reject them entirely, only to recognize and disapprove of some of them; the film lets us cling to the beauty of clichés such as the American dream girl and admire shallow, pretty Angela even though we recognize we *should* prefer sullen but more profound Jane. For Ball, recognition is enough: Even if we see that certain things are beautiful only on a surface level, we may still admire them, and we will almost automatically see a deeper beauty elsewhere. The question is, again, how authentic, how transformative, this ultimate recognition can be. We may get at the answer through metaphor.

The film's title derives from the red roses that Carolyn grows in the Burnhams' front yard. These flowers are the film's central metaphor, a species in fact called American Beauty, and the metaphor's meaning is as showy and obtrusive as the flowers themselves. In its very name, the species points out the hollowness of American concepts of beauty and, by extension, the meaninglessness of the American Dream that the Burnhams embody; in its breeding, it embodies the manufactured culture that Ball laments. And yet it also stands for the erotic feelings Lester has for Angela — showing yet again that Lester's rebellion is conventional and will lead to essentially the same place as his cubicle life.

There is some debate as to what an American Beauty rose really is. In a range of songs performed by artists such as Frank Sinatra and Diana Ross, the American Beauty is usually called a red rose, and the name seems to refer to a specific breed. On the Internet and in gardening books, a search for pictures turns up more pinks than reds, along with descriptions of a range of scents; and garden bloggers have compiled lists of species that might have supplied the roses for the film.[8] There are widespread notions that the "true" American Beauty has been bred especially for long stems that will look good in crystal vases, and that a side effect of that breeding has been a loss of the fragrance for which many people prize roses. It would seem, however, that "American Beauty red rose" is a more generic term, referring to any red rose grown in America; and the film exploits that everyrose quality while making the flowers join the dream girl as symbols for conventional American life and American fantasy.

As to the specific roses in the film, they may be plants, but they don't seem to grow as much as simply appear. They are a very bright, uniform red, almost certainly enhanced in postproduction; they are more artificial than natural. And they have a supernatural longevity: The movie's action supposedly takes place over several months, but the flowers are always blooming in their tidy ranks inside the front yard's white picket fence; they bloom even when the trees are bare of leaves and we are presumably approaching winter. Carolyn's roses seem to be scentless, or at least no one comments on their aroma. A next-door neighbor, Jim, compliments them in general terms early on: "I just love your roses. How do you get them to flourish like this?" (3). What the movie audience sees is all there is to the rose: the bright reds, long stems, apparent lack of thorns. They might as well be scentless, limited to only one kind of sensory appeal. The deliberate and purely visual aesthetic of the flowers is reinforced by the way Lester introduces Carolyn's matching shears and clogs in voice-over (2). Carolyn's aesthetic eliminates accident, and nature, as much as possible; there is beauty — distinctly *American* beauty — in careful choices. The more spontaneous or multisensory pleasure that other flowers might give has been bred out of her flowers, just as Carolyn (despite eventual declarations to the contrary) has bred away whatever was once natural and joyful in herself.

Her "secret" for the flourishing roses says a lot about that aesthetic: "Well, I'll tell you. Egg shells and Miracle Grow [sic]" (3). Miracle-Gro is a popular fertilizer, the name of which seems to push plant growth beyond the natural world and into the realm of the magical and miraculous. Egg shells are empty — one of the first images of emptiness we get in the film — and sterile, drained of the potential life inside. They are a fitting nutrient for the roses that we see Carolyn cut with those gardening shears just after we watch Lester masturbating in the shower; if her relationship to the flowers symbolizes her castration of Lester, the use of empty, female-identified eggshells binds the two of them together in a single symbolic rose.

We will see the roses many times over; they decorate key scenes within the Burnham house in order to remind us, again, that this apparently beautiful life is hollow and sterile. For example, in the first dining-room scene, "RED ROSES are bunched in a vase at the center of the table. Nobody makes eye contact, or even seems aware of anybody else's presence, until ..." (8) — until Jane complains of the "elevator music" Carolyn likes to play while eating. The music is as processed and artificial as the flowers appear to be, and the roses remind us that although every-one seems polite enough, this family has been put together out of shells and held together with a near miracle; it can't help but crumble.

The roses are part of a larger color scheme in the film. The palette is primarily red, white, and blue, with obvious implications. The Burn-hams live in a white house with blue shutters and a red door; even Lester's office folders are red, white, and blue. Lester buys a red Pontiac Firebird; in the early scenes (before her sexual and emotional awaken-ing), Jane's lips are a very bright rose red to match the roses; and the list goes on, until Lester lies in a pool of his own intensely red American Beauty blood, rigor mortis making him smile faintly into his reflection. Mendes admits to choosing red objects to make a "theme" referring to blood (DVD commentary). Simply put, the roses are tied to the Amer-ican flag, which offers a symbolic castration to those who buy into the Dream it represents, and the red flowers ultimately point toward death.

Because of the relationship between sex and death in American cul-ture, it is appropriate to see the roses performing a certain kind of dou-ble metaphoric duty here. Ever since the medieval allegory *The Romance of the Rose*, roses have stood for female genitalia, and this movie exploits that longstanding tradition. From the dewy petals on the poster, arranged to resemble labia, to the petals that pour from Angela's jacket in the first fantasy sequence, to the subsequent fantasies of her lying on a bed sprin-kled with red petals and bathing in a tub full of them, the connection is explicit and in fact overwhelming.[9]

The sexual metaphor is used heavyhandedly to draw attention to its easy surface meaning. In the same way that Lester's and Carolyn's overbright smiles and stilted speech point out the falsity of their happi-ness, the overabundance of rose petals and overdetermination of their meaning seem designed to teach us about the limited American ability to appreciate visual beauty and, incidentally, to decode symbols. The erotic beauty embodied in Angela, the archetypal American dream girl is too easy to recognize, too consumer ready, and its natural destiny is the sterility and disappointment seen in Carolyn — still beautiful in her way, but not likely to please anyone for long.

An Empty Sack and a Brick Wall:
Projecting Images in a Manufactured Culture

The type of beauty embodied in the film's red roses is extrinsic, cal-culated to please the eye but no other senses. They are a mere image of beauty, as opposed to the small and neglected things that Ricky — and, more generally, the film itself — celebrates as beauty itself. Lester is not the only character who yearns to break free of his sedation, but not every-one wants to gain freedom the same way. Carolyn also desires happiness (which she seeks through an erotic connection), but she thinks it will lie within the picket fence; with her three-thousand-dollar sofa and her minivan, she chases happiness by buying into the American consumerist dream in which beauty is something manufactured. The shallowness of consumer culture and the dissatisfying gap between appearance and real-ity are, of course, further intellectual conventions, but the film presents them as earnestly as Ricky presents his plastic bag. To Carolyn and Angela (the budding Carolyn-to-be), image is almost everything that counts; if they appear to live the dream, they *will* live it. And the dream lies within their grasp because both are beautiful. It is important to control one's public image if reality is to measure up to the dream buried in the heart; as Carolyn tells Lester at the beginning of the cocktail party, "my busi-ness is selling an image. And part of my job is to *live* that image" (29). That vision, of course, is of a happy family (she tells Lester to "act happy" at the party [29]) living in tidy, safe suburbia — the facade beneath which we have already been told to "look closer."

The image must be not only lived but also made into a spectacle — hence removing any authenticity imparted by actually living; living is for show. This is what selling means: The salesperson presents the object (or lifestyle) in terms that excite the customer's desire, make him or her recognize that this very object is what his or her life is lacking; the money follows. Über-salesman Buddy Kane, the Real Estate King, understands the game of desire very well. When Carolyn and Buddy get together for lunch (so she can "pick his brain" and learn how to sell as effectively as he does), he explains the breakup of his apparently happy marriage by telling her, "Well, call me crazy, but it is my philosophy that in order to be successful, one must project an image of success, at all times" (51).

The verb "project" has an obvious significance in a movie, particu-larly a movie that includes a filmmaker as a character. It denotes a turning outward, an audience, and an acknowledgment that the image will not match up with the reality behind it. It's no longer a question of living the image, merely of appearing to do so: The image has become almost nothing but a sales tool, and there no longer seems to be a possibility of finding intrinsic happiness. Lester, a reporter for *Media Monthly*, makes the sales strategy even more obvious when he tells the Colonel, "Nope, our marriage is just for show. A commercial, for how normal we are. When we are anything but" (89). Happiness has been replaced with "success," a concept oriented toward the marketplace and the critics and customers who might want to make a judgment and buy into the object. Success is primarily financial; where money is, love and happiness will follow. After all, Carolyn is attracted to Buddy largely because of his sales, perhaps secondarily because he is played by handsome Peter Gallagher. If he had never sold a house, he would be just another attractive background figure at the restaurant.

Carolyn all but melts when Buddy delivers his line. They share the same "philosophy" (of both ethics and aesthetics) and the same reality, the marriages that should be perfect but are crumbling away. And Buddy's line projects another image, that of the brave but heartbroken soon-to-be-ex-husband; it is no wonder that it gets him success in another area, and the next time we see Buddy and Carolyn (that same day), they are having sex in a motel bed and shouting about how good it feels. When they discuss their intercourse, they essentially project an image of success for each other:

> **Carolyn:** Yes! Oh, God! I love it!
>
> **Buddy:** You like getting nailed by the king?
>
> **Carolyn:** Oh yes! I love it! Fuck me, your majesty! (53)

Carolyn "proves" that she's not the frigid wife Lester thinks she is; and Buddy's prowess, his success as both swordsman and Realtor, get ample reinforcement with her pleasure. The slight discrepancies in verbal register ("nailed" — "king," "fuck" — "majesty") highlight the contrast between the image of success and what really might be going on behind the image. A king who performs a gutter-language "nailing" is somewhat less than majestic — and again demonstrates the link Bataille has proposed between the erotic desire to possess beauty and the desire to defile it.

When Lester learns about the affair and Buddy breaks it off (he's afraid of the financial repercussions for his divorce), Carolyn becomes bitter and echoes their mutual philosophy "sarcastically," with a change of inflection and a new pause. The words she uses are Buddy's: "In order to be successful, one must project an image of success. At all times" (79). With the pause before "At all times," Carolyn hints that, until now, she may not have realized there can be no other times, private moments at which it is possible to reveal one's own sense of vulnerability. And the script says she regrets her words immediately; her sarcastic inflection means she's projecting the wrong image, and it is clear the relationship will never start up again.

Whatever her skills as a Realtor, lover, wife, or mother, we have seen that Carolyn is more than the image of success in one area: Her American Beauty roses. In this case, the image matches the reality, and worldly appreciation from her neighbor is the result. Even Carolyn, however, is not in control of the roses' ultimate success: their function as metaphor within the film. The film projects its metaphor the way Buddy projects success, constantly reminding us of the sterile, odorless life the characters are really living, even as they tend to their images of happiness.

As an aspiring model, Angela is all about image. Where there is beauty, particularly with "perfect even features, blonde hair and a nubile young body" (stage direction, 15), there is money from advertisers and magazine sellers. We might "look closer" at a model, but all we see of her is the image she projects; hers is a very limited form of acting, in which the moment the shutter snaps becomes eternal — if the photographer and editor deem the result likely to appeal to the people who will buy the makeup, cars, or magazines that the photo represents. As "the archetypal American dream girl" (15), Angela is the model for an entire culture, destined to sell (at least initially) the American Dream itself.

When she first sells Lester on the dream, as we have seen, it's all about physical image — his as well as her own. Later on, he overhears her tell Jane, "Your dad's actually kind of cute. [...] If he just worked out a little, he'd be hot. [...] I bet he's got a big dick. [...] If he built up his chest and arms, I would totally fuck him" (36–37). Lester immediately starts pumping iron and jogging, and he tells his neighbors Jim 1 and Jim 2, "I need to shape up. Fast. [...] I want to look good naked" (44). He is inspired to reshape his body to conform to her ideal, which is also the general culture's: the well-developed chest muscles, arms, and abdomen. The transformative power of beauty, through the medium of erotic attraction, registers clearly, as does the image of sexual success he wants to project.

A Heart Caves In (Susann Cokal)

Angela projects a carefully fashioned image off camera as well as on, but it's not the image of a pretty, innocent girly-girl of the kind that *Seventeen* (her biggest success to date) usually features. In her mind, success boils down to becoming someone with whom other people want to have sex: "If people I don't even know look at me and want to fuck me, it means I really have a shot at being a model. Which is great, because there's nothing worse in life than being ordinary" (20). She assumes a jaded air and brags about a photographer she slept with on her way to success because "It would have been so majorly stupid of me to turn him down" (25). When one of her listeners reacts by calling her a prostitute, Angela says, "Hey. That's how things really are. You just don't know, because you're this pampered little suburban chick" (26). She claims to know the truth behind the image that the modeling industry projects, and in fact she does—she just hasn't lived that truth yet, as we find out toward the end, when she tells Lester she's a virgin. In this early scene, she maintains her image by insulting a girl who's living the suburban dream-life, and that girl pokes a hole in Angela's projection: "You've only been in *Seventeen* once, and you looked fat, so stop acting like you're goddamn Christy Turlington" (26). Even when there's no clear direct benefit, people are willing to play along with image — but only until it starts to shake the foundations of their own carefully constructed worlds. It is no accident that "Teenage Girl #2" (a fine name for a member of a manufactured culture) compares Angela to Christy Turlington; not only is Turlington one of the most famous and highest-paid models of all time, but she also lends her first name to Buddy's divorcing wife, pointing out, again, that Buddy's life — and the lives of all these characters— has been about image projection.

The model's image is heavily and obviously manipulated to match the culture's definition of beauty. If we look closely at any photograph, particularly one that might make it to the cover of a magazine — or the poster of a film — we see not only the image the model is projecting but also the traces of the photographer, editor, and printer. Airbrushing (or its digital equivalent in Photoshop) is the most obvious of these alterations, as it removes imperfections, evens tones, and pulls objects from the frame. All of these changes remind us that, at least in market-driven America, beauty is not natural or intrinsic.

The movie's poster — the very one that invites us to look closer — is a prime example. The image is striking: a stretch of naked stomach, toned but without much muscle definition, with an oddly shaped navel framed between a hand coming in from the left and the rose that hand holds—thornless, leafless, red, and beaded with dew. The title is in capital letters, with "Beauty" in boldface. The skin of the model or models (it's possible one girl lent her stomach, another her hand[10]) shows no pores, barely even a wrinkle on the knuckles; the photograph has been cleaned up to erase details and quirks that might make the woman individual rather than archetypal. The nails have been perfectly manicured, too, and they lie nearly flat on the stomach as they hold the rose in place. That rose is arranged so that its stem seems to originate around the girl's vagina; though we see a lot of the abdomen, there's no glimpse of pubic hair, and that hairlessness emphasizes the model's youth. The rose is perfect, its petals symmetrically folded, red and curled like the folds of the labia that the stem might be touching. There is dew, a dewy freshness. The hand and flower make a sort of heart shape below the navel, which itself has an odd form: the upper portion of a question mark, without the black dot beneath. The location of the dark circle can be guessed easily; everything in the poster points us toward a young girl's genitals in a carefully constructed image of the "archetypal American dream girl." Seeing this girl, this movie, will allow us to live the image, or at least satisfy some prurient curiosity.

This type of photograph and the aesthetic it embodies are antithetical to what we see from Ricky, the film's most credible philosopher. But with the movie poster, some closer looks reveal the artifice and processing, the careful construction, of the image. Ricky's films appear to do the opposite: The plastic bag footage, for example, is grainy, not as highly processed as the poster or a magazine photograph, certainly not even as sophisticated as the movies he and his father watch. Mendes describes the video as a "bluer, flatter image" (DVD commentary). Ricky doesn't seem to process his films at all, rather to shelve them as soon as they come out of the Digicam; his room is lined with cartridges, accumulated images of the discards he finds beautiful, spiritual, transformative. All his footage is "raw"—hence, presumably, more authentic, closer to a true form of beauty. And yet the key image is of a discarded artifact, the plastic bag that has been processed and used until it would seem to have no further meaning or value, except in the eyes of someone who prizes discards.

Ricky projects images in a very literal way, using his camera, tape player, and other expensive video equipment; but within the film's aesthetic, he manages to capture the "true images" behind the characters' own projections, the real people behind the models. Most of those images are ugly or at least ridiculous—"Welcome to America's Weirdest Home Videos" (39) he mutters while watching a naked Lester work out for the first time — but he also has the ability to recognize, record, and reproduce what he considers beautiful. In general, as we have seen, the film seems to support his aesthetic, letting him speak for a less obvious kind of beauty than what others appreciate, a sort of pure form untapped in our culture — but that aesthetic is ultimately as fragile as the floating plastic bag, and as manufactured.

A Film Caves In: Artifice and Cinematic Experience

Once again, *American Beauty* reminds us that the cinematic experience — and perhaps even our experience of the world beyond the screen — is primarily a passively visual one. The film also explores the limitations of our vision, and the principal vehicle for this reminder is in the repeated framing of images within doorways and windows, and even against square or rectangular spaces— what Mendes calls "a series of jail cells" and compares to paintings by Magritte and Hopper (DVD commentary). The picket fence enclosing the line of American Beauty roses and the Burnhams' front yard is just the beginning; there is also Lester's shower; Jane's window, in which she poses bare breasted for Ricky's Digicam; the doorway of the house for sale, where Carolyn tries to project her image of success— and the list is virtually endless. Essentially, every character is defined within the kind of selective vision that produces images such as the one on the film's poster: a fragmentation of the body and of character itself. This framing insists on the need to look closer, look carefully; for example, Colonel Fitts misunderstands what he sees between two windows— Ricky on his knees, Lester leaning back in a papasan chair — and decides that Ricky must be fellating Lester (rather than rolling a joint for him, as he is actually doing). The wall in between the windows blocks Fitts's view of the scene, and he is incapable of looking closely enough. This misunderstanding, or misviewing, leads him to approach Lester and try to kiss him; Lester's gentle rejection finally pushes the Colonel over some kind of edge (beyond the careful framing of his life), so that Fitts shoots Lester.[11]

Vincent Hausmann considers this framing strategy to be part of the movie's undercurrent of violence: "the film argues that all cinematic viewing entails a measure of violence: the film's obsessive motifs of framings here conspicuously come to underscore the violence of the cinema effect" (122). Given what the Colonel does to Lester, he is probably right. The murder scene, Hausmann writes, "suggests that spectators and the cinema cannot be absolved of what motivates the colonel: the search for a final meaning that might mute a discordant Otherness within the subject by projecting that horror outward, here onto the white wall [where Lester's blood splatters] functioning self-referentially as a version of the film screen" (132). Through our search for a "true" interpretation and "true" beauty, we are all guilty of a kind of violence to the text and the characters; but then again, it is a violence invited with "Look closer." We look so closely that, literally, we see into Lester's brain ... and what we see at the murder scene is so grisly that, perhaps, we would be excused from a more active pursuit of beauty. The passive acceptance of beauty that accompanies death becomes more attractive itself.

The ultimate celebration of beauty within the examined life is found in a series of visual memories that give Lester his last moments of pleasure: his eleven-year-old self watching falling stars, his grandmother's papery hands, his first view of his cousin's red Firebird, a four-year-old Janie dressed in a princess costume, and Carolyn on a teacup ride at an amusement park (not the original amusement-park photo, as some critics have assumed; that picture included all three Burnhams) (98–99). Memory comes in the form of a classic movie montage; even in Lester's own mind, his life unfurls as a film. Moreover, all of these images are in black-and-white, a more old-fashioned form of photography that is meant to draw attention to the status of these images as memories. Black-and-white also, inevitably, reminds us that we are watching film, in which different finishes and processes are possible. That film of memory restores Lester's love for the world and even for Carolyn, as he says her name at last "with love" (99). Again, we see the appreciation of beauty as a series of framing moments, focused on details such as the grandmother's hands or Carolyn's laughing face — a selective cultivation of petal or stem, or blonde hair and a smile. Beauty is essentially a construct, and what lies beyond the bounds of that construct may be too dangerous.

By limiting his view of the world to that frame, Lester implies that there is no natural, primal beauty to be found, and a close look at the film supports that message. We remember that all of Ricky's objects of beauty are dead, bodies emptied of soul, plastic forms with nothing but air inside; and his object of desire, Jane, is likely to be blamed for her father's murder. (The first shot, in which she complains about Lester and asks Ricky to kill him, suggests as much, and in fact the original version of the film included a frame story with an epilogue in which Jane and Ricky were convicted of the killing.) And rather than end with Lester's memory montage, we have that final image of the dancing bag, followed by a flying shot over the neighborhood. Again, the film's carefully established and perhaps overly rigid dichotomy between the manufactured beauty of models and the artifice of Carolyn's world (all bad), with Ricky's raw images (good) breaks down. Perhaps Lester's articulation of his new aesthetic allows us to feel good temporarily, but it demands nothing from us—it allows us to creep back into our "stupid little lives" and wait for death without taking responsibility for the changes that, elsewhere, the film appears to advocate.

Lester's final, self-deprecating words to the viewer also undermine the power of the art object that has made us look closer: "You have no idea what I'm talking about, I'm sure. But don't worry ... You will someday" (100). We have just seen the montage that should have driven home Lester's (and Ball's) message, so we should have a very good idea what he's talking about, if the film has allowed us our vicarious life experience. But here he acknowledges that only our own experience can give us this peaceful sense of beauty—and only when viewed in retrospect. The beauty of *American Beauty*, the Fitts/Burnham aesthetic, is essentially powerless; its effect lies in the future experience of death. *American Beauty* is an empty bag that points the way to beauty but is not beauty itself. If we feel comforted after watching, it's more thanks to the promise of beauty than the actual experience of it.

Thus, in the end, the movie's viewers have to question any response to the artful or the beautiful, including our response to the film itself. Whether we feel despair or joy, *American Beauty* shows that we are so divorced from our feelings that they are no longer our feelings. They are culturally produced artifacts framed and focused in other artifacts—a rose, a movie, a model, a plastic bag; a frame so rigid that even Lester's burst of good feeling cannot transcend it. Instead, trapped by the frame and overburdened by artifice, the heart caves in; the movie, having done precisely and calculatingly what it is bred to do, ends before we can look too closely at what it has made us feel.

Notes

1. Here I'm using Georges Bataille's distinction between the sexual as a biological urge and the erotic as the desire that lies beyond the sexual. See *The Tears of Eros* (19).

2. Alan Ball wrote in the shooting script that he was first inspired by the "Long Island Lolita" story of Amy Fisher and Joey Buttafuoco (113); Angela's last name echoes the one Nabokov gave his Lolita, Haze. For examples of reviewers' references to the *Lolita* element, see Ebert and Guthmann, neither of whom objected to the use of the taboo.

3. As Bataille puts it, "The erotic moment is even the zenith of this life, in which the greatest force and the greatest intensity are revealed" (*Tears* 33). At the moment eros prevails, we are most vibrantly alive; death would, of course, seem to be the negation of life.

4. He has made several overtures toward Jane already—for example, "Janie, what happened? You and I used to be pals" (10)—only to be rebuffed consistently. The movie's very first scene (a flash-forward to one played near the middle of the film) shows Jane complaining to Ricky about her father: "I need a father who's a role model, not some horny geek-boy who's gonna spray his shorts whenever I bring a girlfriend home from school" (1). The problem isn't just her anger about his attraction to Angela; Janie rejects Lester even before he sees the other girl. Perhaps it is, as Lester thinks, that he hasn't "been more available" (10) recently, or perhaps it's simply Jane's adolescent rebellion. In any case, the two have grown apart, and the plot does nothing to bring them together in person.

5. Ricky uses "amazing" sincerely, though just a few minutes earlier in the film, Lester has told the Mr. Smiley's burger store manager, very sarcastically, "I'm sure there have been amazing technological advances in the industry, but [...] It seems unfair to presume I won't be able to learn" (55). The repetition reinforces Lester's exhausted, jaded sensibility and Ricky's lingering capacity for wonder—at the same time as it shows the word is overused in our culture (even Ricky's sense can't completely restore the word's full meaning).

6. The discarded people and objects that Ricky calls beautiful (and Jane is among them) are safe objects of desire, as no one else appears to want them. Ricky's celebration of these objects may point to his own fears. It may be fear that keeps him living with his abusive father, even though his drug-dealing business gives him the means to live on his own. Are we to value certain objects simply because no one else does? It would certainly be a way to establish individuality, to make ourselves special.

7. See David L. Smith for a discussion of this spiritual aspect to the film.

8. See, for example, http://www.au.gardenweb.com/forums/load/roses/msg0800044724881.html (accessed 10 September 2005).

9. Robert Herrick's poem "To the Virgins, to Make Much of Time" springs inevitably to mind, with the line "Gather ye rosebuds while ye may" (Herrick, 30); the virgins to whom that poem was originally addressed may be ready to spill their hoarded buds, and the older man (poet, aesthete) who appreciates virgins and buds-Lester-is ready to collect them again. As the poem points out, death will come swiftly: "this same flower that smiles today/Tomorrow will be dying." Lester, who smiles first falsely, then with some genuine pleasure, dies early.

10. A movie trivia website identifies the hand and stomach as belonging to one woman, Chloe Hunter, but I haven't been able to confirm the information elsewhere. See http://www.imdb.com/title/tt0169547/trivia (accessed 11 September 2005).

11. In earlier versions of the script, Fitts had had a homosexual lover in Vietnam and held him as he died; but he nonetheless repressed his homosexual desires once back in America.

Works Cited

Bakhtin, M. M. *Art and Answerability*. Eds. Michael Holquist and Vadim Liapunov. Trans. Vadim Liapunov, Kenneth Brostrum. Austin: Uuniversity of Texas Press, 1990.

Ball, Alan. *American Beauty: The Shooting Script*. New York: Newmarket Press, 1999.

Bataille, Georges. *Erotism: Death and Sensuality*. Trans. Mary Dalwood. San Francisco: City Lights, 1986 (first published as *L'Erotisme*, 1957).

A Heart Caves In (Susann Cokal)

A Heart Caves In (Susann Cokal)

A Heart Caves In (Susann Cokal)

_____. *The Tears of Eros*. Trans. Peter Connor. San Francisco: City Lights, 1989 (first published as *Les larmes d'Eros*, 1961).

Ebert, Roger. "*American Beauty*." Review. *Chicago Sun-Times*. 24 September 1999.

Gadamer, Hans-Georg. *The Relevance of the Beautiful*. Ed. Robert Bernasconi. Trans. Nicholas Walker. Cambridge: Cambridge University Press, 1986.

Guthmann, Edward. "Breathtaking 'Beauty.'" Review of *American Beauty*. *San Francisco Chronicle*. 17 September 1999.

Hausmann, Vincent. "Envisioning the (W)hole World 'Behind Things': Denying Otherness in *American Beauty*." *Camera Obscura* 19:1: 113–149.

Herrick, Robert. "To the Virgins, to Make Much of Time." *Robert Herrick: Everyman's Poetry*. Everyman, 1996. 30.

IMDb: The Internet Movie Database. http://www.imdb.com/title/tt0169547/trivia. Accessed 11 September 2005.

Lorris, Guillaume de, and Jean de Meun. *The Romance of the Rose*. Trans. Frances Horgan. Oxford: Oxford University Press, 1994.

Mendes, Sam. Director. *American Beauty*. Dreamworks Pictures, 1999.

Smith, David L. "Beautiful Necessities": *American Beauty* and the Idea of Freedom. *Journal of Religion and Film* 6:2 (October 2002). http:www.unomaha.edu/jrf/am.beauty.htm. Accessed 11 September 2005.

"You Have to Develop an Eye For It": Anti-Aesthetic Art in Alan Ball's Vision

Kirstin Ringelberg

In both *American Beauty* and *Six Feet Under*, Alan Ball makes visual artists and the values they represent central to his core themes. Although Ball's own art is mainstream and appeals to a relatively broad audience, the aesthetic stance he promotes through characters like Ricky Fitts, Claire Fisher, and Billy Chenowith is much more challenging. It shows the influence of the most avant-garde art of the 1960s through the 1980s— art that deemphasizes traditional notions of beauty and emphasizes instead the *experience* of the aesthetic through the visceral, the performative, and the banal. Photography in particular is featured as the way to access both this experience and the nostalgia Ball seems to connect to it. As the art medium most familiar to the general public and the one in which they encounter Ball's own visual representations, photography allows Ball to tie together his vision, the artistic sensibilities of his artist characters, and the major themes of both *American Beauty* and *Six Feet Under*: death and the dysfunctional family. Representing visual imagery as participatory, intimate, and idiosyncratic, Ball's vision of beauty recuperates the kalliphobia of postmodern art and relates it to the typically atypical American family experience. In doing so, he accomplishes two impressive feats: teaching more mainstream audiences the importance (and pitfalls) of avant-garde art's desire to generate self-reflection and change, and reminding us that traditional notions of beauty (the beauty we've come to expect in our movies and television shows) are over-rated — and perhaps even damaging.

Anti-Aesthetic Art: A Brief Historical Overview

Kalliphobia is a concept introduced by Arthur C. Danto in *The Abuse of Beauty: Aesthetics and the Concept of Art.*[1] Rooted in the WWI-era Dada movement's anarchic rejection of traditional artistic approaches and results (because they felt traditional values had led to the atrocities and hypocrisies of the war), Danto sees many twentieth century avant-garde artists as kalliphobic — fearing or hating traditional notions of beauty as the goal of art making and experiencing. The coin of phrase is recent, but the idea isn't. Perhaps the most cited source for this issue would be Hal Foster's anthology *The Anti-Aesthetic: Essays on Post-Modern Culture.* Foster and Danto occupy two of several positions on the spectrum of contemporary art criticism: Foster sees the fundamentally anti-bourgeois and anti-capitalist critical art practices of anti-aesthetic artists as both the defining feature of Post-Modern (or any avant-garde) art and necessary to society. Danto, when he's in a good mood, sees Post-Modernism as pluralistic both formally and philosophically, but, like many more recent critics, he believes we have entered a new phase in which beautiful images are once again relevant and to be strived for. The basic argument breaks down like this: fans of the anti-aesthetic tend to desire art that is politically and socially critical, avoiding the seductions of beauty that either serve the dominant paradigm/power or distract the viewer from thought and action for change. For them, art is at its best when it fosters social change for the better of humanity by drawing attention to society's injustices; beautiful art, they argue, never does this because its beauty is our focus in seeing it. Fans of the so-called return to beauty occupy three basic positions: our troubled world needs the catharsis provided by a focus on sensual effects; anti-aesthetic fans are just jealous because most people "on the street" prefer beauty to conceptualism; and (Danto's position) you can have both beauty and criticality in the same object, so why not make art this way?

The majority of the canonized art of the twentieth and twenty-first centuries is anti-aesthetic. A rather elementary but common understanding of the art of this period proceeds with the story that in the nineteenth century, artists began to break away from the formal art schools (the academies) that had as their basic philosophy an emphasis on rigorous, scaffolded training in mimetic skills—learning how to draw, paint, and sculpt in the most realistic way possible, so that your apples look almost like real apples and your happy faces look different than your sad faces. This was coupled with a valuation of historical content (religious, historical, or ennobling subject matter) over mundane content. You could paint only apples or taxi drivers, but if you did, you wouldn't be as successful and lauded as your peer who paints people in Roman togas fighting for their ideals. This kind of art we now call academic—in the worst way. From the nineteenth into the twentieth centuries, increasing numbers of artists rejected sitting in a room with 35 other people sketching a plaster cast of a Roman copy of a Greek sculpture for several years so they could get it just right. They started painting, drawing, and sculpting in ways that showed their work (think of the surface of a Monet painting or Rodin sculpture, where you can sometimes literally see where the hand of the artist has been); in ways that showed they had a different idea of what looked "real" (think of a Van Gogh painting in which the sky or fields of wheat seem to move in a swirling dance); and with subjects that were not particularly ennobling (prostitutes, fruit, the corner of your studio) or completely absent (Kandinsky's floating colored shapes and lines). This emphasis on originality and increasing abstraction was coalesced (largely artificially and inaccurately) into a dominant theory of twentieth-century art: Modernism. Modernist theorists considered certain other forms of Modern art, such as Dada, Surrealism, and Social Realism, anathema because they involved either works not created manually by the artist, works that emphasized representation of objects or people, or works that showed specific social and political events and concerns rather than "pure" shape, color, and line. What both Modernist and non–Modernist works from this period have in common is their avant-garde courage: artists from all of these moments were making art that had not been seen before — art that redefined what art might mean. As such, they all de-emphasized beauty as previously defined because they thought it symbolized the academic, bourgeois, traditional, and unoriginal.

Dada art in particular de-emphasized beauty for a particular purpose: the beauty of ennobling art was supposed to create a better, even utopic, society. Yet there had been vast amounts of it, and still the trench warfare, mustard gas, and mutilation of WWI was occurring. So Dada artists rejected not just traditional approaches to art, but art itself, creating rather "anti-art." Utilizing random chance, picking up scraps of trash from the street or photographic images from newspapers and gluing them into chaotic, nonsensical forms, or selecting objects already made by others (especially if factory-produced and ordinary), like Ricky in *American Beauty*, they found beauty in the banal.[2] Dada artists were the most anti-aesthetic of the early twentieth century. In the 1950s and '60s, when most of their teachers were Modernists who believed fully in abstract, "pure" formalist art, some artists began to recuperate Dada and other critical approaches. This was in part because Modernism had become the new beauty — Jackson Pollock and Mark Rothko paintings were seen as beauty for the twentieth century in the same way that an Ingres *Odalisque* was in the academy of the nineteenth.[3] So Jasper Johns, Robert Rauschenberg, Claes Oldenburg, Andy Warhol, Eva Hesse, and a number of other artists looked to the unfinished, unpure, mixed-media, mass-media, and found-object works of the Dada and Surrealist artists for inspiration. Since then, the institutions of art have supported more and more what we now call Post-Modern art — art that might question originality through appropriating the work of a previous artist or question purity by including a wide variety of materials normally kept distinct or utilize mass-media graphic styles to critique consumer culture or require audience engagement to question authorship and ownership or be known only through documentary photographs to question commodification or emphasize contingency.[4] These very values will be touted by Claire and her art school teachers in *Six Feet Under*—that art should shock, rebel, be real, not pretend to false purity or meaningless beauty.

Visual artists began to see their media and approaches as unlimited by standard expectation or tradition — after all, even avant-gardists like Piet Mondrian made oil paintings on canvas to be hung on gallery walls. Most of the art produced in this renewed environment was staunchly anti-aesthetic — Joseph Kosuth's *One and Three Chairs* (1965), for example, consisted of an ordinary chair, a grainy black-and white photograph of that same chair, and a grainy black-and-white blown-up photocopy of a dictionary definition of the word *chair*, presented in a line along a gallery wall. Mining the meaning and intricacies of representation, Kosuth's work focused on the concept (Which, if any, of these "chairs" is the real/meaningful one? What and how does "chair" mean?) rather than the chair itself as an interesting or beautiful object made by his own craft skills. One of the most famous Post-Modern artists of the last 25 years is Cindy Sherman. Among her works is a photograph (*Untitled #175*, 1987) of what appears to be a party gone horribly wrong: the viewer sees, close up, a floor strewn with smashed cupcakes and vomit, with a pair of sunglasses reflecting the artist's horrified face in her trademark disguised self. Beauty is a subject of Sherman's work, certainly, but this viscerally nauseating image does not use the traditional means of beauty to maker her point.[5]

In the year in which *American Beauty* was released in theaters, the dominant vocabulary in the contemporary art world was this anti-aesthetic, critical style. Even if, like Jeff Koons' giant flower *Puppy* outside the Bilbao Guggenheim, some artists were embracing kitschy cuteness, irony and a dislike of the overtly aesthetic were the common postures of successful contemporary artists. The "return-to-beauty" movement was beginning, though — Peter Schjeldahl, *New York Times* and *New Yorker* art critic, had already written "Beauty is Back: A Trampled Esthetic Blooms Again."[6] Engaging the problematic of beauty at precisely the point when critics were gratefully hailing its return, Alan Ball took a side in the aesthetic debate — a side more common to the avant-garde artist than the Hollywood producer and writer.

American "Beauty": Video, Plastic Bags, and Not So Much Happiness

Perhaps the most memorable moment of anti-aesthetic avant-gardism in Alan Ball's work occurs in *American Beauty*, when Ricky shows Jane the video he made of a plastic bag swirling through the air and brushing the leaf-covered ground of a parking lot near a wall. Ricky explains why such a mundane, even unattractive set of subjects captured his attention.

> That's the day I realized that there was this ... entire life behind things. And this incredibly benevolent force that wanted me to know that there was no reason to be afraid. Ever. Video's a poor excuse, I know. But it helps me remember. I need to remember. Sometimes there's so much ... *beauty* ... in the world, I feel like I can't take it. And my heart is just going to cave in.

First, he sees the beauty in this image as revealing the presence of some benevolent force of good in the universe. That's a pretty standard association with an aesthetic image throughout the history of Western art, but particularly in the last two hundred years, when art's place in society became solidified as one that was to be isolated from other purposes and seen as a sign of great cultural (and therefore moral and political) achievement. To give an example, Vassily Kandinsky's non-objective paintings made between WWI and WWII, showing no references to the world of known objects but rather emphasizing color and line as unique and expressive elements, were intended by him and received by many as fundamentally spiritual images that could, if properly made with colors and forms in ideal balance, create a harmonic convergence in the universe (Taylor 69–75). To that point, Ricky is relatively traditional in looking for signs of "God" in beautiful things. However, what reveals this to Ricky is not the kind of image true traditionalists, or even most early-twentieth-century Modernists, would see as appropriate. An image of a plastic bag floating in the air, captured by a shaky hand-held video camera,[7] satisfies the aesthetic tastes of neither the extreme traditionalists who prefer representational painting and sculpture from before the twentieth century nor those of the Modernists with their desire for "pure," transcendent paintings or sculptures.

The aesthetic vocabulary that allows for Ricky's work to be considered "art" and "beauty" is one that comes from the more kalliphobic movements of the last century. Rather than focus on creating an object to be fetishized as beautiful, whole and complete, original and unique, these movements have emphasized ideas over objects, process over completion, repetition or appropriation over individuality, and fragmentation over wholeness. Utilizing banal objects or imagery, often not made but rather found by the artist, and technologies that de-emphasize the hand-made or craft-based aesthetics of previous arts, these movements pry open a space for Ricky's video— one that has only been mainstream within the avant-garde art world itself, and only then in the last 45 years.[8] Ricky's videotaping of dead birds and Jane giving him the finger would all make sense to viewers familiar with the conceptual, performance, and video art of the 1960s, '70s, and '80s. In these, recording whatever you come across, with little apparent editing or control on the part of the artists, with lighting and grainyness that is not as beautiful and slick as *American Beauty* itself, was both normal and ideal.[9]

What is perhaps most interesting is the tension between Ball's own relatively mainstream approach to his art and the much less mainstream perspectives of his artist characters. *American Beauty* was released within a year of Todd Solondz's *Happiness* (1998), a movie that explores many of the very same issues (family and personal dysfunction in the extreme, including the desire of an adult with children for a friend of his child's; murder; voyeurism; etc.) but in a much starker way. Solondz's movie is both visually and textually less appealing — less beautiful — than *American Beauty*: with its flat lighting, seemingly genuine lower-middle class interiors filled with kitschy tchotchkes, and largely ordinary-looking actors (older, overweight, sweaty, wearing droopy underwear and bland prints), *Happiness* does not shrink from showing the "real" dysfunctions of the American family in an unvarnished way. I heard of no viewer walking out on the fantasy and foreplay scenes between Lester and Angela, despite the fact that she is clearly below the age of consent; *Happiness'* much less beautiful scenes of pedophilic longing were much more controversial.[10]

Solondz' *Happiness* is undoubtedly even more anti-aesthetic, more avant-garde, than *American Beauty*. Although both share ironic titles, Solondz presents an unremittingly bleak (although often darkly funny) view of the Americans whose stories he tells. In addition to making them look more "normal" and thus relatable (with the blunt exception of Lara Flynn Boyle playing Helen Jordan, whose beauty does nothing to assuage her emptiness, but does give her an ugly self-righteousness akin to Angela's in *American Beauty*), the characters in *Happiness* have none of the "I've finally figured it out" excitement of Lester and Jane Burnham. Instead, they make stumbling, ineffective attempts to change their lives, but Solondz never allows them to succeed. Joy (ha ha) Jordan's every attempt at intimacy with her family and with men ends in tragicomic failure; Allen, whose lewd anonymous phone calls to Helen Jordan seem to be winning her over, is rejected within minutes of revealing his true physical self to her; Lenny Jordan tries sleeping with another woman after "separating" from his wife and discovers he doesn't "feel anything." The only sweet and effective relationship in the entire film seems to be that between Bill Maplewood, the pedophiliac therapist, and his young son Billy. As Billy begins to discover masturbation and other sexual issues, he seeks out his father for advice and information. In these night-time family-room chats, Bill is perfectly candid, encouraging his son to ask questions and giving him truthful answers in a gentle way. The occasional "would you like me to show you" from Bill, a more chilling part of the conversation given our knowledge of his rapes of two of Billy's classmates, is brushed off by Billy and results in nothing more sinister. Bill is warm and affectionate, not creepy, with his son, and Billy seems to genuinely appreciate his father's love and honesty, even in their final conversation (in which Billy asks if his father would molest him, and his father replies, "I'd jerk off instead"). More direct, more blunt, less beautiful in every way, *Happiness* is the *American Beauty* for the anti-aesthetic in-crowd.

It is easy to see why *American Beauty* might be more successful on a broad scale. Perhaps by adopting the anti-aestheticist's devotion to truth over beauty, Todd Solondz received critical acclaim (*Newsweek* awarded it #1 Movie of the Year and it won awards at film festivals at Cannes, Toronto, and São Paolo, as well as winning a Golden Globe) like Cindy Sherman but not widespread, Thomas Kincaid–level fame and money. *American Beauty*, while not quite mall art, is certainly more palatable in its depiction of dysfunction. One could argue that the slick, well-received *American Beauty* was made more so by director Sam Mendes than by Ball; however, by making his pedophilia more culturally acceptable because it was between a man and a beautiful teenage girl (a cheerleader and teen model, no less) rather than a man and an elementary school boy, Ball chose to create a scenario in which Lester's longing and actions, while easy to criticize, are also easy to understand for the average (straight male) viewer.[11] Additionally, Angela's clear distinctions (her appearance, attitude toward the opposite sex, and actions) from Jane keep Lester from seeming to break the incest taboo in his desire for his daughter's best friend. Unlike in Solondz's film, the cast of Ball's film is almost uniformly attractive (save perhaps Colonel and Mrs. Fitts, who are by no means as culturally unacceptable in their appearance as are the characters played by Camryn Manheim, Philip Seymour Hoffman, and Louise Lasser in *Happiness*). Even Angela achieves a certain self-awareness, unlike Solondz' mirror character Helen Jordan, and Colonel Fitts also has his moments of tenderness in which we can pity, if not like, him. Perhaps Ball's point in choosing to show his dysfunctional American families as beautiful and redeemable, given the right circumstances, is a nod to the requirements of Hollywood and future success.[12] Equally likely, and somewhat more fair, is the possibility that Ball wanted to emphasize the *Beauty* in his title. While Solondz shows us just how ugly we are, Ball wants us to see how beautiful we are on the surface, how that beauty is often merely skin-deep and deceptive, but how a different appreciation of beauty is possible if we "just look" under the surface. In other words, the surface visual beauty of his characters and the filmic work of those who present them to the viewer are necessary precisely because they seem at first so slick, so false, so Hollywood. As the audience for film and television comes increasingly to expect visual perfection in both actors and cinematography, it backs further away from the kind of self-awareness required to generate meaningful change in our patterns of dysfunction. Ball makes us first relate to Lester's desire for Angela — one that is created and satisfied by mainstream media; then, he points out that her type of beauty is a ruse beneath which lies nothing meaningful or satisfying. *American Beauty* uses the tools of its own machine to point out the flaw in that machine — our fantasies of life keep us from solving our actual problems. As contemporary artists Victor Burgin and Barbara Kruger use the look and language of advertising to point out social, political, and economic injustices related to consumerism, Ball uses our expectations for pleasure in the superficial to point out their emptiness. Look at the plastic bag, not the roses; the blood, not the family photo; Jane, not Angela. Look at what you normally ignore; don't allow yourself to be swayed into mindless catharsis by well-crafted surface.

"This Drawing Instantly Makes Me Feel Nauseous"

Six Feet Under gives Ball the opportunity to expand on his vision of the true artist as a recorder of real experiences; it also reveals a much more explicit embrace of the anti-aesthetic. The first artist we encounter is Billy Chenowith, but by the end of the second season, Claire has decided to go to LAC-Arts (presumably a twist on Cal Arts or CCA) for college. Claire, Billy, and the other artists in the series (Claire's teacher Olivier Castro-Staal, her friends Russell Corwin and Edie, and the occasional visiting artist or friend of her aunt's) all represent this more anti-aesthetic approach to art in either their work, their attitudes, or both.[13] Most notably, Olivier, while teaching a class in which the students are doing fairly traditional charcoal drawings, states the position: "But the way I tell if something is good is— does it make me want to throw up?

78

This drawing instantly makes me feel nauseous. You can tell if something is truthful, even if you don't understand it, if it affects your body. Your liver and your bowels are more important as an artist than your eyes, because they are so far away from your brain" (3.3). Excoriating a student for a sweet drawing of a pretty girl in a hat, Olivier praises Claire's work for making him want to vomit. This visceral response is prized by artists who are not interested in creating beauty in the traditional sense, but in making art that generates a strong response in the viewer, often even negatively. Perhaps the most obvious examples in the art world include the work of Chris Burden, whose performances included having himself shot in the arm (*Shoot*, 1971) and nailed to the hood of a Volkswagen Beetle (*Trans-fixed*, 1974), or William Pope.L's literally retch-inducing installations of organic materials (if you can call ketchup and hot dogs organic) that decompose in the gallery during the course of an exhibition (as in his retrospective traveling exhibition *eRacism*, 2002–04). Such artists view the primary purpose of art not as soothing catharsis but as visceral, vital, forcing one to think or react and thus change.

Following politically invested anti-aesthetic artists of the 1960s and '70s particularly, *Six Feet Under* represents commercialism as a negative value in art in several episodes. Artists of the '60s and '70s often made performance and body works or merely provided photographic or textual documentation of experiences already past or works destroyed after their making as a way to avoid the inherent exchange of goods (and therefore economic systems of oppression and injustice) in the art market. Art that involved more than one author, including anonymous participants, was seen as a way of avoiding the dominant Modernist myth of the solitary genius creating work in a vacuum (à la Jackson Pollock). In "Nobody Sleeps" (3:4), Claire and classmate Russell Corwin go to see a talk by visiting artist Scott Philip Smith on "The Responsibility of Art." Smith, ardently arguing the value of politically-based, shocking art, shows a work in which he had homeless people wipe their feces on an American flag (called the "skidmark flag" according to the DVD commentary by episode director Alan Poul). On the white board behind Smith, he has scrawled: "Art = Politics, Awareness alone = Bullshit! Apathy! Action! and Boredom." Although Claire and Russell initially think Smith is great because he is "so unafraid, so committed to what he believes in," they end their night at the Watts Towers, celebrating the even less commercial work of "outsider artist" Simon Rhodia, the construction worker who, in his spare time, built the towers out of found objects, then gave the title for the land to a neighbor and left. Throughout the episode, artists who are merely narcissistic and self-aggrandizing (and thus automatically in and of the system) are compared unfavorably to artists who care more about expressing themselves honestly. Over drinks, Olivier states that Claire is going to be a great artist who "can change the world" and Russell is going to be rich and famous—clearly contrasting the two. This constant blunt comparison between Russell and Claire seems to be one of Olivier's purposes as a character, as he enacts it regularly and always to remind the viewer whose tastes might not be so discerning that there is a qualitative difference between them. In "Making Love Work" (3:6), Olivier invokes (somewhat inaccurately) the critical terms of art and film critic and painter Manny Farber, "elephant art" and "termite art," to denigrate Russell's sculpture and praise Claire's. It's a neat trick, because Russell's sculpture is the first in the class to be given a term other than "mediocre," "terrible," or "redundant"; what begins as praise for Russell quickly turns sour (for him), as Olivier points out Claire's less obvious work and says that "termites work secretly at night, but they can tear down a house as fast as an elephant can. But they don't stop. They infest. Good job."[14]

In "The Opening" (3.9), Claire is asked to include one of her works (*Life on Earth*) in a big exhibition (that, without identifying it, includes a work by Catherine Opie, known for her photographs of lesbian couples and S&M practices, as well as banal images of strip malls).[15] Claire presumably underprices at $75 her duratrans-and-lightbox image of a skinny man and a plump woman in bathing suits, sunning themselves in lawn chairs on either side of a cemetery marker that says only "husband." Throughout the episode, she watches nervously as it fails to sell, while around her works that include cleaning products placed on the floor sell for four and five figures. When Russell's lame formalist sculpture *Single Helix* sells, one of the comments Claire makes is that "it's a really beautiful piece" (Claire's is described as "dark," "awesome," "magnificent" and "incredible"). Russell consoles her by saying that "disturbing work always takes longer to sell. Most people want something that's just pretty." As no clear difference is made between Claire's work and others in terms of quality (other works in the exhibition are not pretty also), the gist is that art sells by how overpriced it is—presumed rather than real value. This argument is amplified in Season Five when Claire's gallery dealer establishes that he's only interested in selling her work when it matches the kind he took her on for (photocollages not entirely dissimilar from those of the The Starn Twins), not when she tries something different.[16] So the idea that there is a consumerist art market like any other kind of economic force, and that this market is to be resisted with integrity and work that is meaningful, fully connects Claire's world to Alan Ball's as well as to the broader idea that superficiality is fundamentally dissatisfying.

The role of Federico "Rico" Diaz is relevant here. As an artist aestheticizing death, he makes the ugly beautiful again, and he's widely touted for it. Certainly his skills are appreciated by both the Fishers and their clients; many episodes make brief or extended reference to his ability to make the dead look radiant and whole, whatever disfiguring event placed them in his care. But Rico's art is clearly not considered in the same class as that of the "real" artists in the series, because he is covering up, not revealing, the truth. In "The Eye Inside"(3:3), Rico admits to Nate that, while he is great at the kind of work he has to do downstairs, it doesn't come naturally to him to do what needs to be done upstairs, like comfort a crying client (as Nate has just done unaffectedly). This scene, I think, reiterates the core Ball concept that often those best known for making things look beautiful on the surface (like Rico and Carolyn Burnham and Angela) are not capable of handling the bigger, more real issues of life successfully — as if the skill for aestheticizing cannot exist easily in equal parts with the skill for coping. Rico cleans up death, and as such denies its truth and cannot handle its pain. Although every character in *Six Feet Under* at some point or in some way denies or mishandles their problems, Rico is the most consistently likely to live in a false world of his own construction: he thinks a gay man is having an affair with his wife, he tries to ignore first his wife's addiction and then her need for help overcoming it, he doesn't see his separation coming, and he imagines a false intimacy with several other women.[17]

"You Have to Develop an Eye For It."

Alan Ball believes that art, like human nature and family dysfunction, is not something that leaps clearly to your vision and is immediately understood in traditional ways. Rather, it's something for which we must develop an eye, a way of looking beneath the surface. Ball's familiarity with the visual arts gave him the ability to select from a wide variety of references; his choice to emphasize the anti-aesthetic, the narrative, the critical, the visceral, and the banal in the art and artists he includes in his work challenges us as viewers to reject superficial or traditional notions of beauty and by extension the values they support. Like Ricky, Claire, and Billy, we want to see more, to see more deeply, and to not be fooled by the seductions of the merely beautiful or the easily consumed. Especially when the beautiful, like Angela, or Carolyn's roses, or Rico's embalming, barely mask the much messier, uglier, more real truth underneath. It is appropriate that Lester is shot while looking at the black-and-white photograph of his family in happier times—although the voice-over suggests his nostalgic remembrance of what a good life he had actually led, signified by this charming picture of smiling faces, one of the real points here is that picture is *not* true—it isn't an accurate representation of the Burham family. More beautiful and meaningful, as Ricky shows us, is the blood pooling under Lester's head and his dead face—the messy reality of Lester's actual life and inevitable death.[18]

Anti-aesthetic art is what Ball himself is engaged in. Although *American Beauty* was indeed beautiful to look at, the underlying meaning of the film was to pay attention to what is wrong with the American family and, by extension, our culture—to see typical beauty as always false. In *Six Feet Under*, Ball pushes the notion further—beauty of any kind is almost impossible to find here, and the problems of the Fishers often seem unrelenting. With more control over the finished product as executive producer than he had as writer in *American Beauty*, Ball seems to have pushed for less glamorous settings and cinematography. The Fisher house in *Six Feet Under* is indeed painfully normal, only its Craftsman exterior (and the bodies in the basement) revealing any character. Compared to the clean, tastefully and expensively decorated cream and blue interiors of the Burnham home, the Fishers are surrounded by older, dingier household goods in dusty off-whites, faded greens and browns. Certainly no one would get outraged over potential spilled beer on a couch at the Fishers' the way Carolyn does at the Burnhams.' Ruth Fisher dresses more like Mrs. Fitts than Carolyn Burnham. The most Hollywood-glamorous family in *Six Feet Under* is Brenda's—and they are inarguably the most dysfunctional on the show. Rather than gather around a formal dinner table, the Fishers congregate at the kitchen table, idly pulling food out of the cabinets to nibble while discussing their problems. Admittedly, some problems in the extended Fisher household can feel soap-operatic, but most have the ring of truth. By not denying those problems, which mimic those in our own families, to make a more standard, T.V.-appropriate, more-beautiful-than-true series, Ball supports the anti-aesthetic notion that understanding, representing, and working to change our problematic society is much more important than hiding behind cathartic beauty, even if that might make us feel better for a little while.[19] After all, you never know when it's all going to end.

Notes

1. Danto coins the phrase by using the Greek root kalos, usually translated as "beauty." For a more brief and direct discussion, see Danto's "Kalliphobia in Contemporary Art," *Art Journal* 63:2 (Summer 2004): 24–35. This volume of *Art Journal* contains several articles (stemming from a session of the annual College Art Association conference) addressing the growing cry among some artists and critics in the last decade for a "return to beauty" and the conflicts this creates with the previous century's emphasis on the deliberately un-beautiful, through abstraction as well as conceptualism. An earlier volume, *Art Journal* 56:1 (Spring 1997) contains a similar cluster of essays on aesthetics.

2. Although Marcel Duchamp claimed at some points to be searching for an aesthetic numbness or disinterest rather than attraction to the ordinary objects he assembled into his readymades, his choices and his earliest statements belie this widely accepted interpretation. It would appear Duchamp recast his goals in light of the over-fondness of some viewers to read objects like *Fountain* (1917), a white porcelain urinal turned to lie flat and signed pseudonymously *R. Mutt*, as abstracted objects akin in their beautiful effects to the photographs of an arch-formalist like Edward Weston.

3. I wish to reinforce that this is neither my nor a wholly accurate interpretation of the work of most artists embraced by formalist critics; much art historical analysis throughout the last 100 years shows these works to have more significant meaning politically, religiously, and as social critique than was accepted by critics and encouraged by teachers from 1945 on. Modernists themselves used works by Pollock and Rothko to argue the United States' ideological supremacy in comparison to the USSR during the 1950s; see Eva Cockcroft, "Abstract Expressionism, Weapon of the Cold War," *Artforum* 15:10 (June 1974): 39–41.

4. The literature on Modernism and Post-Modernism in art history is vast, and I have radically simplified some very complex issues in order to provide the unfamiliar reader with a helpful framework for the art-historical context of Alan Ball's work, of which he is evidently well aware. Readers wishing an introductory but intelligent study of these issues would do well to read any of The Open University art history textbooks, published by Yale University Press, but particularly the *Art of the 20th Century* series of four books.

5. In "I'll Take You" (2:12), the flyer for LAC-Arts, Claire's school, advertises Sherman as one of their former graduates. In the tour of the school, the guide compares Billy Chenowith's works unfavorably to those of Gregory Crewdson. Jill Soloway, who wrote the episode and provides commentary on the DVD, was supplied with the reference by Alan Ball (she had never heard of the artist). Crewdson apparently liked the homage and became the photographer for the Season Three promotional advertisements, creating the flower-strewn, oddly lit images fans tried to read for clues of upcoming plot twists.

6. Schjeldahl, like Danto, believes in a redefined notion of beauty for our era-one that, interestingly enough, would include a lot of what most non-art-institution people would consider pretty un-beautiful.

7. Although some of the hand-held video shots in the film had to be re-shot by a full film

crew, Mendes gave Will Bentley (the actor portraying Ricky) a working video camera and encouraged him to shoot whatever interested him. According to Mendes' DVD commentary, some of the most intriguing imagery in the film came from Bentley's experimentation; the bag scene was, however, fully scripted by Ball before the film was shot, and (again according to the commentary) Mendes shot that scene almost exactly as written.

8. An interesting occurrence in my classrooms is my students' initial discomfort and confusion when faced with Modernism (now more than 50 years "old"), followed by complete disbelief when we get to Post-Modern anti-aesthetic approaches. This leads me to believe that although Ricky's video would raise no eyebrows in the arts community, it would still be seen as avant-garde among those in the general viewing audience for *American Beauty*.

9. One of the widely touted first moments in video art occurred when Nam June Paik took a Sony Portapak out to record a visit of the Pope to NYC in 1965. Other incarnations that might share Ricky's perspective include Vito Acconci's videotaping of himself lying on the floor of his apartment, addressing the video lens (and thus the viewer) from only a few inches away as if he is trying to get us to have sex with him (*Theme Song*, 1973); or Sophie Calle and Gregory Shephard simultaneously videotaping their every conversation as they cross the U.S. on a roadtrip (*Double Blind*, 1992).

10. The film was originally produced by October Films, which, when taken over by Universal Studios and their parent company Seagram, was forced to drop it (no official word was ever given on why, although rumors suggested CEO Ron Meyer was offended by the pedophilic content). *Happiness* was then picked up by two of its producers and distributed by them under their company Good Machine.

11. In fact, in the audio commentary on the DVD, director of photography Conrad L. Hall, initially disconcerted by the relationship between Lester and Angela, is persuaded by Alan Ball to see it as normal-Hall realizes that, although he would never act on them, he does see fantasies about his childrens' teenage female friends as "normal." I doubt we'd hear the same admission in Solondz's film commentary-showing the clear sexist and homophobic distinctions our society makes between some kinds of pedophilia and others.

12. In Ball's original screenplay, Lester does have sex with Angela; Ball claims to prefer the film version of events, however.

13. Just as this essay was due to the editor, the *Six Feet Under* website introduced a new segment, "Claire's Artwork" (www.hbo.com/sixfeetunder/artwork/), in which you can see many of the individual works presented as Claire's throughout the run of the show. In the commentary we learn that the artists responsible for those works are Doug Hyun, Danny Feld, John Johnston (all photographers), Kim Dane (responsible for the drawings and paintings in Claire's class), Margot Lovinger (who made the "Medusa" portrait of Claire), Rusty Lipscomb (the set decorator), Lara Porzak (who created the photographs at Brenda and Nate's wedding), David Meanix (the artist responsible for the collaged photos that make Claire briefly successful), and Matt Burlingame (maker of the family diorama). I list them all here both to ensure they get the credit for all their hard work and to point out the wide variety of artists and media that are shown as "Claire's Artwork." This diversity is common in art school as students learn the various media and approaches, but it is also part of the general trend in Ball's aesthetic, in which Claire must experiment and doesn't limit herself to only one medium or style. In the website commentary, several of the "real" artists remark on the collaborative nature of making the work for the show-another part of the non-traditional approach common to the aesthetic view promoted in the series.

14. Olivier says that the terms were invented by "the Fluxists," a significant conceptual art movement (loosely so) of the 1960s and '70s that included among its members Yoko Ono. Farber's essay, largely film criticism, contrasts films, even avant-garde ones, that are bombastic or obtusely symbolic in their approach to other films, even commercial ones, that appeal with smaller, more subtle cues. When Olivier introduces these terms, none of the students know what they mean, and as a professor I love his response: "Who are you people, don't you guys read?" The essay is indeed well known in film circles and some art circles.

15. The Opie photograph *Self-Portrait* (1993) from the episode, shown several times, is a poignant choice. In this image, Opie has had someone make a drawing on her back that she photographs, revealing both the drawing and her own back, shoulders, and head in larger-

than-life-size scale. The drawing depicts what seems like a typical second-grade child's image of a happy couple holding hands in front of a gabled house, the sun shining from behind a cloud as birds fly by. Upon closer inspection, the viewer sees both that the happy couple consists of two women, and that the red lines constituting the drawing are the bloody cuts from a sharp object pushed into Opie's freckled skin. Opie's dream of a happy lesbian family is thus written literally in blood and pain and is both self-revealing and revealing of our shared desires (the familiarity of the drawing instantly connecting its viewers to the concept). This photograph connects thematically to the Fishers' various hopes for family happiness and stability, but particularly David's struggles in a heteronormative society.

16. Throughout the series, one wonders just where the line is for Ball-he seems to enjoy presenting art both as one of the only ways to achieve real enlightenment and also as the province of over-dramatizing, lazy, emotionally unstable, manipulative liars. Unlike the processes of most accepted performance, conceptual, and video artists, Ball's artists seem to stumble upon their beauty, with little awareness of what they are trying to do until someone else points out that it's good. This attitude is expressed directly in "Everyone Leaves" (3:10).

17. Some readers may argue that Nate is equally problematic in his marriage to Lisa and constant rationalizations and escapes. However, Nate regularly introduces the *most* aware interpretations of events, particularly with clients. Rico's blind spots are perhaps less dramatic than Nate's (or David's in the carjacking episode, for example), and he does improve his ability to manage clients, but Rico's illusions are more fundamental to the fabric of his character.

18. For a quite different critical reading of the role of photography and video in *American Beauty* based in psychoanalytic theory, see Vincent Hausmann's excellent essay "Envisioning the (W)hole World "Behind Things": Denying Otherness in *American Beauty*," *Camera Obscura* 19:1 (2004): 112–149.

19. The HBO series *Sex in the City* is an example of the more typical approach: when gorgeous, designer-clad, hardly-ever-working Carrie's biggest problem is whether to move to Paris with her world-famous artist boyfriend or stay in New York with her incredibly wealthy longtime lover (nick-named for his impressive genitals), it's hard to think, "Oh yeah, that's just like what happened to me."

Works Cited

Cockcroft, Eva. "Abstract Expressionism, Weapon of the Cold War." *Artforum* 15/10 (June 1974): 39–41.

Danto, Arthur C. *The Abuse of Beauty: Aesthetics and the Concept of Art.* Chicago and Lasalle, IL: Open Court, 2003.

Danto, Arthur C. "Kalliphobia in Contemporary Art." *Art Journal* 63/2 (Summer 2004): 24–35

Farber, Manny. "White Elephant Art vs. Termite Art." *Negative Space: Manny Farber On The Movies.* Da Capo Press, 1998 (first published in *Film Culture Magazine* 1962).

Foster, Hal. *The Anti-Aesthetic: Essays on Post-Modern Culture.* Port Townsend, WA: Bay Press, 1983.

Schjeldahl, Peter. "Beauty is Back: A Trampled Esthetic Blooms Again." *New York Times* (September 29, 1996): 161.

Taylor, Mark C. *Disfiguring: Art, Architecture, Religion.* Chicago and London: The University of Chicago Press, 1992.

Meet the Chenowiths:
The Therapeutic Drama
of *Six Feet Under*

Robert F. Gross

The imagination boggles at a culture made
up mostly of virtuosi of the self [Rieff 32].

Although healthy persons communicate and enjoy communicating,
the other fact is equally true, that *each individual is an isolate,
permanently non-communicating, permanently unknown,
in fact unfound* [Winnicott 187].

In 1966, sociologist Philip Rieff looked backward with nostalgia and
around him with dismay. He contrasted the demise of *religious man*,
who was characterized by his reliance on tradition, social institutions,
and "a consensus of 'shalt nots'" (15), with the rise of *psychological man* —
a figure of rampant individualism, fundamentally anarchic in the way
it imagined itself as the innately good individual struggling against the
powers of a repressive and evil social order. In *The Triumph of the Therapeutic: Uses of Faith after Freud*, Rieff lamented the advent of a modern culture that had given rise to a plethora of new-fangled beliefs and
practices, "all aiming to confirm us in our devastating illusions of individuality and freedom" (10). Although one may take exception to the
conservative aspects of this elegy for the passing of a retrospectively idealized order based on renunciation and its supersession by an age of
deluded self-indulgence, there is no doubt that the book focused on a
significant development in modern culture.

In the decades that have followed *The Triumph of the Therapeutic*, sociologists and cultural historians have continued to refine and elaborate on Rieff's basic insight. Often replacing the term *psychological man* with the less totalizing (and sexist) term *therapeutic culture*, Frank Furedi, Ann Swidler, Eva Illouz, and Philip Cushman (to name only a few) have charted the effects of an ideology that prizes self-affirmation and growth above all other values. Furedi articulates the fundamental premise of this ideology: "Therapeutic culture regards the affirmation of self as the central element of the good life" (147). This therapeutic self is not that of the nineteenth-century *Bildungsroman*, whether Goethe's *Wilhelm Meister's Apprenticeship* or Charles Dickens's *Great Expectations*. In those novels, the protagonists work toward the harmonious realization of self within the conventions of the society. In the *Bildungsroman*, the world is a school; in *Six Feet Under*, it is group therapy. The therapeutic self, as Rieff feared (and others might celebrate), puts self-affirmation above harmonious social integration. As Ann Swidler explains, the therapeutic self is "the seat of authentic feelings and needs that must be explored, brought to life, and expressed" (246).[1]

So it is with the characters of *Six Feet Under*. If they sit down with a book, chances are they are reading self-help literature— *Now That You Know*, *Hunger for Love*, or *The Whole Child*. Whether they are involved in a visit to Essalen or a wilderness weekend, a sexual addiction twelve-step group or an EST-like weekend seminar, premarital counseling or a stay in a psychiatric ward (complete with medications, intensive "talk" therapy, and electroshock), the characters of *Six Feet Under* are constant shoppers in the therapeutic marketplace.

Indeed, the focus on the therapeutic is so intense that one cannot help but sense a lack of interest in the world beyond the most immediate relationships, even to the extent that the world dwindles to little more than a vehicle for self-realization. When David is coerced into resigning from his deaconship in a local parish because of homophobia, he does not speak from the pulpit about the church's need to have a conscience on matters of social justice, but rather his own shame and inability to fully love himself. These characters do not discuss history, science, politics, economics, social issues, philosophy ... there is very little room for any topic that does not focus on personal growth and the immediate personal relationships that effect it. In this respect, they are the "virtuosi of the self" that so boggled Philip Rieff's imagination decades earlier (32). This limitation of the dramatic universe to issues of personal growth contributes to the overall failure of the series to address political concerns, which Robert Deam Tobin has discussed (90–91).

The therapeutic ethos is so deeply ingrained in the perspective of *Six Feet Under* that events not usually thought of as therapeutic become so. When Ruth takes a course in flower arrangement, it becomes far less the acquisition of a skill than a therapeutic exercise in the benefits of respiration (1:11). Blocked and frustrated in her attempts to produce a satisfying arrangement, Ruth is advised by her teacher to be aware of her breathing as she works. Concentrating on her breath, she soon creates an arrangement that dazzles everyone in the classroom. In this scene, art is produced through connection to one's emotions, and there are techniques, easily mastered, that can emancipate the inhibited self and result in creativity. Ruth does not learn to arrange flowers by studying color relationships or principles of composition; she intuitively finds these aesthetic principles within herself by learning how to breathe, and the result is a work of art that is instantly accessible to everyone in the classroom. The personal, when revealed, turns out to be the universal. The lesson is clear: any task, rightly approached, can become a therapeutic exercise.

The dominant means of therapy in *Six Feet Under*, however, is the cultivation of intimate relationships. Ann Swidler has identified three ideologies about intimate, committed relationships at work in the United States today: (1) American individualism, with its idea of a relationship as a contract; (2) American fundamentalism, with its idea of obedience to God's will; and (3) the therapeutic ethic, with its idea of responsibility to one's deepest self and its potential. In this series, relationships are repeatedly judged by the extent to which they help the individuals in that relationship to grow. As Swidler explains:

> The therapeutic ethic helps individuals discover their true selves, so they can make authentic choices that reflect what they "really" want. Its underlying assumption is that individuals who have "gotten in touch with" their real selves, freed of the inauthentic residues of family pressures, social roles, or others' expectations, will be able to forge genuine bonds to others, ties that will be strong because they satisfy genuine needs (not just arbitrary preferences) of both parties [143].[2]

This notion of the therapeutic relationship is articulated most fully and directly by Rabbi Ari, who introduces Nate to the notion of the "soulmate." She defines it as "the person who makes you the most you could possibly be" and "the person who challenges you to grow." The other person in the relationship becomes, in effect, a means for furthering your therapeutic growth. For Rabbi Ari, the therapeutic quest is nothing less than salvational: "If anything is going to save you," she tells Nate, "that will" ("Back to the Garden," 2:7).

Six Feet Under develops as a skein of intertwined narratives of personal growth, with *growth* defined as a deepening acceptance of self and openness to others. The process of growth is mostly dramatized through the ups and downs of intimate relationships. The primary questions the series develops include: Will Nate and Brenda develop a strong, committed relationship? Will Keith and David? Is Nate acting in his best interests by marrying Lisa? Is Claire setting herself up for trouble by getting so close to Gabe? To Russell? Will Ruth let Hiram enter her life, will Nikolai let her enter his, and is the emotionally reticent George the right choice for her as a husband?

Six Feet Under is marked as an artifact of the therapeutic culture, not only through the potential expansion of the concept of therapy to virtually all human experience and the understanding of intimate relations as vehicles for personal growth, but also through a variety of more narrowly defined, usually professional, psychotherapeutic experiences undergone by the characters in the series. The frequent appearance of therapy is not merely the result of the series's attempt to realistically depict American middle-class life, but is more importantly a reflection of the therapeutic ethos that pervades the series. Examining some examples of the role that therapy plays in the series will reveal the ambivalences of contemporary therapeutic culture toward the therapy it both seeks and fears.

Professional psychotherapy first makes its way into the reserved world of the Fishers in the wake of the patriarch's death. Following what might be psychoanalytically described as an episode of "acting-out" (she puts the foot of a corpse in a classmate's locker at school), Claire is sent to Gary, an itinerant psychotherapist who works a circuit of five local high schools ("An Open Book," 1:5). Sensing Claire's melancholia and frustration, Gary urges her to talk about her feelings. Responding to her talent and interest in the visual arts, he recommends that she consider entering a conservatory after high school, rather than a college. Overall, his effect on Claire seems to be positive.

From the beginning, however, Claire's experience with therapy unfolds within severe constraints. Since the Fishers are not wealthy, Claire's sessions are little more than brief conversations with an overworked employee of the school district, who at first even has trouble remembering her name, and whose session with Claire and her mother is so brief that Ruth is astonished — "That's all?" Ruth remarks with perplexity ("An Open Book," 1:5). As time goes on, other problems emerge: Gary has his own problems with personal relationships; he may have been sexually involved with one of Claire's high school friends; he violates the confidentiality of the therapeutic relationship by calling in a police detective when Claire's boyfriend Gabe is in trouble; and once he learns that his position is being terminated, he is incapable of responding to her with empathy. Realistically drawn with both strengths and weaknesses, Claire's sessions with Gary are simultaneously helpful and disturbingly limited. Watching this plot unfold, we are shown that psychotherapy is no panacea. Limited by both structural and psychological factors, it creates its own troubled dynamics.

Therapy is viewed with affection and wry amusement when Ruth attends a weekend self-help program called "The Plan" and is temporarily swept up in the exhilaration and promise of autonomy it offers. "It teaches you how to feel really good about yourself and get what you want out of life" explains Ruth's co-worker Robby ("Out, Out, Brief Candle," 2:2). The Plan seems to be a thinly disguised version of Landmark Forum, Inc. "Forum," as it is casually called by many of its adherents, is a highly lucrative repackaging of EST, a therapeutic program that enjoyed considerable vogue in the '70s and early '80s, particularly on the West Coast.[3] Ruth's counterculture sister Sara gives a history of The Plan that mirrors that of Landmark Forum, albeit in slightly more scandalous terms:

> I did it myself back in the 70s when it was still called "Transitional Focus," before Ernst Vollhofer was busted for tax evasion and sold it to the Canadians. That's when it became "The Plan" ["In Place of Anger," 2:6].

Daniel Attias, the director of an episode during Ruth's involvement with The Plan, describes it as an "EST-like" program ("Back to the Garden," 2:7, audio commentary). The Plan, like Landmark Forum, is made up of intense weekend workshops in which the participants are urged to "get complete" by coming to terms with painful experiences in their lives. They are called upon to get up and "share" their stories, after which the group invariably responds with applause. There are banks of phones available for the participants to call important people in their lives, as Ruth does, and forgive them for the suffering they have caused. At the end of the program, participants go through a "graduation" to which they are urged to invite friends and relatives. Robby invites Ruth to attend his "graduation," and she is moved by the experience of liberation that it offers.

Riffing on the root metaphor of Landmark, The Plan presents its vision of the self in architectural images. Asking Ruth if she is merely "a guest in her own house?" the leader of the session calls upon her "to renovate" her life ("The Plan," 2:3). At The Plan, Ruth is rewarded for opening up and sharing her "real feelings" with a roomful of strangers who pay attention and applaud her honesty, even when she vents frustration with the group. The foundation of The Plan is one frequently encountered in therapeutic culture: that repression is crippling, and the best thing one can do for oneself is express one's repressed emotions (a belief so absolutely fundamental to psychotherapy that it could already be satirized by Rachel Crothers as a cliché of the nascent therapeutic culture in her 1924 Broadway comedy *Expressing Willie*).

Like Claire, Ruth seems to benefit from her therapeutic experience. It leads her to express her anger, communicate more openly and freely with her children, and re-establish contact with her estranged sister. But her adoption of the building metaphors bewilders her children and leads to comic moments. After only a few episodes, Ruth has derived some benefits from The Plan and jettisons it. In the therapeutic marketplace, there is little room for full and extended involvement. Therapies are commodities, meant to be used and discarded like any other purchase. Enthusiastic commitments are generally qualified and short lived. In therapeutic culture, the high modernist notion of the psychoanalyst as guru has deteriorated, as clients have learned to be shrewd consumers. Rieff had noticed this development, though he seems to have been unaware of its economic underpinnings: "Indeed, the therapy of all therapies, the secret of all secrets, the interpretations of all interpretations, in Freud, is not to attach oneself too passionately to any one particular meaning, or object" (59). Ruth, for all her naiveté, seems a sufficiently savvy therapeutic consumer not to fully identify any particular therapy with the larger therapeutic project of her life: as it once was with flower arranging, so now it is with The Plan. Momentary immersion is necessary for growth, but so is distance, and the objectifying comic perception that goes with it.

What are we to make of Claire's sessions with Gary and Ruth's immersion in The Plan? Neither is a panacea, nor a total fraud. Watching them, we are left with an uncomfortable mixture of critical detachment and grateful belief. As Ashley Sayeau amusingly (and accurately) puts it, "So, what do we make of our times when all this supposed nonsense actually works?" (97). As viewers, we are left to judge each therapy, and be aware of our own feelings toward each, as well as our feelings about therapeutic culture as a whole.

What Philip Rieff did not perceive in 1966, and what has become increasingly clear through later analyses, most notably the work of Philip Cushman, is how therapeutic culture has been shaped and maintained by the capitalist marketplace in ways that are at least as manipulative and controlling as any institution in traditional societies. The criterion for judging the value of a particular therapeutic regimen in *Six Feet Under*, as in much of contemporary life, is totally pragmatic — and since each regimen is judged solely by its immediate effect, there is no adherence to any particular psychotherapeutic school. The characters of the series, like much of the American middle-class today, navigate their way through a bewildering bazaar of ever-proliferating psychotherapeutic tools and techniques and utilize them without meticulously scrutinizing their scientific, philosophic, and ideological underpinnings. Life is rough, and our desire to assuage our suffering may lead us to make various therapeutic choices that may at best be incoherent and at worst conflicting. Most insidiously, however, we have become vulnerable to the manipulations of a therapeutic marketplace, rife with hucksterism, that tantalizes us with the prospect of a more complete and satisfying existence through continuous and promiscuous therapeutic consumption (Cushman 271, 275).

But, while professional therapies are presented in a way that elicits our ambivalence, the whole-hearted and uncritical acceptance of the therapeutic ethic of intimate relationships is perhaps the most fundamental unexamined premise of the series. *Six Feet Under* so thoroughly assumes that viewers subscribe to the therapeutic ethic that involvement with the series would become virtually impossible without it. That premise is not questioned here. Indeed, I have discovered that my own overall acceptance of the therapeutic culture and its understanding of intimate relations is too strongly inculcated in me to allow me to find an Archimedean point from which to critique it. Perhaps the greatest value for me in studying *Six Feet Under* is that it has made me aware of the extent to which I operate within its assumptions—a lesson learned not without irritation. Does the show create a world far too self-absorbed for its own good? Am *I* too self-absorbed for my own good? But would it be good to dismiss all the compassionate and civilizing discoveries of the therapeutic culture? It may be egotistical to focus on personal growth too exclusively, but it may be brutal to ignore it.

The ambivalence I feel is embedded in the series itself, nowhere more clearly than in the Chenowith family. The Chenowiths are established from their first appearances as the embodiment of the therapeutic culture at its most perverse, self-dramatizing, and self-deluding. They are the antithesis of the Fishers, who are presented as a family that is hesitant to express its feelings, drawn into therapy only by emotional turbulence in the wake of the patriarch's demise. So it is no coincidence that the day of Nathaniel Fisher's death coincides with the entrance of Brenda Chenowith, the series's ultimate therapeutic character, into its relatively staid and repressed existence. Brenda is the character who not only comes from a family of therapists, but who in turn invites analysis, resists analysis, and uses analysis both as an aid and a weapon in her dealings with others. And it is through Brenda and her family — brother Billy and parents Margaret and Bernard — that the nightmare side of therapeutic culture makes its presence felt most strongly.

Brenda is quickly characterized in the first episode as a person given to casual sexual encounters and psychotherapeutic discourse. Wounded by both psychotherapy and psychotherapists, and canny enough to play the analytic game herself, she becomes the most intensely conflicted figure in the first two seasons of *Six Feet Under*, an embodiment of all the series's fascination with and fears about therapeutic culture. A practitioner of shiatsu, she reads trauma through the body, interpreting a tense, knotted muscle in Nate's back as an old psychic wound ("The Will," 1:2). Quickly perceiving his fear of mortality, she calls him on it and provokes his frustrated response "Are you a shrink?" "No! God, no! No!" she responds with alarm, adding "Both my parents are." He accuses her of indulging in "psychobabble." He asks defensively, "You analyze guys on the first date?" ("Pilot," 1:1). She arranges for Nate and David to ride on the bus that hit their father's car and caused his death. As the second episode ends, the brothers are riding the bus, overcome with grief, as Brenda looks on with a pleasure that could be benign or maleficent. In a later episode, Connor, an old boyfriend of Brenda's, says he broke up with her because he grew tired of her playing "Fucking Freud" all the time ("Life's Too Short," 1:9). "For Brenda, there are no coincidences," observes Margaret archly, alluding to Freud's famous denial of chance ("An Open Book," 1:5).

It is only in the Chenowiths' shadow world of psychotherapy that we encounter references to the high priest of therapeutic culture, Sigmund Freud. For all the various therapies encountered in *Six Feet Under*, none of them are, strictly speaking, psychoanalytic. Even for Rieff in 1966, Freud, however impressive, was already passé. "Freud has already receded into history" he observed. "His problems are not ours" (21). And yet the Chenowiths are marked with signifiers still popularly associated with Freudian psychology: they are affluent, sexually transgressive, and defined in relation to the incest taboo.

Brenda's capacity for using the insights of therapy as tactics to control her personal relationships is explained when we meet her mother and father. Brenda had already described her parents not as healers, but as "whores" who would do anything for money ("The Foot," 1:3), and their affluent, designer surroundings, so removed from the middle-class world of the Fishers, indicates they have flourished in their prostitution. From early on, psychoanalysis was seen as a luxury item, expensive for its clients and lucrative for its practitioners. Kenneth Rice, the Machiavellian psychoanalyst of S. N. Behrman's 1936 high comedy, *End of Summer*, explains why he changed his career from physician to psychoanalyst: "I gave up tonsilectomy for the soul. The poor have tonsils but only the rich have souls" (182–183). Despite the proliferation of self-help manuals, group therapies, and television shows, this early perception of psychotherapy as an indulgence for the rich persists, and it resurfaces in its depiction of psychotherapy here. This, of course, is not a false perception. The access to quality health care in twenty-first century America is largely determined by wealth, and mental health care is a part of that. But the perception also resonates with much deeper, almost mythic fears about psychotherapy that the Chenowiths embody, in which psychotherapy, sexual license, and wealth become signifiers of a dangerous decadence.

American popular culture has long shown a deep ambivalence toward psychotherapy, with images of the psychotherapist-as-healer alternating with images of the psychotherapist-as-exploiter — sometimes within a single work, such as Alfred Hitchcock's *Spellbound*.[4] In *Six Feet Under*, the Chenowiths contrast not only with Billy's brilliant and invisible Dr. Hanover, but with all the other therapeutic figures. The Chenowiths, apparently the most wealthy and successful of the lot, are also the most purely destructive.

The Chenowith clan owes its existence to a violation of ethical boundaries. Although there is some disagreement about the details— Brenda says her mother was Bernard's patient, Margaret says she was only his intern — both agree that the relationship was transgressive. "The second I laid down, I knew I wasn't going to get off that couch!" Margaret crows ("The Secret," 2:10). The psychiatrist's couch becomes a place not of healing but of illicit sexuality. *Lying down on the couch* has long been a popular double entendre. In the popular imagination, the libidinous drives that psychoanalysis (and by extension, all psychotherapies) sets out to explore undergo a displacement and become identified with the analytic process and the analyst, making them both the cause and the embodiment of the very drives that psychotherapy sets out to treat. The powerful attraction of this metonymic slippage can be seen not only in *Six Feet Under*, but in Augusten Burroughs's bestselling 2002 memoir, *Running with Scissors*, in which a mentally disturbed mother entrusts her son to the care of her psychotherapist, who turns out to be the head of a household defined by a host of libidinous transgressions, including sexual abuse and incest.

The violation of the ethical boundary between Margaret as patient and Bernard as therapist resonates with the theme of incest that runs through the Chenowith family. The repetition of inappropriately sexually charged interactions among the Chenowiths raise the specter of incest. When Nate first encounters Billy as an intruder in his girlfriend's apartment, this young man, clad only in a towel and disconcertingly familiar with Brenda, feeds Nate's jealous suspicions. His explanation of his relationship to Brenda only worsens matters. "She's my sister. My mother. My sister. My mother." ("An Open Book," 1:5.). This riddle, accompanied by self-inflicted blows on the head, is a reference to the climactic scene in Roman Polanski's *Chinatown*, in which Evelyn Mulwray's repeated "She's my sister. My daughter" leads to the revelation of incest. The conflation of categories in incest produces riddles: how can a person be both sister and daughter, mother and sister?[5] Now it is clear that Brenda is not sufficiently older than Billy to actually be his mother, but the intertext with *Chinatown* foregrounds suspicions of incest that are never laid to rest. "Do you think I fuck my brother?" Brenda angrily challenges Nate in an argument ("Brotherhood," 1:7), a gauntlet that she will throw down again in her knockdown-dragout confrontation with Nate near the end of the second season — a challenge which, significantly, Nate will refuse to address on both occasions.

But whether the relationship between Brenda and Billy was ever overtly sexual, it is presented as sufficiently close to damage them. Bearing matching tattoos in the small of their backs, they are shackled together with bonds that remain darkly unarticulated. Nate interprets Brenda's deep concern for Billy as co-dependency: "You're letting him manipulate you" he tells her ("Brotherhood," 1:7). Brenda explains how she went to Europe after her graduation from high school, planning to attend Yale in the autumn, when Billy, she believes, tried to kill himself, necessitating her return to Los Angeles ("The New Person," 1:10). While such self-sacrifice might be lauded in another culture, the therapeutic culture of *Six Feet Under* views it suspiciously. In this series, taking care of others is often a way of running from self-care. Similarly, Ruth is not praised for taking on the responsibility of caring for her grandmother, but is pathologized for it. Claire, in her caring relationship for the psychologically wounded and suicidal Gabe, is shown to be seriously out of her depth and dangerously vulnerable. In a culture that holds "the affirmation of self as the central element of the good life" (Furedi 147), acts of renunciation are construed as symptoms.

In this context, Brenda's decision to commit Billy to the psychiatric ward is shown as her healthiest and most courageous act, but also, surprisingly, the beginning of her deterioration. Margaret, in a rare moment of acute insight, sees the desperateness of Brenda's situation:

> You've spent thirty-two years being your brother's nursemaid to avoid having any emotional life of your own. And now that he's been put away, you're going to have to face your own demons, and sweetheart, they're legion ["Driving Mr. Mossback," 2:4].

Brenda, stung by this brutally accurate piece of truth-telling, slaps her mother. Future events confirm that Brenda's committing Billy was not a sign of her emergence but, rather, the cause for greater suffering and unrest. Having lived far too intimately with her brother for too long, the act of separation becomes devastating.

Bernard and Margaret make their first appearance beside their swimming pool, in which Brenda and Nate are cavorting amorously. Surprising the lovers—and the viewers—they seem to take a distinct pleasure in Nate's discomforture. After introductions are made, the parents sit patiently, waiting for the (apparently) naked and (probably) aroused Nate to step out of the pool, which he never does. Is this unsettling encounter the result of the parents' voyeurism, the daughter's exhibitionism, or some insidious collusion of both? In this clever but deeply disturbing sequence, the Freudian primal scene is reversed, as the parents observe their child's sexual activity.

The traumatic scene of psychotherapy in the contemporary imagination may not actually be the parents' sexual act, but the violation of the client/child by the psychotherapist/parent. Do the accusations of incest that initiated Freud's explorations become reinscribed in the spectacle of the pioneers of psychoanalysis practicing on their children? If Evelyn Mulwray's incestuous riddle is "My sister. My daughter," and Billy Chenowith's is "My mother. My sister," perhaps there is also a place for "My parent. My analyst." Consider the spectacle of Freud analyzing Anna, Melanie Klein analyzing her children and, above all, Hermine Hug-Hellmuth analyzing her nephew Rolf, who subsequently murdered her and then approached the Viennese Psycho-Analytic Society asking to be compensated, asserting that he had been the subject of psychoanalytic experimentation (Appignanesi and Forrester, 196–202).

How often have we observed a comment, in casual conversation, about an exasperating and maladjusted individual met with the rejoinder, "Well, his mother/father *was* a therapist, you know." At this pseudo-explanation, eyebrows are raised, faint smiles play across the faces of the group, and there is an immediate, unspoken consensus that this one fact accounts for all the problems: who, after all could survive the endless mindfuck of a therapist parent unscathed? That this response can so readily occur (even among people who themselves visit therapists and are deeply grateful for the help they have received) suggests that the figure of the therapist parent is one with deep roots in fantasy, not experience or learning. That fantasy seems to be sufficiently powerful to elicit anxiety in otherwise confident adults who are members of the therapeutic culture. It promotes the paranoid suspicion that if we have been able to keep any secret whatsoever from our parents, it was only because they lacked the professional expertise to ferret it out.

For British psychoanalyst D. W. Winnicott, the fear of psychotherapy is the totally justifiable fear of violation. It is, he writes, "a protest from the core of me to the frightening fantasy of being infinitely exploited" (179). With the Chenowiths, the fear of an incestuous family is combined with the fear of an intrusive and exploitative psychotherapy. While Ruth and Nathaniel Fisher are the absent parents of *Six Feet Under*, the Chenowiths are their malignantly omnipresent opposites. Even when they are physically absent from their children, they remain present as psychic scars. Better too distant than too close, the series leads us to infer. The desire to be intimately known in therapeutic culture is shadowed by the terror of being known. As Winnicott observed, "Rape and cannibalism are trivial compared to the intrusion upon the secret self" (187).

Sara expresses a similar fear of violation, though in a lighter tone, when she tells Ruth about her meeting with The Plan's founder, Ernst Vollhofer:

> [...] he came on to me, but I had just dropped acid for the first time and I thought he was some Mayan death priest who wanted to cut out my heart and throw it into a pit ... so I blew him off ["In Place of Anger," 2:6].

Echoing psychiatrist Martin Dysart's nightmare of sacrificing children as a sort of Aztec priest in Peter Shaffer's immensely successful and influential 1973 therapeutic drama, *Equus*, Sara's drug-induced perception is not random; it resonates precisely with an anxiety that pervades *Six Feet Under*.

Is the series's apparent preference for group therapy and self-help over one-on-one psychotherapies a sign of wanting the benefits of psychotherapy without risking domination by a person who knows all too much about you? The therapeutic culture insists on the importance of self-revelation as a means of achieving growth, but in so doing, arouses increased anxiety about the possibility of psychological violation that accompanies such revelation. As a result, the self-help book becomes less threatening than group therapies and the more diffuse dynamic of group therapies less threatening than the intensity of one-on-one therapies. In the therapeutic culture, we learn to love therapy but fear the therapist. While Rieff was able to define many aspects of the therapeutic culture with insight, he was unable to sense the deep resistance his psychological man had toward the therapeutic, resistance that leads to increasing ambivalence.

But this fear of the therapist is only part of a more general fear of the demand to divulge personal aspects throughout therapeutic culture. While the traditional entry to the public realm was predicated on the individual's ability to leave behind the psychological and spiritual issues that constituted the private realm, the entry to the new, therapeutic society requires that its members divulge details of their private lives, since the public realm now constitutes itself increasingly through shared acts of personal revelation (Furedi 37–43). Reticence was once seen as an essential part of civility; now it is a pathological symptom. "We are, I fear, getting to know each other," observed Rieff sardonically (21). *Six Feet Under* repeatedly dramatizes both the need for therapy and its concomitant dangers, a variation of the series's broader theme of the need for intimacy and its dangers. When does intimacy become co-dependency, threatening self-esteem and autonomy?

The results of psychic violation are dramatized in *Six Feet Under*'s children of parent therapists. Billy and Brenda both express a perilously diminished sense of self. Brenda tells Nate that she wakes up feeling empty ("An Open Book," 1:5), has no idea who she is ("In the Game," 2:1), and suffers from "a fear of feeling something real" ("I'll Take You," 2:12). Billy, a photographer, is troubled by his inability to produce self-portraits that satisfy him, but his ruminations on the subject quickly move from the aesthetic to the psychological:

> That's the thing about Narcissus. It's not that he is so fucking in love with himself because he isn't at all; he fucking hates himself. It's without that reflection looking back at him, he doesn't exist ["Someone Else's Eyes," 2:9].

Naked and tearful, Billy stands before Claire, having asked her to photograph the scar of the self-inflicted wound in the small of his back, the result of his manic effort to hack out the tattoo that stood as a sign of his profound link to his sister. Severely damaged in themselves, neither brother nor sister has the secure sense of self that the series postulates as necessary for intimacy.

Surprisingly, the Chenowith family includes the most unambiguously hopeful therapeutic narrative to be found in the series. Although positioned on the periphery of the dramatic action and often vanishing from the screen altogether for long stretches, Billy Chenowith is at once one of the most psychically damaged characters in the series and one of the most successfully rehabilitated. Although he is described by Brenda early on as a manic-depressive who occasionally neglects to take his medication ("Pilot," 1:1), it quickly becomes clear that his bipolar condition is only a small part of his problem. Often erupting onto the scene with inappropriate and even threatening behavior, his possessive attitude toward his sister makes him dangerous to the tentative and troubled relationship of Nate and Brenda, as well as to Claire, who in her youth and vulnerability could become, it is suggested, the innocent object of Billy's jealous rage against Nate.

Billy is a common character type in American popular culture — the psychopath as villain — and he is drawn with mysterious touches that endow him with an almost preternatural force. When Brenda and Nate visit Las Vegas, for example, they return to Los Angeles to find that Billy has somehow been able to take photographs of them together in their hotel room. As the first season reaches its conclusion, his behavior becomes increasingly threatening. Brenda is pressured to commit him to a psychiatric ward, a course of action that she resists until he attacks her with a knife and forces her to see the extremity of his condition. In the final episode of the first season, Brenda visits her brother in the ward, where he expresses his deep love for her, his hatred for himself, and acceptance of the reality of his mental illness.

After this scene, Billy vanishes for several episodes and reappears late in the second season as a changed person. The process of this transformation is kept off screen and remains almost totally unknown to us, though we are told that he underwent electroshock therapy and now visits Dr. Hanover, a psychotherapist whom he describes as "a total genius" ("Someone Else's Eyes," 2:9) three times a week. Accepting whatever diagnosis he has been given as a fundamental and permanent aspect of his existence — "I'm still sick. I'll always be sick" he admits ("It's the Most Wonderful Time of the Year," 2.8) — and still troubled, he nevertheless seems totally purged of his violent and possessive impulses, is able to accept his parents' foibles with tenderness, and shows he has gained some insight into his "really toxic" relationship with his sister (2:9). Respecting boundaries and eschewing "negativity" ("I'll Take

You," 2:12), Billy has embraced the values and vocabulary of the thera-peutic culture and in so doing, has been transformed from the shadowy, psychopathic villain of the first season to a sensitive guy. Billy stands at one extreme of *Six Feet Under*'s characterology as a figure who can, under the pretext of an off-screen therapeutic intervention, be completely transformed. Situating Billy within an unambiguous narrative of heal-ing, his story demonstrates the power of psychotherapy at its most potent and unambiguous.

Billy's rehabilitation is presented in idealized terms, but the process is scarcely dramatized. This is no doubt in part because he is a minor figure in the series, but it may also be that the rehabilitation can only remain idealized by transpiring off screen. In *Six Feet Under*, the more we see of a professional therapeutic relationship, the more flawed and limited it appears. The invisible Dr. Hanover can transform Billy in a way that neither Gary nor The Plan could.

Although we are told very little about the specifics of Billy's child-hood and the damage he sustained (with the exception of his unusual closeness to his sister), we are given a much fuller biography of Brenda and the violation she endured. A child of exceptional intelligence, she was quickly made the subject of psychological inquiries and treated as, in her own words "a fucking lab rat" ("An Open Book," 1:5). The result of these studies was a book written by the fictional Gareth M. Feinberg, PhD, *Charlotte Light and Dark*, which has become a canonical case study, rendering Brenda, much against her will, a minor celebrity of the ther-apeutic. Claire has read the book, as has a dinner guest of Brenda's who informs her hostess that one of her psychology professors in graduate school described "Charlotte" as a "classic example" of borderline disor-der ("In the Game," 2:1). Brenda responds that she, brilliantly preco-cious child that she was, had researched borderline disorder and enacted its symptoms to mislead the doctors. But, later in the evening, she con-siders the ironic possibility that enacting borderline symptoms may have rendered her so.

Borderline is a psychoanalytic term coined to account for patients who seem not to fit in the Freudian categories of *neurotic* or *psychotic*. They are called *borderline* because they "must be considered to occupy a borderline between neurosis and psychosis" (Kernberg 3). Defining a concept that lies on the threshold between two others is not without its problems, and Laplanche and Pontalis have judged it a term that "has no strict nosological definition" (54). Turning, however, to "The Boy Scout Handbook" of psychotherapy, officially known as the *Diagnostic and Statistical Manual of Mental Disorders*, one can find a definition of borderline disorder, followed by a crisply worded list of nine diagnostic criteria. The entry begins: "The essential feature of Borderline Personality Disorder is a pervasive pattern of instability of interpersonal relationships, self-image and affects, and marked impulsivity that begins by early adulthood and is present in a variety of contexts" (650). A number of the criteria describe Brenda: "markedly and persistently unstable self-image or sense of self," "extreme sarcasm, enduring bitterness or verbal outbursts," "problems controlling anger," "chronic feelings of emptiness," and — particularly important for Brenda in the second season — "impulsivity in at least two areas that are potentially self-damaging"(651).[6] Brenda's increasing attraction to casual sexual encounters and frequent use of alcohol and marijuana add up to the requisite "two areas" of impulsivity. It is difficult to read this entry without imagining *Six Feet Under*'s scriptwriters hard at work with the *DSM-IV* in hand.

Objectified into a case study and transformed into a narrative in the therapeutic marketplace, it is no wonder that Brenda's sense of self is beleaguered. She tries to keep Nate from knowing about *Charlotte Light and Dark*, fearing that if he reads it, he will be misled into believing he understands her. She attempts to counter *Charlotte Light and Dark* with her own text, a highly explicit memoir of her casual sexual encounters, but while proclaiming her freedom from that earlier, confining text, it actually documents the very impulsivity identified as a symptom of borderline disorder. Brenda is incapable of freeing herself from the pathology that has officially defined her since childhood.

Brenda's diagnosis, however, shifts as the second season approaches its end, and we are encouraged to view her not as an example of borderline personality disorder but as a sex addict. The concept of sexual addiction arose in the late 1970s not out of psychoanalysis but out of the twelve-step programs that had developed to help people addicted to substance abuse. In that context, people who felt intense sexual compulsions while recovering from substance abuse came to see these compulsions as no different from those that had led them to abuse alcohol, marijuana, or hard drugs.[7] The psychoanalytic diagnosis of borderline personality is replaced with the behavioral diagnosis of sex addict.

Impulsivity, one of a cluster of symptoms defining a personality type, becomes addiction, a behavior to be modified.

There is, however, no evidence that Brenda is about to wholeheartedly embrace the identity of a sex addict. Rather, she encourages us to wonder whether shopping in the therapeutic bazaar may not merely be an exercise in self-deception. When Margaret announces that she has at long last discovered her spirituality and begins spouting New Age psychospeak, Brenda, the veteran of therapies responds, "Great. So someone completely not in touch with herself now has a whole new vocabulary to be not in touch with herself with" ("I'll Take You," 2:12). In one compact, devastating utterance, Brenda challenges all of the many therapeutic ventures of *Six Feet Under*—from The Plan and *The Whole Child* to the language in which all the series's relationships is couched.[8] What if all of these therapeutic tools can as easily be used to foster self-deception as insight? As psychotherapeutic concepts circulate ever more briskly through our society, leading us to glibly render our daily experiences in terms such as *bipolar identity*, *trauma triggers*, *toxic relations*, and *boundary issues*, the search for self is increasingly threatened with the possibility of winding up in a blind alley of trendy clichés. In an age of endless psychological volubility, has the promise of depth psychology worn paper thin? *Six Feet Under* draws a disconcerting cultural map of the therapeutic culture, in which we ceaselessly navigate between Scylla and Charybdis—if therapy is facile, it is pointless; if it is profound, it is dangerous.

Six Feet Under begins with a rupture in the Fisher family marked by the death of the father and the near-simultaneous appearance of Brenda as the entry into therapeutic culture. The second season ends with the Fisher family banding together around Nate's surgery to treat a potentially lethal circulatory problem in his brain. Nate's cranial "wound" not only hearkens back to the "wounds" that Brenda discovered during a shiatsu session, but it also embodies his increasingly perilous intimate relationship with the series' ultimate damaged therapist/client. At this point in the series, the consolidation and healing of the Fisher family seems to require the temporary resolution of the Chenowith plots: Margaret and Bernard have survived their marital crisis and publicly celebrated their marriage in a recommitment ceremony, Billy has responded to his therapeutic regime and accepted his parents, and Brenda is scapegoated and expelled for her pathology. As the Chenowiths disappear, so do the formal therapies: Ruth has repudiated The Plan and Claire has moved beyond her all-too-fallible high school therapist. Brenda has packed up her belongings and driven away. She is the last of the Chenowiths to disappear, taking with her the shadow side of the therapeutic culture that they have embodied.

Of course this ritual explusion is only the ersatz closure of a continuing television drama's season finale. No sooner does the action resume than new therapies and therapeutic figures spring up: Keith and David find themselves in couples therapy, Claire finds therapeutic discourses linked to artistic creation in the classrooms of LAC-Arts, and so it goes. In time, even the Chenowiths return. Even though they are used as scapegoats for the therapeutic culture, the fact that Six Feet Under is a therapeutic drama makes it impossible to exorcise them (and their ilk) definitively.

The excesses of therapeutic culture need to be expelled in the figures of the Chenowith, just as the capitalist excesses of the funeral business need to be regularly expelled in the representatives of the Kroehner Corporation. The reasons are similar. Just as the ruthless acquisitiveness of Kroehner deflect whatever unease we might feel about the profit-making venture of Fisher and Sons, so too the alternately amusing and appalling adventures of the Chenowiths help deflect whatever unease we might feel about the therapeutic ethos, not only of the Fisher family but of Fisher and Sons as well. For the funeral home is the series's primary therapeutic space, a site for short-term, intimate interventions in a highly emotional crisis situation. Corpses are cared for, and, when necessary, restored. The friends and family of the deceased bring their sorrow, rage, guilt, doubts, and personal histories to the home, and the Fishers are often called upon to address them. As Mandy Merck observes, "Throughout the series, good grieving, like good living, requires the release of repressed feeling" (69). It was the therapeutic side of the business that led Nate into the family business in the first place.

And yet, as is the case in therapeutic culture, the business is not self-sacrificing, and the dynamics are not purely altruistic. Nate returns in an attempt to break through a dead end in his own life, and the deceased often play the role of therapist toward the staff, as when David tends to a gay man murdered in a hate crime or Nate struggles with his own fears of mortality at the death of a young athlete. The potential for dangerous self-absorption, grotesque projection, or insensitive misidentification, along with the mixed motives of a profit-making, self-oriented business presenting itself as a therapeutic enterprise for the good of others, cannot bear too meticulous an examination and Kroehner and the Chenowiths, each in their own ways, help to siphon off a good deal of ambivalence. In the world of such excesses, the Fishers appear relatively benign. The writers of *Six Feet Under* split these dangerous impulses off from the Fishers and embody them in villains, rogues and pathetic victims. While these impulses cannot be expelled from the series, they can at least be somewhat contained.

Notes

1. For a theme closely related to therapeutic culture, the American self-help tradition, see Ashley Sayeau's insightful essay.
2. For a similar description of the role of therapeutic discourses in contemporary American life, see Illouz, 198–200.
3. For this and further information on Landmark Forum, Inc. and its history, see Grigoriadis.
4. For a detailed overview of the representation of psychotherapy in American movies, see Gabbard. For a similar overview of the Broadway stage (though only until 1953), see Sievers.
5. For riddles and incest in drama, see Shell and Pitcher
6. Actor Brenda Griffiths's skewed smile and sly gaze, use to indicate Brenda is moving into the more pathological side of her nature, is a cinematic indicator of mental instability that goes back at least as far as ZaSu Pitts's 1924 portrayal of the pathologically greedy Trina McTeague in Eric von Stroheim's *Greed*.
7. For the history of the sexual addiction movement and twelve-step therapies, see Irvine.
8. In the audio commentary on this episode in the DVD set, writer Jill Soloway says that Brenda's subversive wisecrack was not in the script, but was written on the set by the director of the episode, Michael Engler. It is interesting to reflect that this subversion came as an intervention from outside the usual writing team, whose general tone toward therapeutic culture is less acid.

Works Cited

Appignanesi, Lisa, and John Forrester. *Freud's Women.* New York: Basic Books, 1992.

Behrman, S. N. *End of Summer: A Play in Three Acts.* New York: Random House, 1936.

Cushman, Philip. *Constructing the Self, Constructing America: A Cultural History of Psychotherapy.* Reading: Addison-Wesley Publishing, 1995.

_____. *Diagnostic and Statistical Manual of Mental Disorders.* Fourth edition. Washington, D.C.: American Psychiatric Association, 1994.

Furedi, Frank. *Therapy Culture: Cultivating Vulnerability in an Uncertain Age.* New York: Routledge, 2004.

Gabbard, Glin O., and Krin Gabbard. *Psychiatry and the Cinema.* Washington, D.C.: American Psychiatric Press, 2005.

Grigoriadis, Vanessa. "The New Me Generation." *New York* 34:26 (July 9, 2001): 18–25.

Illouz, Eva. *Consuming the Romantic Utopia: Love and the Cultural Contradictions of Capitalism*. Berkeley: University of California Press, 1997.

Irvine, Janice M. "Regulated Passions: The Invention of Inhibited Sexual Desire and Sexual Addiction." *Deviant Bodies: Critical Perspectives on Difference in Science and Popular Culture*. Eds. Jennifer Terry and Jacqueline Urla. Bloomington: Indiana University Press, 1995. 314–337.

Kernberg, Otto. *Borderline Conditions and Pathological Narcissism*. Northvale: Jason Aronson, 1992.

Laplanche, Jean, and J. B. Pontalis. *The Language of Psychoanalysis*. Trans. Donald Nicholson-Smith. New York: W. W. Norton, 1973.

Merck, Mandy. "American Gothic: Undermining the Uncanny." *Reading Six Feet Under: TV to Die For*. Eds. Kim Akass and Janet McCabe. London and New York: I. B. Tauris, 2005. 59–70.

Pitcher, John. "The Poet and Taboo: The Riddle of Shakespeare's *Pericles*." *Essays and Studies* 35 (1982): 14–29.

Porter, Cole. "Make a Date with a Great Psychoanalyst." In *Cole*. Ed. Robert Kimball. New York: Holt, Rinehart and Winston, 1971. 187.

Rieff, Philip. *The Triumph of the Therapeutic: Uses of Faith after Freud*. New York: Harper and Row, 1966.

Sayeau, Ashley. "Americanitis: Self-Help and the American Dream in *Six Feet Under*." *Reading Six Feet Under: TV to Die for*." Eds. Kim Akass and Janet McCabe. London and New York: I. B. Tauris, 2005. 94–105.

Shell, Marc. *The End of Kinship, "Measure for Measure," Incest and the Ideal of Universal Siblinghood*. Stanford: Stanford University Press, 1988.

Sievers, David. *Freud on Broadway*. New York: Hermitage House, 1953.

Six Feet Under: The Complete First Season. Created by Alan Ball. 4 videodiscs. HBO Video, 2002.

Six Feet Under: The Complete Second Season. Created by Alan Ball. 5 videodiscs. HBO Video, 2004.

Swidler, Ann. *Talk of Love: How Culture Matters*. Chicago: University of Chicago Press, 2001.

Tobin, Robert Deam. "Politics, Tragedy and *Six Feet Under*: Camp Aesthetics and Gay Mourning in post–AIDS America." *Reading Six Feet Under: TV to Die For*." Eds. Kim Akass and Janet McCabe. London and New York: I. B. Tauris, 2005. 85–93.

Winnicott, D. W. "Communicating and Not Communicating Leading to a Study of Certain Opposites." *The Maturational Process and the Facilitating Environment: Studies in the Theory of Emotional Development*. New York: International Universities Press, 1965. 179–192.

Strangers in Blood:
The Queer Intimacies
of *Six Feet Under*

Lorena Russell

Alan Ball's *Six Feet Under* presents a fragile notion of family through its consistent interest in how people alternately manage and botch their relationships with those whom they love. Throughout the show's run, each character strives repeatedly for stable and meaningful intimacies, only to run headlong into complications and frustrations. As a family group, the Fishers come to be marked by their individual differences more than by any meaningful biological connection. As much as they seem to need each other, the family members function more as strangers than as kin through much of the five-year series. It is only in the final moments of the show that the family manages any sense of a traditionally expected unity, and even here the intimacy is qualified by reminders of the fleeting nature of life. In all of their relationships, the characters struggle to move beyond their destructive and limiting patterns, yet remain trapped in patterns of urgent and troubled intimacies.

Such personal failings are the stuff of numerous TV serials, especially those fashioned with attention to character development. Many of these serial shows — and soap operas are a good example here — thrive on exploring the complexities of social relationships. Mandy Merck usefully offers the term *serial melodrama* to talk about the level of narrative deferrals that propel much of the *Six Feet Under's* storyline, resulting in an "oscillation between isolation and community" (Merck 65). It is here, through the extended mapping of characters' lives, that desires and fears can come alive, as they so often do in *Six Feet Under*. As Merck puts it, "Drama or comedy, *Six Feet Under's* ruling genre is the family saga, affirming the centrality and continuity of kinship itself" (64). But part of what distinguishes this show from others is the level of complication that this central concern of kinship and intimacy receives. This is, after all, a show that takes place in a funeral home, and the business of undertaking exerts a series of unique pressures on how the characters, and by extension the viewers, come to consider intimacy, kinship and love.

Six Feet Under explores the intense and unpredictable impact of death on intimacy. When viewed in the shadow of loss, love takes on a new aura of urgency and possibility. Time itself seems to take on a different quality, as perceptions and attitudes towards the future and the past shift.[1] Characters respond to death and loss in a range of unpredictable ways, and simple moral judgments no longer seen adequate. These complications are part of what accounts for the show's appeal, but they also invite viewers to suspend narrow judgments about proper relationships and to imagine instead a broadening array of identities, sympathy, attachment, pleasure and love, a dynamic I call queering.

Clearly, the notion of recognizing mortality as a path for appreciating life is nothing new. Such recognition stands behind the time-worn concept of "Carpe Diem," as individuals are often challenged to reckon with the sometimes positive and transformative potentials of loss. While part of the concept of queering builds from this paradox of productive loss, I am specifically interested in how such transformations, and the narrative contexts in which they are presented, might be read as fostering queer imagination. The use of *queer* here thus focuses less on sexual identities per se and more on a conceptualization of queering as an anti-normalizing impulse — one that works on several levels to resist the expected, and often limiting, stories of family, intimacy and kinship. I am making an argument here for a particularly queer resonance in the ways in which death functions in *Six Feet Under*, one that extends beyond the mere presence of gay or lesbian characters to attend to meanings that emerge from the narratives themselves. The thematic pressures of death in *Six Feet Under* not only clear a space for thinking about alternate kinships, but the show invites viewers to exercise what might be described as a "queer imagination."

How might an audience begin to enter a space conducive to developing queer imagination? In the case of *Six Feet Under,* this invitation emerges through the shows varied and repeated encounters with death and its associated imagery. The show's catchy title sequence builds through a series of iconographic images of death to set the scene. Death enters here through association, not through direct contact, as viewers encounter bits and pieces of a larger whole: edges of brightly shined coffins, a bit of a hearse, a time-lapse wilting lily. As Celia Wren describes it, the metonymic sequence performs a kind of seduction as it "evokes death, morgue work, and burial with a hallucinatory chain of exquisitely macabre imagery" (19). As with *American Beauty,* Ball invites us to suspend our typical repulsion towards the morbid and to consider instead its potential link to beauty. We not only engage images of death, but we are further invited to consider their aesthetic value and to reconsider our (often reactionary) relationship to those symbols and what they represent.

Every episode begins with a death narrative. The opening death story, even though it is fully "expected" by the viewer, often plays out in surprising ways. The deaths are typically written so that viewers anticipate one possible scenario only to have it turn to another. For example, the episode entitled "You Never Know" (3:2) opens with a distracted man on the phone fiddling with matches and a gas stove. Viewers are invited to expect that this man will provide us with the opening death, as each match he lights seems sure to ignite an explosion. In fact, the death that does occur strikes the telemarketer with whom he is speaking on the telephone. This playful treatment of death, where viewers are invited to consider both the inevitability and the surprise of death, mirrors the ambivalent way death often enters our lives: it is an inevitability we each live with, yet something few can predict with any sense of certainty.

This element of surprise relates to queer theorist Eve Kosofsky Sedgwick's thoughts on the reading process. In her introduction to *Novel Gazing,* Sedgwick challenge readers to consider the emotional states that lie behind the different ways we approach meaning in stories. Some of us approach stories with an attitude that might be described as "paranoid," insofar as we are always guarded and on the lookout for nasty surprises. Sedgwick proposes that such paranoid readers shift towards an affect that is less closed and guarded.[2] She suggests that a better reading

109

position might be curious and more open to surprises. Death is perhaps the penultimate nasty surprise and could in some ways be considered the lasting justification for any paranoid positioning. But there is at the same time a decided inevitability to death that makes paranoia in an odd sense redundant. While one might expect that a show on death would result in more, not less, paranoia among its viewers, in *Six Feet Under* elements of surprise paired with death's inevitability shift our attitudes away from the paranoid and towards the more open position Sedgwick describes as "reparative."

The story lines of the individual shows further the relationship of the viewer to death, as each hour unfolds beyond and in some ways in response to the "opening death." In *Six Feet Under* the viewers begin in paranoid anticipation of that ugly surprise of death, but as the hour stories unfold, viewers are invited to shift positions towards acceptance. Death may be inevitable, but life does go on. And the way that it goes on in *Six Feet Under* often proceeds from one surprise to the next. As Alan Ball commented in an August 2004 NPR interview, "The appeal of the show ... was that it didn't take you where you expected to be taken" *(Fresh Air)*. Viewers are subtly shifted from paranoid to reparative positions not only in their weekly encounters with death, but through a range of surprising narrative shifts within the story lines themselves.

Most of us in contemporary America live our lives effectively removed from reminders of death.[3] Such a life is not available for the Fishers, who are in the business of death. This point is made early in the series' pilot. When Ruth, Claire and Nate return from viewing their father's body at the morgue, David greets them, fully expecting the body to be in tow, and is harsh and critical when he realizes they have forgotten their professional duties in the face of their grief. Viewers might forgive this lapse of professionalism given the difficult pressures of grief. Most American families would enjoy and expect that relief from death: viewing the body of a loved one would be enough, and one would then leave the corpse to be tended by a professional, using that distance to mitigate the shock of the loss. But for the Fishers, death remains a constant presence, something that it is impossible to avoid or escape.

An often-quoted line from that same pilot episode illustrates the intensity of the Fisher's relationship with the abject, and the unbecoming familial intersection their occupation demands. In another outburst, David comments, "I just got through stuffing formaldehyde-soaked cotton up my father's ass to keep his insides from leaking out." One of the reasons that this line stands out is because of the taboos the narrative represents. On one emotional level there is the challenge of the bereaved encounter with the death of a loved one: a reality check with loss of the kind nobody could easily endure. But even beyond this sense, the viewer is presented with an iconography of anal penetration between son and father that opens the associative door to sodomy and incest. Let alone that David must intimately handle a dead body, here the son is figuratively fucking the father. In *Six Feet Under,* the challenge to death taboos often leads to other radical reformations of social order.

The Fishers' private lives also encompass the lives of those families who are seeking their professional, yet highly intimate, services. There is always a body to be prepared in the basement, family or friends to be managed in the parlor, as clientele and the dead are soothed, consoled and tended. The aura of death brings its own set of insights to the Fishers, serving as a constant reminder that life is a fleeting and precious thing. As Ruth puts it at one point, life is best viewed as "a fleeting gift" (4:1). This central element of *memento mori* comments most frequently on the lost and fumbled relationships, making those interpersonal mistakes stand out with a harsh contrast. The finality of death signifies an irretrievable, irreparable loss. When our lives are lived facing such loss, we are challenged to take stock of our shortcomings and to find ways to live and love fully.

This invitation to "seize the day" and to live fully in the face of death is not a charge that comes naturally to the Fishers, who are each marked by various levels of repression. As the show progresses through various seasons, each character evolves to move beyond these inhibitors, and in doing so, changes quite dramatically. From the beginning of the show, though, their general characteristic of repression is offset by occasional emotional outbursts: moments when a typically restrained Fisher lets go in uncharacteristically volatile styles. In the pilot episode, for example, the tightly-wound mother, Ruth, screams upon hearing of her husband's death and flings the pot roast skittering across the kitchen floor in her grief. Nate explodes unexpectedly in the grocery store and David will later surprise with his impassioned speech at the undertaker's convention in Las Vegas. Aside from these uncharacteristic outbursts, the characters each struggle towards change, evolving through each season in substantial and sometimes unexpected ways.

Ball comments that the characters were intentionally scripted to highlight their individual repressions: "They're sort of living 'six feet under,' if you will" (Magid 71). As the series progresses, they emerge. Change for each character is often precipitated by a death, and characters carry away some lesson from the "death *du jour.*" David, who starts the show as a deeply closeted gay man, certainly begins as one of the more uptight, repressed characters on the show. His process of coming out forms one of the persistent narratives of the series and one of the more obvious points of queering in the show.

In "Telepistemology of the Closet; or The Queer Politics of *Six Feet Under,*" Samuel A. Chambers usefully links the progression of this narrative in the first few shows to the general politics of the closet, noting how David's painful emergence offers useful insight into how American society operates according to presumptive heteronormativity. Chambers praises the show for its "subtle, sophisticated, and deft approach to the subject matter of identity and sexuality" (24). In a later article Chambers explores the show's complex treatment of the closet and maintains that "*Six Feet Under* has been the only show on television to investigate the issue of closeting" ("Revisiting the Closet" 175). David's painful emergence offers useful insight into how American society operates according to heterosexual norms.

While Chambers praises this aspect of the show, David Bergman considers David's repressed and troubled sexual identity as one of the weaknesses of the show, one of the ways it might be said to perpetuate homophobia. Bergman sees *Six Feet Under* as a part of an insidious trend in films whereby homophobia is absent socially yet present in an internalized form, problematically carried by the gay character himself.[4] According to Bergman, the show presents homophobia away from a broader social context, so that for David, his "sexual paralysis seems to be his own doing" (15). For Bergman, this focus on the psychological complexities of internalized homophobia is socially irresponsible, as it seems to invite a kind of "blame the victim" mentality.

Issue can be taken with Bergman's analysis on several levels.[5] For one thing, David Fisher's situation is quite typical: a conservative man who is so compelled to "do good" might quite understandably internalize much of the negativity around homosexuality he encounters through his church and culture. From this perspective, then, the show offers an educational glimpse into the workings of internalized homophobia.

Bergman does note that David's primary incentive for coming out evolves from the brutal and unprovoked gay bashing of a young man (Mark Foster, who bears a close resemblance to Matthew Shepard). Yet for Bergman this plot element — the fact that David's growing political sensibility is provoked by social violence — is not enough to mitigate what he sees as an insidious trend of placing homophobia inside the psyche of the gay character.

The impact of Mark's violent death and his haunting presence illustrates the link between an individual's psyche and the social reality of homophobia. The fact of Foster's impact on David's coming out cannot be bracketed as incidental, as Bergman would argue through his dismissive treatment of the show's logic and David's psychology: "To be sure, one of the episodes in the first season depicts a young man murdered by homophobic thugs, a murder that impels David to tell his fellow deacons at his up-tight church that he's gay. But David's sexual paralysis seems to be his own doing" (15). Rather, a close reading of the character emphasizes the social element implicit in the notion of "internalized homophobia"—i.e., that the process of internalization implies a movement from the outside in, and logically presumes the social pressures of living gay, lesbian, bisexual, transgendered, and/or queer (glbtq) in a homophobic society.

For David, as for so many of the other characters in *Six Feet Under,* the fact of death serves to bring home any number of social points and life lessons. It is through the case of Mark's violent demise by gay bashing that David is challenged to move towards self-acceptance and coming out. David's discomfort with Mark's death becomes literalized through his ghosting: through his projection of Foster's ghost, David creates a mirror image of himself through a gay, battered character who jeers, punishes and taunts him. His projection of Foster thus externalizes and quickens his internalized homophobia.

In his DVD commentary to Episode 13, Ball remarks that Mark appears as David's "idea of himself." The show's use of "ghosts" to illuminate what is transpiring within the minds and emotions of the living is one of the ways that the series reminds viewers about the complex dynamic between the living and the dead. It is not so much that these ghosts exist as true revenants, but rather that their presence signals the response of the living to their deaths. As Ball comments, the ghosts are "a literary device to articulate what's going on in the living character's minds, so I don't want them to seem supernatural" (Magid 71). With the exception of one brief appearance by Nathaniel Fisher at the end of Episode 13, ghosts in the series appear as projections: a visible link between the interior states of living and the effects of the dead.

The changes that take place in Mark's appearance highlight this device. It is only after David has successfully comes out to his church that Mark appears whole, relaxed and smiling. Healing and political progress thus are linked to death, in a problematic dynamic that is all too familiar for the queer community. In the same way that Matthew Shepard's 1998 death became the impetus for reconsidering homophobia in America, Mark becomes a kind of martyr of remembrance for the fictionalized David and the glbtq community members who gather to publicly mourn their loss.[6]

While *Six Feet Under* does seem to replicate the somewhat homogenous portrait of gay identity in its use of Mark Foster, it does find ways to go beyond this simplification in other ways. For one thing, the show has taken on an exploration of any number of forms of "deviant" or at least non-normative forms of sexuality: incest, dominance, voyeurism, and promiscuity, to name a few. Most obvious, perhaps, the show makes an effort to at least engage diversity through its inclusion of David's African-American partner Keith and the family's Latino partner Rico. Even here, though, inclusion may not be sufficient. Robert Tobin discusses the complexities of the series engagement with race, noting how "At times the depictions of these characters verge on the orientalist fetishizations of the dark-skinned male, along with a sentimental nostalgia for the more traditional family life of the Puerto Ricans, but the show should be credited for trying to analyze racial difference in earnest" (Tobin).

There is much to agree within Tobin's reading of the show. He too feels that the show is best understood as queer in part due to some of the reasons cited above, such as its linking of death and community through AIDS/HIV. He further discusses the show's engagement with patriarchy, signaled through the show's beginning story with the death of the father to posit a post-patriarchal world:

> As it exposes this world without fathers, *Six Feet Under* asks the most basic, fundamental, human questions and makes an ambitious effort to answer them in the new modes required after the death of the patriarch. These questions include: How do we know each other, when we insist on

our privacy? How can we care for each other, when we want to be left alone? How can we affirm that our lives and death are worthwhile, when we know we've been cheated out of a full existence? Does God exist? Why do children die? Why do we die? How, in short, are we to live, when, as Claire says in one of her therapy sessions, our shadow is death and silence?

For Tobin, then, the focus on death in the show becomes linked to these broader, philosophical questions of life and death, and the ways in which the show engages many of these life questions through a camp humor forms another aspect of its queering.

The relationship between death and queering extends beyond these particular points to consider other ways that the show invites us to balance our love against our losses, and in doing so, extends the possibilities of kinship beyond the bonds of blood or state legitimacy.[7] In *The Undertaking: Life Stories from the Dismal Trade,* poet and undertaker Thomas Lynch notes: "The meaning of life is connected, inextricably, to the meaning of death; that mourning is a romance in reverse, and if you love, you grieve and there are no exceptions" (25). For Lynch, the relationship between death and love seems to be a logical bond that is part of the human condition, and certainly he speaks to the kind of loving service that morticians (like poets) provide: "Undertakings are the things we do to vest the lives we lead against the cold, the meaningless, the void, the noisy blather, and the blinding dark. It is the voice we give to wonderment, to pain, to love and desire, anger and outrage; the words that we shape into song and prayer" (xviii).

In their resistance to institutionalizations, the Fishers certainly represent this humanist calling. The show often reminds us of the loving and tender respect the family offers both the bereaved and the dead. Much care and effort — even love — get put into the corpses through cleansing, massaging, and restoration. While attention gets put towards the dead, the show nevertheless also reminds us of the way death brings its effects primarily to the survivors: "Only the living care ... This is the central fact of my business— that there is nothing, once you are dead, that can be done *to you or with you* or *about you* that will do you any good or any harm; that any damage or decency we do accrues to the living, to whom your death happens, if it really happens to anyone" (Lynch 7).

Even in shows where it seems the focus of the relationship is clearly on the dead, viewers are left each week contemplating the living. Season

115

Two introduced us to Emily Levine, "The Invisible Woman" (2:5) who lived alone and died alone. Her solitary existence sparked Ruth's concern and compassion, and the show concluded with the immediate Fisher family as attendees at her service. Even without family or mourners, Levine's death ended up having an impact on those living — in this case the Fisher family, inspired through Ruth to at least momentarily seek community and stave off solitude.

But it is in their dealings with the dead that people do come to be most changed. The logic of this transformation can be linked to another dynamic with significant implications for queering: the complex relationship between love, shame and disgust. In *Anatomy of Disgust,* William Miller links our emotional affects to our ethical sensibilities, making the case that the human emotions of disgust and contempt actively inform the way we relate to others:

> I look at the emotions — disgust mostly, but also contempt — that confirm others as belonging to a lower status and thus in the zero-sum game of rank necessarily define oneself as higher. The emotions that constitute our experience of being lower or lowered — shame and humiliation — exist in a rough economy with those passions which are the experience of reacting to the lowly, failed, and contaminating — disgust and contempt [x].

Miller's position thus links our emotions or affects to our hierarchical sensibility, making the case that the emotions of disgust and contempt are implicated in the ways we rank ourselves as somehow superior or inferior to others. Rather than explaining social action in terms of how it relates to self-interest he offers "a more anxiety-ridden account, privileging defensive and reactive passions" (x). This affective economy in turns implies a rough equation between love and disgust: when disgust is suspended, love becomes apparent. Miller asks: "Doesn't love (sexual and non-sexual) involve a notable and non-trivial suspension of some, if not all, rules of disgust?" (xi). According to Miller, "Disgust rules mark the boundaries of self; the relaxing of them marks privilege, intimacy, duty and caring" (xi).

The emotion of disgust is quite obviously linked to death. For some theorists of disgust, the emotion serves in part to veil the harsh realities of our animal selves and their mortal nature. In *Hiding from Humanity: Disgust, Shame, and the Law,* Martha C. Nussbaum considers that "perhaps we cannot easily live with too much vivid awareness of the fact that we are made of sticky and oozy substances that will all too soon decay" and goes on to make the broader argument that throughout history disgust has served "to exclude and marginalize groups or people who come to embody the dominant group's fear and loathing of its own animality and mortality" (14).

It is with this latter point that the link between disgust and queer sexual practices becomes apparent. Nussbaum argues her points on disgust in the context of her work as a legal ethicist and links her points on disgust and shame to indicate ways that these emotions have been (mis)used in legal cases to justify violence against marginalized groups such as glbtq people. While legal appeals based on disgust date from the trials of Oscar Wilde, Nussbaum sets out to debunk such appeals, in part by noting disgust's irrational link with our fear of mortality and with death: "Because disgust embodies a shrinking from contamination that is associated with the human desire to be nonanimal, it is frequently hooked up with various forms of shady social practice, in which the discomfort people feel over the fact of having an animal body is projected outwards onto vulnerable people and groups" (74). It is here, in this link between the psychological fear of mortality and the social alienation of groups that the connection between death and glbtq politics might be said to potentially emerge.

In "Death, Liminality and Transformation in *Six Feet Under*," Rob Turnout makes a similar argument about social effects of "death pollution" and the social intervention work of the TV series. Although Turnout is not explicitly concerned with queer politics, he nevertheless notes how the show's close engagement with death interact with our almost obsessive avoidance of the topic: "In a sphere where the privatized and isolated experience of death might still be acutely felt, *Six Feet Under* can make a radical intervention and propose profound social change" (49). For Turnout as well as Nussbaum, our psychological inhibitions surrounding death link with the ways we act in the world. The stories of *Six Feet Under* might somehow facilitate political work by challenging our fears of mortality and our associated emotions of disgust.

The job of undertaking, if done well, demands that one resist the negative passions of disgust that may arise in the presence of decay. A couple of the episodes in *Six Feet Under* make this point (alongside social commentary about burial practices). When Nate's wife, Lisa, dies, he and his brother David drive to pick up the badly decomposed body at the morgue. Nate's unrelenting narcissism has eroded audience confidence in his character, but it is hard not to have sympathy for an individual in this particular situation. David returns with the body and Nate, struggling to maintain control, shifts to the driver's seat. The script describes the moment when the smell of the body reaches him: "It's a horrible moment: the unspoken admission that there's a disgusting body in the back, and it's Lisa, but like any other badly decomposing body, it stinks" (hbo.com) Most episodes of *Six Feet Under* avoid the association of decay, typically presenting death as innocuous or at least everyday, and sometimes, as the opening sequence reminds us, as something aesthetically valuable. But here the abject is highlighted and the inadequate widower must face his disgust. The website commentary on the scene glosses the psychological adjustment the moment represents: "Death ends up being bigger. And it comes and gets him. I think that's what this beat is about. The reality of death sort of vanquishing Nate's self-aggrandizing."

This scene, and the following sequence where Nate illegally buries Lisa's body, make additional points about the strained economy of love and disgust. One could certainly consider that Nate's sense of duty to Lisa comes too late, as he honors her request for a natural burial in defiance of her family's wishes for cremation, thus placing his need to honor the dead over that of the living. But the sequence comes to have broader meaning when considered against the backdrop of Nate's fear of death and his obsession with his own mortality. It is not so much that Nate fails by reacting to Lisa's body with disgust, but rather that he manages to honor their relationship, however rocky it was in life, though overcoming what Miller might call "disgust rules." And once again, the dead are quite beyond caring; it is only the living who can change.

David himself will face a similar challenge in a life-changing close encounter with death. The fourth season of the show reaches a climax in "That's My Dog" (4:5). While David's boyfriend Keith is struggling to stay closeted in his new job as bodyguard, David falls victim to a violent assault and carjacking. While the violence of the event was not a gay bashing per se, the episode in some sense mirrors the early violence against Mark Forster from Episode 12. Like Foster, David finds himself at an automatic teller machine and victim to violence. While homophobia is not directly linked to the assailant's motive, David picks up the guy out of a mix of motivations, not least of which is as a cruising gesture. He fantasizes sex and flirts with his captor, and even comes out as gay before things turn violent. Homophobia further helps to account for the deep sense of shame that David comes to feel around the episode. The extended torture he endures and his near-execution trigger a traumatic response that will last for the duration of the series.[8]

Death comes to form a point of tension between David and Jake. At one point in his abduction, the assailant, Jake, discovers that the van carries a dead body. He reacts with psychotic glee and treats the remains violently. David in turn reacts strongly and reminds the man (despite the fact he has a gun), "This body was somebody's sister, somebody's daughter! How dare you treat it like this!" In his compassionate appeal, David asks Jake to consider the dead body as kin, as a woman with whom this man might have been connected in some meaningful way. The ethical demand predictably falls on deaf ears, the body is painfully dumped from the van, and the torturous spree continues. David is finally left in emotional extremis, kneeling in an alley, badly beaten, waiting for an execution that never comes.

In the final episode of season four, David decides to confront Jake in an effort to rid himself of the terror he is suffering. Jake, who has been recently imprisoned, remembers David after some prompting as the guy who rode him around with a dead girl farting in the back, and wants to blame his assault on the way that he was "tricked" into having a close encounter with death. "What did you expect, man?" he asks, as though the only reasonable response to sharing space with a corpse would be a violent crime spree.

Season Four ends with David badly shaken, struggling to find his balance and reconnect with those he loves. The episode with Jake placed David in a vulnerable position, full of conflicting elements of rage and helplessness, and long-lasting fears and insecurities. Jake may have left David with the "fleeting gift" of life, but David emerges from the encounter with a new sense of his vulnerability as a victim and as a mortal. In the remaining episodes of the show, David will repeatedly do battle with this fear, which comes to a pitch following Nate's death and is only resolved when David turns aggressively on a shadowy figure, only to end up confronting his own self wearing Jake's clothes.

In his narrative commentary of the episode, director Alan Poul describes how the abduction is meant to be read as a relationship ("a complex relationship"), as David and Jake's time together tracks various stages of intimacy, dominance and dependency. As with the show's engagement of variants of intimacy, such as incest and pornography, the story of David and Jake leads viewers into a consideration of an alternate, even taboo, relationship. This violent, non-consensual bondage, however, is not held up as any kind of social model. Rather it complicates and extends the ways we might think of the boundaries of relationships and normality, pushing the edges in ways that one might consider queer.

Such complications and challenges, however, coexist with traditional narratives of family, or at least are staged against the promises of unity, support, love and stability. Death provides the ballast here; it keeps the show afloat and keeps the narrative tensions in place. While in many ways the show's storyline demands audience appreciation of traditional values associated with family, at the same time the show's refusal to lose sight of death provides the narrative with a queer force. For theorist Lee Edelman, much of queering's radical force comes in its challenge to the security of civil society, a security achieved in part from its vision of a futurity not contaminated with death. To seek a reality grounded within full realization of death represents a queer position that resists what he describes as "the compulsory narrative of reproductive futurism" (21). *Six Feet Under* somewhat ambiguously qualifies as "queer" under Edelman's analysis. In many ways, its grounding in death provides a radical alterity, but in other ways its ultimate investment in futurity might be said to undermine its resistance to "reproductive futurism."

The series' conclusion best represents this tension between death and futurity. The final sequence of the show begins with an affectionate family dinner in the home's kitchen, a space ever-resonant with promise of kinship. The old home has undergone a tasteful remodeling under the gay aesthetic eyes of Keith and David, but the old kitchen table remains. The scene is warm, the camera circles lovingly and all is forgiven through a sequences of fond remembrances and toasts. The next morning, Claire prepares to depart for her new life in New York City and takes a photo of the remaining Fisher family on the steps. This resolution is briefly interrupted by Nate, who appears over Claire's shoulder with a reminder that photography might be understood as an impossible effort to capture time: "You can't take the picture." He warns, "It's already gone." Death, as it were, seems to hang in the wings, and deflates the sentimental potential of this Norman Rockwell moment.

The final montage provides a nod to both futurity and to death. As Claire drives east in her new hybrid car we see time flash forward to the deaths of the various characters. Much of the future that we see is devoted to family time: weddings and meals and children. But each of the main characters lives we follow ultimately ends in a death. The conclusion is thus carefully crafted to provide us with a sense of narrative closure and promise, leaving the audience to ponder the hope of the future alongside the finality of death.

There are many possible variations and shades of queering. *Six Feet Under's* queering oddly happens alongside a rather traditional humanist value system, one that reiterates the importance of kinship and family. Even the gay couple in the show, Keith and David, end up modeling a clearly recognizable and traditional form of family. Gay, yes. Interracial, yes. But still solidly middle class, centered on the futurity of children, and conservative in many ways. Yet, despite this clear presence of what Halberstam might describe as "reproductive time" (4–5), the fact of their gay relationship amid the pressures of death provides a radical strain within the show.

Samuel Johnson once allowed that "the imminent prospect of hanging concentrates the mind wonderfully." In *Six Feet Under,* death becomes an opportunity for the living to reconsider the preciousness of life and the centrality of our relationships to the process of living. This most human of realities cannot in itself been seen as queer. But insofar as the show presents itself through the lens of death, it skewers our view of life and tilts our reality. It invites us to consider the unthinkable, and in giving expression to this silence, *Six Feet Under* parallels a coming-to-knowledge not unlike that of the closet. It reminds us to consider alternatives to futurity, and, in the words of Eve Sedgwick, to live every day with full knowledge that "there's no time to bullshit" (27).

Notes

1. Judith Halberstam describes "a middle-class logic of reproductive temporality" and considers ways that "queer time" might interrupt the ways that dominant culture conceptualizes time (4). Part of my argument about queering in *Six Feet Under* develops from Halberstam's theorizing, to note ways that the show engagement of death and futurity challenges traditional models of reproductive temporality.

2. Sedgwick's ideas on reading positions go on to make a link with our political positions in the world. She argues, as I do in this article, that affects of openness and curiosity might serve the queer community well, insofar as they invite new alliances.

3. For a thorough discussion of Americans' relationship to death, see Jessica Mitford, *The American Way of Death Revisited,* 1st ed. (New York: Alfred A. Knopf, 1998).

4. Bergman only discusses this phenomenon in terms of gay men.

5. It is interesting to note that Bergman centers his case around *Big Eden* (2000), a film I

would argue ironically posits the unlikely and utopic phenomenon of a homophile small American town to make a point about the broad presence of social homophobia.

6. My discomfort with this dynamic of martyrdom within the U.S. queer community, most memorably marked by the deaths of Brandon Teena and Matthew Shepard, relates in part to my frustration that political progress should depend on such violence. For a discussion of how such deaths tend to replicate sexual, racial and class bias and existing systems of privilege, see Halberstam, 16–17.

7. Judith Butler defines kinship practices as "those that emerge to address fundamental forms of human dependency, which may include birth, child-rearing, relations of emotional dependency and support, generational ties, illness, dying and death (to name a few)." See Judith Butler, 15.

Works Cited

Alan Ball: A *Six Feet Under* Postmortem. 2004. Radio. Terry Gross, 8 August.

Bergman, David. "Closet-Dwellers of the Mind." *Gay & Lesbian Review* 11:6 (2004): 15.

Butler, Judith. "Is Kinship Always Already Heterosexual?" *differences: a journal of feminist cultural studies* 15:1 (2002): 14–44.

Chambers, Samuel A. "Revisiting the Closet: Reading Sexuality in *Six Feet Under*." *Reading Six Feet Under: TV to Die For.* Eds. Kim Akass and Janet McCabe. London and New York: I. B. Tauris, 2005. 174–89.

_____. "Telepistemology of the Closet; or The Queer Politics of *Six Feet Under*." *Journal of American Culture* 26:1 (2003): 24–41.

Edelman, Lee. *No Future: Queer Theory and the Death Drive.* Series Q. Eds. Jonathan Goldberg, Michele Aina Barale, Michael Moon, Eve Kosofsky Sedgwick. Durham, NC: Duke University Press, 2004.

Halberstam, Judith. *In a Queer Time and Place: Transgender Bodies, Subcultural Lives, Sexual Cultures.* New York: New York University Press, 2005.

hbo.com. "Hbo Online." Internet. (2005). 18 March 2005. http://www.hbo.com/.

Lynch, Thomas. *The Undertaking: Life Studies from the Dismal Trade.* First Edition New York: W. W. Norton, 1997.

Magid, Ron. "Family Plots." *American Cinematographer* 83:11 (2002): 70–79.

Merck, Mandy. "American Gothic: Undermining the Uncanny." *Reading Six Feet Under: TV to Die For.* Ed. Kim Akass and Janet McCabe. London and New York: I. B. Tauris & Co. Ltd., 2005. 59–70.

Miller, William Ian. *The Anatomy of Disgust.* Cambridge, MA: Harvard University Press, 1997.

Mitford, Jessica. *The American Way of Death Revisited.* 1st ed. New York: Alfred A. Knopf, 1998.

Nussbaum, Martha Craven. *Hiding from Humanity: Disgust, Shame, and the Law.* Princeton: Princeton University Press, 2004.

Sedgwick, Eve Kosofsky. "Paranoid Reading and Reparative Reading; or, You're So Paranoid, You Probably Think This Introduction Is About You." *Novel Gazing: Queer Readings in Fiction.* Ed. Eve Kosofsky Sedgwick. Series Q. Durham, N.C.: Duke University Press, 1997. vi, 518.

Six Feet Under: The Complete First Season. Created by Alan Ball. 4 videodisks. HBO Video, 2002.

Six Feet Under: The Complete Second Season. Created by Alan Ball. 5 videodisks. HBO Video, 2004.

Six Feet Under: The Complete Third Season. Created by Alan Ball. 5 videodisks. HBO Video, 2005.

Six Feet Under: The Complete Fourth Season. Created by Alan Ball. 5 videodisks. HBO Video, 2005.

Tobin, Robert. "*Six Feet Under* and Post-Patriarchal Society." *Film & History: An Interdisciplinary Journal of Film and Television Studies.* Historian's Film Committee and the Film and History Center, 2002. 87–89. http://www.h-net.org/~filmhis/reviews/32_1/film/six_feet.htm.

Turnock, Rob. "Death, Liminality and Transformation in *Six Feet Under*." *Reading Six Feet Under: TV to Die For.* Eds. Kim Akass and Janet McCabe. London and New York: I. B. Tauris, 2005. 39–49.

When We Living Awaken

Craig N. Owens

If Alan Ball did not become a household name as the screenwriter for the film *American Beauty*, a wry commentary on the deadening influence of modern, middle-managed suburban life on the spirits of those who inhabit it, then he certainly has since the advent of his HBO series *Six Feet Under*. Both the film and the series, however, offer peculiar challenges in the way its viewers perceive the characters and events depicted. In doing so, though, they also challenge the way viewers conceive of their own at-home lives, as well. For, unlike the many films that reserve quiet, reflective, and mournful tonalities for period films and American films set in foreign countries,[1] in both *American Beauty* and *Six Feet Under*, Ball treats contemporary America and its denizens with a light touch that asks its audience to adopt a contemplative, rather than consuming, attitude toward the filmic and televisual text.

In the three sections that make up the body of this essay, that these two texts situate themselves within two of three main literary traditions built on centrally considering death: the Oedipal and the Absurdist. But, more significant, in my view, *Six Feet Under* represents an attempt to portray a kind of middle-space, a no-man's land in the contemporary American psychological and cultural landscape. In this way, it works in relationship to its culture much like Samuel Beckett's *Absurdism* did to its: by investigating life as we know it as a kind of death, as a kind of automatic, routinized, and directionless wandering that demands disorientation, pain, and effort as the price of living. These considerations account for both the particular tone of Ball's pieces and the formal narrative devices they deploy in presenting their characters and their stories.

Unity

All narrative may be in essence obituary [...].
— Peter Brooks, *Reading for Plot* (95)

Peter Brooks's view of narrative death grows out of his reading of Sigmund Freud's theory of the death drive. Embedded in the human psyche is a tendency toward stasis, equilibrium, and motionlessness that remains always at odds with the ego instincts, which, desiring, maintain the behaviors and beliefs necessary for living. Brooks sees, in literary narrative, an analogue to this psychological tension in the tendency of narrative resolution to restore equilibrium to a fictive world disrupted by conflict, crisis, and disorder (96).

If, as Jacques Lacan asserts, literature and the psyche share a common structure, then we can read narrative as the literary negotiation between two kinds of forces: desire for increasing complexity, for the repeated introduction of failed objects and encounters that sustains narrative, moving it inexorably forward, on the one hand, and a drive toward closure and equilibrium. Thus, we might call this kind of narrative, in which death always wins out in the "dualism" of desire and drive, thanatotropic — tending toward *thanatos*, death.

Many of what are often considered the great works of the Western literary tradition mark the narrative death Brooks examines with the literal death of protagonists or main characters. Aeschylus' *Agamemnon* (458 BCE) provides an early example of such a narrative death-drive. The hero Agamemnon's return to Argos with his trophy concubine Cassandra, along with his hubristic gesture of stepping on the carpet whose purple color was traditionally reserved for divine celebrations, commits Agamemnon to his own death. That is, the inciting incidents of the play's plot and its complications already have Agamemnon's death built into them.

In this way, such narratives in complicating themselves according to the demands of narrative desire also lay the groundwork for the literal and narratological death that will resolve those complications in the end, if only temporarily. The witches' prophecies early in Shakespeare's *Macbeth* serve a similar function: to move the narrative toward death by way of desire-producing complications.

This double nature of narrative complication clarifies what is at the heart of Aristotle's notion of "Unity of Action." In his *Poetics*, Aristotle claims that, among plots, "the episodic are the worst" because they lack such unity. Aristotle explicitly favors the tragic narrative whose

> action [...] is complete and whole and has some magnitude. "Whole" is that which has a beginning, middle, and end. "Beginning" is that which does not necessarily follow on something else, but after it something else naturally is or happens; "end," the other way round, is that which naturally follows on something else, either necessarily or for the most part [so], but nothing else after it; and "middle" that which naturally follows on something else and something else on it. So, then, well-constructed plots should neither begin nor end at any chance point but follow the guidelines just laid down [30].

Aristotle's privileging of "naturally" and "necessarily" progressing events as the hallmarks of unity is more than just an adherence to the mathematics of syllogistic logic. If it were so, then the guidelines for well-constructed plots, if properly followed would allow the reasonable reader, spectator, or thinker, given only the initial circumstances, to deduce the outcome. Narrative, in such a system, would become a process of deciphering, rather than of unfolding. The sense of unity emerges from Aristotle's poetics precisely because it deconstructs the apparent binary of narrative desire and the death drive. It demands a narratology that finds traverses desire toward its own undoing: death.

Importantly, Brooks's theory confuses drive with desire. For he claims that, because narrative drives toward its closure, all of the crises and complications in what he calls the middle stretch of "dilation" and "postponement" actually incite a "desire for the end" (90–112 passim). But desire plays in the open spaces and is sustained in the crises and obstacles; drive toward finality seeks to put an end to desire. They are, in fact, impulses at odds with each other. Brooks's conflation of desire and drive seems to emerge from an adherence to a notion of Aristotle's guidelines for unified plots so naturalized that Brooks himself does not perceive the duality of the narrative trajectory. This confusion, however, enables our inquiry because it reveals how compelling the apparent unity of the thanatotropic narrative can be: death is so deeply involved in the dilating crises of the classically unified narrative that desire and drive seem to collapse into a single phenomenon. This seeming collapse will become important later, as we consider the narrative structure sustaining *Six Feet Under* specifically and television series in general.

Perhaps, however, the clearest example of this deconstruction of the desire/drive binary comes in Arthur Miller's celebrated anatomy of the failure of the American Dream, *Death of a Salesman*. In it, Willy Loman finds himself unable to continue as a successful traveling salesman and encounters a series of complications that grow out of his increasing obsolescence: as brother, father, lover, friend, and employee. His own suicide marks not his resignation from that narrative, but rather his acquiescence to the narrative itself: His decision to kill himself makes his dead body—notably unrepresented in the final funeral scene—the embodiment of a both psychological and narrative drive toward death, itself already bound up in the dynamics of personal and narrative desire.

Alan Ball's *American Beauty* seems to engage the same logic for negotiating the often elided tension between the death drive and desire. Introduced as a man almost without desire—a an automaton resigned to his middle-class, apparently stable lifestyle—Lester enters into the dynamics of desire at precisely the same moment he enters into the dynamics of death. In an early scene of the film, having left his job and frustrated with the facade he feels he must re-erect over the banality of his own existence, Lester flings a plate of asparagus against the perfectly painted wall of a perfect dining room in which the American middle-class family has seated itself around a perfectly set table. The splatter of asparagus flung from one table sounds Lester's prescient death knell, foreseeing a final splattering from another table when Lester, sitting in his kitchen, will be shot. The fact that, between these two splatterings, he enters into equally automatic and unfocused routines (such as weightlifting) and even takes a job at a fast-food restaurant, the element of desire enters into his existence with the element of unpredictable instability. His murder itself grows out of that unpredictability, as the film out-Aristotles Aristotle by elevating the coincidental and the improbable to the level of narrative unity, revealing by the end that what is random does not go nowhere, just nowhere foreseeable. Of course, it is foreseeable, but only in retrospect: at Lester's death we recognize that the film had always been unraveling itself toward death from the very beginning.

Split

The God commanded clearly: let some one
punish with force this dead man's murderers.
—Sophocles, *Oedipus the King* (15)

In contrast to story lines that culminate and resolve in death are the stories that arc between literal death as the plot's inciting incident and narrative death in the resolution. Sophocles' *Oedipus the King* serves as the prototype of just such narrative. Beginning in the play's prehistory with the murder of King Laius of Thebes and structured by the oracular imperative, quoted above, to find the murderer and banish him from the city, the narrative trajectory of *Oedipus the King* seems, if anything, circular, working to unite the two kinds of death at each end of the plot into a monad. This move from an initial split in the death motif toward its eventual unity is essentially unlike the thanatotropic narrative. For the thanatotropic structure arrives at narrative death and character death simultaneously; the unity of the death motif is already built in. The Oedipal narrative's objective, however, is to traverse the temporal and spatial distance — Brooks's "dilation" and "postponement," again — between these two deaths and thereby reunite the two halves of the death motif.

In doing so, *Oedipus the King* also serves as the archetypal murder mystery. For the murder mystery, and particularly the hard-boiled *noir*-style narrative — such as Dashiell Hammet's *Maltese Falcon* — needs to reunite the discovery of the deed and the discovery of the doer in order to locate its protagonist reliably in a stable subject-position. Like Oedipus, Sam Spade (or Marlow or Hitchcock's various vicariously implicated protagonists) must, at all costs, get out of the no-man's-land between murder and murderer where the identity of the investigator bleeds into the identity of the object of investigation. While Spade success in this task, Oedipus fails.

When Oedipus discovers, at the end of his inquiry, that he himself is the murderer, he immediately sheds the role of investigator/enforcer and submits fully to the power of the oracle, even to the point of allowing Creon the empty gesture of banishing him, when it is clear by then that Oedipus would impose exile on himself anyway. Likewise, when Spade finds himself implicated in the murder of his partner, Miles Archer, and the increasingly convoluted conspiracies in which it entangles him, he must work to extricate himself from his partial position of suspect in order fully to reclaim his identity as investigator, the hard-boiled objective observer who neither judges nor is judged. Different as the hard-boiled hero may seem from the classical tragic hero, they have this in common: both succeed in extricating themselves from the problematic middle ground where they cannot fully conceive or experience a unified identity.

Again, though the narrative trajectory is a more complex one than the thanatotropic narrative's, the need to sort out how individual identity and subject position are shaped by one's relationship to a death, and to narrative death, remains a central concern. For the period of investigation, inquiry, and exploration that stretches between the inciting death and the narrative resolution is an interstitial space in which identities, relationships, and even individuals' existences are in flux. It's not precisely a liminal space, because it has not been opened up by an intentional act, such as the performance of a ritual. Rather, it is a gap, a rift that attests to the failure of the killing and the killer to remain united together in a single figure that would, in their singularity, allow the individuals affected by the death to preserve stable positions for themselves in relation to it. The Oedipal imperative, then, is "Mind the Gap": keep out of the middle-space, what T.S. Eliot has called the "Shadow" between the sundered fragments of an act split apart in time and space.

Because both the thanatotropic and the Oedipal narratives seek to elide the gap between narrative resolution and death, both privilege closure and singularity over the openness and multiplicity that emerges when unities fall apart. That tendency toward closure, more significantly, also reveals a Cartesian bent that perceives the human subject as centered on a stable, deeply interior, immutable "self." It's no surprise, then, that a third kind of narrative trajectory, the Absurdist, has the effect of dislocating and destabilizing subjective coherence precisely when it begins to disrupt the role of narratological and bodily death as unifying and stabilizing elements of a work.

Interstice

I don't know when I died.
— Samuel Beckett, "The Calmative" (27)

The Absurdist literary tradition, particularly as it emerged and evolved through the works of Samuel Beckett, triangulates the relationship between narratives tending toward death, on the one hand, and narratives emerging from it, on the other. In doing so, it tries to reclaim this middle position of uncertainty and flux as something other than a no man's land from which the subject must extricate itself. This reclamation also characterizes *Six Feet Under*'s narrative and formal trajectory. Thinking of the series as an elaboration on this strain of the

Absurdist tradition may clarify for us how *Six Feet Under* has begun to chart new thematic territory on television, and may have the added benefit of illuminating some salient features of Absurdism not often acknowledged. For, in the Absurdist tradition, death does not function as the negation of living subjectivity; that is, it does not function as a foil for the living subject, a foil that validates bodily life as the zero-point of individual identity and agency. Rather, this third tradition makes agency not one of two poles in the life/death dichotomy, but questions the way we conceive of agency, identity, individuality, and subjectivity in the first place. It is the literature of the not-quite dead.

Samuel Beckett's short story "The Calmative" — the opening sentence of which serves as the headnote above — wrenches being from living. The narrator, "alone in [his] icy bed" finds himself "too frightened to listen to [him]self rot, waiting for the great red lapses of the heart [...] and for the slow killings to finish in [his] skull" (27). Dead, he decides that, to comfort himself during decomposition, he "will tell [him]self a story." But no sooner than he resolves to do so does he begin to doubt the relationship between the story he is about to tell himself and his own mortality: "Or is it possible that in this story I have come back to life, after my death? No, it's not like me to come back to life, after my death" (27).

Importantly, the dead body still harbors a "me" capable of judging whether a story is "like me." Some vestige of identity, a point of self-identification from which actions can be considered as in or out of keeping with character, remains in the "skull" and in the "caecal walls" subject to "tearings" (27). This vestigial identity, however, does not enact its agency so much as resist it: It refuses to "come back to life," struggling against the impulse to re-animate itself narratologically. Thus, the not-quite dead subject emerges as the resistant subject, withstanding the (natural?) urge to think itself back into the living world.

Later, we might do well to ask what about the living world warrants such resistance. For the time being, however, narrative becomes a "calmative" for the narrator inasmuch as it offers a place of refuge from the world of the living, on the one hand, and of the quite dead, on the other. That is, it allows him to experience a middle ground of not-living that nevertheless is not not-being. However, narrative repeatedly fails as a calmative for Beckett's narrator. Beginning with a story from the point of view of a narrator — a second-order, or *narrated* narrator — being expelled from his home, the dead meta-narrator aborts his first

130

attempt only to begin another, and then another. In each case, the tensions and crises— in short, the props of narrative desire — keep escalating, and in doing so undermine the intended calmative effect.

This recoiling from desire, from the forward momentum we as living readers and viewers have come to expect as our due from narrative, offers us some insight into Beckett's narrator's reasons for resisting his own resurrection, if only in a fiction within a fiction. For desire — whether as a narrative device or as a psychoanalytic dynamo— relies for its genesis and sustenance on disequilibrium: something out of balance in the psychical or narratological hydraulics. And since narrative works like what Gilles Deleuze and Félix Guattari have called "desiring machines," disrupting the Freudian drives toward repression and balance, it fails to serve as a calmative (50 passim); for it depends on the mechanism of increasing and increasingly urgent imbalances to propel itself forward.

We might conclude then that reality — that is, the living reality that stands rather blandly as an alternative both to death and to not-quite death — is, unlike even realist narrative, a field of experience in which desire and the various imbalances that engender it remain, if not entirely unresolved, then only provisionally resolved. And the provisional nature of those temporary resolutions, caught as catch can, itself serves as an imbalance once removed: an imbalance of context rather than of events.

This version of death, as both a process and a position from which a kind of speech other than the fatuous yack of daily life may issue, does not emerge as a bodily state, but as an identity category unconcerned with the precise state of bodily integrity. Thus, many of Beckett's characters apparently quite alive, clinically — such as Krapp of *Krapp's Last Tape*, Didi and Gogo in *Waiting for Godot*, and the title character of his novel *Molloy*—can avail themselves of this not-quite-dead positionality. And they do. But, like Nate of *Six Feet Under*, they do so at the price of living fully.

This longing for a place where stability and resolution, eventual though they may be, become thinkable in their finality is what characterizes the Absurdist strain in *Six Feet Under*. Absurdist narrative, even broadly construed, does not offer us characters who, in the jostle and disorientation of their daily lives, seek and often find some temporary equilibrium conveniently placed at the story's denouement, as death-tending narrative structures do. Rather, such narrative gives us insight into the fundamental unreality of an existence that might, conceivably, hold out the promise of a resolution that characters can experience as final: death thinkable as an experience, not as the end of experience. Moreover, death, as articulated experience, is constructed, in absurdist texts, as an assemblage of brute facts and carefully considered interpretations of them: "It always seemed to me I died old, about ninety years old, and what years, and that my body bore it out, from head to foot" (Beckett, "Calmative" 27).

Thus, a theorem: Narrative is the chronicle of the living; reportage is the chronicle of the dead.

And reportage is precisely the mode in which the opening sequences of every episode of *Six Feet Under* operate. Even disregarding the credits sequence—culminating in a schematic quadrilateral grave plot sketched as an empty place from which a living tree seems to sprout upwards, brute in its facticity and proclaiming the potential fertility of death as a site of generation—the last moments of a soon-to-be-dead character's life are shot from an objective, omniscient point of view. The camera is the obituarist, chronicling without affect the death by mass transit, swimming pool, autoerotic asphyxiation, electrocution, automated kneading, celebratory beheading, and gang-turf warfare, among other means to an end.

The objective, unaffected style of the opening death sequences contrasts sharply with the engaged, subjective, and at times mysterious quality of the rest of each episode. For if the initial deaths chronicle the end of a human life, the scenes that follow throw us back into the thick of life, with all its messy unresolved conflicts. David, for instance, in the first season struggles with coming out, with his religious calling, with his boyfriend Keith's temperamental and impetuous nature, with his brother Nate's apparent unconcern about the future of their father's business, with the grief and demands of each episode's bereaved, and with the hostile takeover attempt launched by a large industrial death-care provider. Even as these crises get provisionally resolved, more emerge, not just for David but for the whole Fisher family as they struggle to regroup after the elder Nathaniel's death.

The difference, however, between the narrative threads that sustain *Six Feet Under* and those of other television serials—here, HBO's *The Sopranos* is instructive—is that, unlike most, they depend upon death to sustain them. They do not move inexorably toward death as the final resolution, as many of the character lines do in *The Sopranos*, nor do they simply deploy death as a jumping-off point for revenge or investigation narratives. The possibility of death does not even function as a potential finality against which the characters must struggle. Rather, death haunts the entire narrative sequence.

One obvious way in which death cohabitates with life occurs when the victim of an episode's initial death seem to return to comment on the lives of the living. Paco, a gang member killed by his rivals when he is caught on their turf at the beginning of the "Familia" episode (1.4), seems to have been a hot-headed, brash, and violent character in life. But, in death, he returns to advise David, gently chiding him for remaining closeted, afraid to face his own sexuality. Though the tenor of his advice — advocating for unapologetic self-realization — seems in line with his own territorial behavior in life, now dead, Paco makes a gift of this attitude to a man with whom we cannot imagine he would ever interact while alive. In other words, death has been a life-changing experience for Paco, who is now able to see and speak in ways that were unavailable to him before his assassination.

Likewise, the elder Nathaniel's occasional return, as a Parrot-headish spectator at his own funeral, say, or as a wry commentator on his own embalming, underscore the critical distance death affords the dead in *Six Feet Under*. But this distance, we should emphasize, is not the same as the complete separation death brings in other kinds of stories. When Big Pussy seems to return from the dead in *The Sopranos*, for instance, we learn later that his return has been unambiguously the figment of Tony Soprano's deranged imagination. In *Six Feet Under*, we get no such unequivocal certainties about the status of the dead as they apparently haunt the living. Rather, though we see the returned dead as if from a living character's point of view, the question of the dead's ontological status remains open.

If, however, death functioned only as a kind of subject position other than living, albeit privileged in its perspective over it, *Six Feet Under*'s appeal would have worn thin quite early. For such a device, if it does not develop or comment on other narrative developments, remains little more than a gimmick or a piece of spectacle. Such, fortunately for viewers and critics, is not the case. For the return of the dead as not-quite dead in *Six Feet Under* reveals to the characters and the audience the degree to which they and we are also not quite alive. And being not quite alive is more like being dead, in the Absurdist universe, than being not quite dead. The not-quite dead, that is, is an excessive state of being. It is the ontology of the dead who exceeds his brief, who is too much with us to be quite dead. The not-quite alive, however, are mired in deficiency: they are the living being who nevertheless fail to live, who are not quite alive enough.

David's various anxieties seem symptomatic of this deficiency, of being not quite alive. But Nate, particularly in the first two seasons, is more clearly positioned in this state of deficient living. For Nate seems not to be driven by a sustained and sustaining set of principles, or even policies, but to rather to drift along a current of coincidences and acci-dents: working as a manager for a co-op; giving in to the temptation of an impromptu tryst in the airport; reluctantly taking part in a business thrust upon him by his father's death; entangling himself in an unhappy marriage. All else being equal, Nate's *modus operandi* seems to be to operate without any *modus* at all. Improvisational, impulsive, and unconsidered, Nate's daily existence seems an existence without desire. Rather, he is impelled by drives, animal in that they do not admit to resistance, reflection, or even regret.

Even when Nate's first relationship with Brenda turns stormy and its inherent dysfunction surfaces, Nate resists making sustained personal and emotional investments, and thus acts (when he acts at all) in what existentialist philosopher Jean-Paul Sartre characterizes as "bad faith" (8). When Nate does resist, then, the forces against which he does are the forces of desire, commitment, and ambition. In this light, his resist-ance begins to look and feel more like inertia. No wonder Nate is so often depicted obsessively running, for he seems always to be running away.

Tellingly, the possibility of his own death from a congenital mal-formation of blood vessels in his brain hastens his awakening to a more invested life. Like the threatened metaphorical death of his father's (and now his) funeral business, his looming mortality reveals to Nate that he might, in fact, have something to live for — though it will be some time before we begin to see what that something might be. Resistance — against Kroner Industries and against his medical condition — becomes, for Nate, an act of will, an act motivated by desire, rather than an act of flight or avoidance.

Later, in "Falling into Place" (4:1), when his wife Lisa dies, Nate asserts his own agency in a striking show of resistance against her family's insis-tence that she be cremated. Knowing that Lisa would have preferred to be buried in an unmarked grave, allowed to return to the earth and rejoin the cycle of nature's regeneration to which she was so devoted in life, Nate substitutes the remains of an unclaimed body for Lisa's, and buries Lisa according to her wishes. Lisa's death, as a kind of return, a re-entry into narrative (she had been missing before her body was discovered), rather than a plucking out of it emphasizes the inadequacy of linear notions of narrative (such as the Oedipal or thanatotropic models) for accounting for Absurdist narratology.

In this sequence of events, the agency of the not-quite dead merges with Nate's agency as he more and more fully enters the world of desiring life, in several significant ways. First, Nate is acting on Lisa's wishes; that is, he becomes her "agent," carrying out acts impelled by her agency from beyond (or not quite to) the grave. However, Nate also exercises agency of his own that emerges from an increasingly clear trajectory he perceives for himself. On the one hand, his choice to act on Lisa's behalf takes into account, and attempts in small measure to rectify, what he rightly thinks of as his often boorish treatment of her while they were married. On the other hand, the act commits him to a future in which some pretenses can no longer be sustained: namely, the pretense that interpersonal, familial, and societal demands can be marginalized, brushed aside and forgotten. In this way, Nate and Lisa together seem to choose a course of action that will bind them together and bind Nate's present with his past and his future. Nevertheless, even that "trajectory" gets depicted as a failure, or a dry run, for a trajectory yet to take its place, again underscoring how his development, and the series' progress more broadly, depends on a mode of unfolding other than a single, sustained, and unified plot line.

Nate, of course, is not the only character impelled by death to awaken from a deficient state of not-quite living to a mode of living in desire. Ruth undergoes a similar awakening, though much sooner, and David seems to undergo a series of such (re)awakenings. Nate's case is instructive, though, because it reveals in depth the condition of insufficient life. Ruth's and, perhaps more starkly, Claire's case anatomize the space between acknowledging desire as an enabling, rather than debilitating, force and acting fully and intentionally upon that desire. Ruth's love affairs and eventual second marriage, her early insistence on taking part fully in the management of the funeral home, and her effort to experience a life beyond the home and its demands show us a woman determinedly, if at times tentatively, testing the limits of the insufficiency she sees retrospectively as having beset her until her husband's death. Claire, similarly, makes frustrated and frustrating attempts to act upon some authentic, genuinely desiring impulses early in the first season, though she seems to do so preemptively, to ward off the future of insufficient living she has watched her mother live out for may years.

In all three cases, though, *Six Feet Under* offers its viewers a living analogue to the partial state of the not-quite dead who repeatedly haunt its episodes. Both seem temporary, between states that tend toward something more to be hoped for: death, on the one hand, and desire, on the other. All of this is not to sum up *Six Feet Under* with a moral lesson, however: "The life half-lived is the unlived life" or some such kitschy pseudo-philosophical palliative. Rather, *Six Feet Under* offers us a diagnosis of the more general state of life in a world where subjects must finally choose between the messy, dangerous, unpredictability of a life impelled by crises and frustrations or the safe, static, and calmative life impelled by inertia and avoidance. That the series does not come down on one side or another is evidenced by the fact that, in acting upon their desires, characters like Brenda and Ruth can be as frustrating and annoying as characters, like Nate, who do not, or characters like David, who often cannot.

Indeed, as the series approaches its end, the final season has begun to re-open the middle spaces of not-quite-life that we had been lured into to thinking closed. Brenda spends her wedding to Nate in a half-drunken, pain killer-induced stupor after a miscarriage. The marriage that ensues proves not to offer either one the refuge from instability and confusion they long for. Indeed, Nate's death does not even provide an end to his life; for despite the fact that he no longer exists bodily, he seems more present than ever in the anguish and grief his family experiences. Likewise, Ruth's second marriage collapses under the weight of George's increasingly paranoid depression, holing up in the family bomb shelter, undergoing electric shock treatment, and finally moving into an apartment of his own. David and Keith's decision to have a child through a surrogate precipitates for them a crisis of fidelity and sexuality. In these cases, and plenty of others besides, the series continually reminds us, formally, that our desires depend upon the very obstacles and setbacks we believe we wish to overcome.

It might be worth mentioning, too, by way of concluding, that the serial form the narrative takes, depending on open-endedness and required to sustain viewer's desire from one episode and one season to another, seems to depend on not explicitly espousing one of two modes of being alive, but rather by charting out a middle space, the space of indecision and indirection where the possibility of valid and valuable experience remains open. Yet the series, too, must end, and how we orient ourselves to that end, just as how we orient ourselves to the crises and frustrations that sustain our desire along the way, asks us to consider the quandary of the Absurd. And, perhaps by extension, it asks us to consider the question of just what kind of place we occupy, as agents and subjects, in a world in which action and inertia seem at times equally attractive — and equally fearful — alternatives.

Notes

1. I'm thinking here of Stephen Daldry's *The Hours* (2002) or Merchant-Ivory's many sepia-toned period films, and of Sofia Coppola's *Lost in Translation* (2003).

Works Cited

Aeschylus. *Agamemnon. Aeschylus I: Oresteia*. Trans. Richard Lattimore. The Complete Greek Tragedies. Eds. David Grene and Richmond Lattimore. Chicago: Pheonix-University of Chicago Press, 1969.

Aristotle. *Poetics*. Trans. and intr. Gerald F. Else. Ann Arbor: University of Michigan Press, 1967.

Ball, Alan, writer. *American Beauty*. DreamWorks, 1999.

_____, dir. *Six Feet Under*. HBO, 2001–2005.

Beckett, Samuel. "The Calmative." *Stories and Texts for Nothing*. New York: Evergreen-Grove Weidenfeld Press, 1967.

_____. *Krapp's Last Tape. Krapp's Last Tape and Other Dramatic Pieces*. New York: Evergreen-Grove Weidenfeld Press, 1957.

_____. *Molloy. Molloy, Malone Dies and The Unnamable: Three Novels*. New York: Grove Press, 1959.

_____. *Waiting for Godot*. London: Faber and Faber, 1965.

Brooks, Peter. *Reading for the Plot: Design and Intention in Narrative*. New York: Alfred A Knopf, 1984.

Coppola, Sofia, dir. *Lost in Translation*. Focus Features, 2003.

Daldry, Stephen, dir. *The Hours*. Paramount, 2002.

Deleuze, Gilles, and Felix Guattari. *Anti-Oedipus: Capitalism and Schizophrenia*. Trans. Robert Hurley, Mark Seem, and Helen R. Lane. Minneapolis: University of Minnesota Press, 1983.

Freud, Sigmund. "Beyond the Pleasure Principle." 1920. *The Standard Edition of the Complete Psychological Works of Sigmund Freud*. Ed. and trans. James Strachey, et al. Vol. 18. London: Hogarth P; London: The Institute of Psycho-Analysis, 1955. 7–64.

Hammett, Dashiell. *The Maltese Falcon*. New York: Vintage-Random House, 1989.

Lacan, Jacques. "Seminar on 'The Purloined Letter.'" Trans. Jeffrey Mehlman. *The Purloined Poe: Lacan, Derrida, and Psychoanalytic Reading*. Eds. John P. Muller and William J. Richardson. Baltimore: John Hopkins University Press, 1988.

Sartre, Jean-Paul. *Truth and Existence*. Trans. Adrian van den Horen. Ed. and Intr. Ronald Aronson. Chicago: University of Chicago Press, 1992.

Six Feet Under: The Complete Fourth Season. Created by Alan Ball. 5 videodisks. HBO Video, 2005.

Sophocles. *Oedipus the King*. Trans. David Grene. *Sophocles I*. Intr. David Grene. The Complete Greek Tragedies. Eds. David Grene and Richard Lattimore. Chicago: Pheonix-University of Chicago Press, 1954.

Shakespeare, William. *Macbeth. The Norton Shakespeare*. Eds. Stephen Greenblatt, Walter Cohen, Jean E. Howard, and Katharine Eisaman Maus. New York: Norton, 1997.

Bridesmaids, Bosoms, and Booze: Visibility and the Veiling of Conservatism

Johanna Frank

Since its première in 1993, Alan Ball's play *Five Women Wearing the Same Dress* has appeared on countless college, university, and regional theatre stages around the United States. The play's popularity in these particular venues is astounding when one considers the politics of season scheduling, the demands of subscription consistency and box office sales, and the requirements of repertory staples for student training and/or general audience viewing. The attraction of Ball's work as a more recent play among a sea of other possibilities warrants attention. Because one is never necessarily privy to the planning process of a theatre venue's artistic director, the reasoning behind season scheduling often remains open to anyone's guess. There are a few clues, however, that may reveal the attraction to *Five Women*. Alan Ball, after all, is the award-winning creator of the *American Beauty* and *Six Feet Under*. Name recognition in this marketing-driven, consumer culture goes a long way for new "products," including drama. Moreover, taking heed from Ball's dramatic oeuvre that critiques contemporary society's excessive consumerism, shallow relationships, and generic gender and sexual behaviors, one might concede that the institutions programming *Five Women* embrace the play's biting look at social customs and their less than apparent flaws.

By making visible a previous invisible, *Five Women* seemingly offers a critique of the roles available to women. The main action of the play revolves around the revealing of secrets. In its simple notion of visibility, *Five Women* assumes a duality between the visible and invisible. Moreover, it offers the illusion that the maneuver of making the invisible visible can and will be politically and socially empowering to women. It suggests that identity is a construction that can be embodied or enacted; that such embodiment or enactment can serve epistemological ends; and that such epistemology can lead to change. The theater as "a seeing place"—as an optical playground for revisions and new visions—is an enticing venue for Ball because it offers the suspended utopian illusion of the possibility for tangible and malleable intervention and invention. Visibility appears to be one of Alan Ball's play's strengths. As a group, the five women engage in lascivious acts of excessive alcohol consumption, of the public baring of breasts, of lewd conversation objectifying men and sex, of disrespect for family and religion, and of anger and resentment for opportunities lost. Each character represents a variety of differences among women as well as gives voice to the gendered oppressions women experience at the hands of others. In this manner, *Five Women* reveals the diverse secrets, desires, loves, and traumas residing among an otherwise singular group of brides-maids. Albeit simplistic, Ball's play appears to delve beneath the taffeta of pastel dresses and matching shoes to uncover the flaws and less than per-fect drives that co-exist alongside social mores and cultural institutions. Ball reveals the illusion of the pure bridesmaid is precisely that: an illusion.

Ball is attempting to write women as realistic and powerful people — the pursuit is admirable and being rewarded in and through the play's production history among college and regional theatres. Yet this deploy-ment of the trope of visibility — as both the architecture and the motiva-tion of the play and its characters— reinforces the very binaries and conservative social institutions it aims to disrupt. Rather than challenge, bypass or undermine the heteronormative narratives of love, beauty, fam-ily, and religion, *Five Women* employs stock characters who operate within strict binaries (even the "locker room" banter in which the women par-take merely flip-flops stereotypical gender roles rather than dismantles them), engages the literal visibility of the female body as an essential body, and presents consciousness-raising as the primary means to achieve strength and empowerment. The ultimate lesson it teaches is that women are insecure until they realize they are not alone in their feelings.

While this essay is not intended to make straw men of contemporary plays, it is vital to acknowledge there are serious limitations to the trope of visibility and visibility politics. Even as visibility remains at the heart of feminism's contested claims to subjectivity and the constructedness of representation, a reliance on visibility as a tactic to bring the issues of gender, sexuality, race and multiple oppressions to the fore has three pitfalls: (1) essentialism; (2) the reiteration of difference; and (3) the portrayal of contexts as transparent and value free. The trope of visibility as a performative technique has a tendency of reducing identity to corporeality, and thus has the potential to result in these significant liabilities, the first of which provides anchored referents to read any given identity category/label as either an authentic identity or a perversion of a naturalized norm. The second reduces politics and policy to a question of cultural visibility and necessitates corporeal-signifying practices to reflect sexual and other identity-based practices. Finally, the third elides historical and sociopolitical specificity, ignoring how ideology reinforces power structures.

Of course, it's unreasonable to demand of all contemporary plays that they engage visibility critically or bypass it all together. But visibility is a loaded trope. In the most visual of popular culture media, feminist film scholars have identified the risk involved with the trope of visibility. For example, Teresa de Lauretis argues in "Aesthetic and Feminist Theory" that the most productive feminist texts are those that shift from focusing on content (i.e., images of women) to that of the axis of vision itself. Borrowing words from Adrienne Rich, de Lauretis articulates radical change as that which displaces "the critical emphasis from 'images of' women 'to the axis of vision itself — to the modes of organizing vision and hearing which result in the production of that image'" (164). For de Lauretis, the project of formulating a feminist aesthetic is a project of redefinition:

> The emphasis must be shifted away from the artist behind the camera, the gaze or the text as origin and determination of meaning, toward the wider public sphere of cinema as a social technology: we must develop our understanding of cinema's implication in other modes of cultural representation, and its possibilities of both production and counter-production of social vision [162].

In calling for cinema theorists to "articulate the conditions and forms of vision for another social subject, and so to venture into the highly risky business of redefining aesthetic and formal knowledge," de Lauretis turns the viewfinder back on itself, makes the mode of vision visible, and suggests that we "formulate the condition of representability of another social subject" (162). A project of re-vision is not merely "the act of looking back, of seeing with fresh eyes," as Rich suggests, or of "reclaiming vision," as de Lauretis would suggest. Instead both Rich and de Lauretis imply a project in which one must change the *conditions* of seeing.

Moreover, not all art need be political. While politics is not necessarily the criterion by which we (should) judge or assess art, politics has become the dominant criterion by which popular culture measures feminist art (where feminist equals politics and art equals aesthetics).[1] Politics, of course, is a volatile criterion: the value and/or meaning of a given work of art becomes dependent on the socio-political sways and fluctuations of any given society and/or community. One only needs to turn to the example of the public reception and controversy surrounding Judy Chicago's *The Dinner Party* to see how public and political reception, as well as aesthetics, changes and fluctuates over the course of several decades. What was celebrated at the 1979 premier of *The Dinner Party* as a positive embrace of assertive and powerful female sexuality caused congressional outrage more than ten years later: (Scherzer 5) as documented in the *Congressional Record* and quoted in newspaper articles throughout the months of July to December 1990, Republican congressmen perceived the art as "weird sexual art" that presents "genitalia served up on plates" (5).[2]

What all of this and other forms of public invocations of visibility reveal, however, is that visibility itself, particularly in relation to art, *is* political. In addition, visibility operates within specific and fluctuating states and depends upon specific conditions of given environments. Just as Chicago's *The Dinner Party* has affected and experienced different receptions at different periods in time, so too does drama and performance. What is curious about Alan Ball's *Five Women Wearing the Same Dress* is how it can be perceived as simultaneously "radical" and apolitical. Keeping in mind that historically, visibility has served as a crucial political strategy for feminist political organizations, the distribution of female-specific information and knowledge, the development of a literary and artistic tradition, and the articulation of aesthetics, it is important not to disregard all together performance that engages the trope. What began in the '70s as radical politics should continue to develop culturally and technically in scope. After all, a generation of politics and theorizing of aesthetics has enabled artists to challenge the evolving notion of what constitutes the relationship between politics and aesthetics.

However, as we move further into the twenty-first century, there are serious limitations to visual representation as a political end or goal in and of itself. While the visibility of identity should be, at most, a starting point for expressing artistic and feminist politics, there is a vital social and artistic need to continue creating projects of redefinition. To change the conditions of seeing, as Adrienne Rich and Teresa de Lauretis advocate, such projects must move beyond visibility. While there are several stakes in such work — disrupting notions of the body as an original, authentic site of experience; of the materiality of the body as a site of feminist politics; of a politics based on the legitimating narrative of consciousness-raising as self liberating — the potential benefits outweigh the risks.

Looking at Five Women

Five Women Wearing the Same Dress is a full-length, two-act play. Five different women, who seemingly have nothing in common except for their dislike of the bride and the fact that they have all slept with or have had a pass made at them by the same man, find they have more in common than they realize. Crisis-transformation-resolution defines the larger trajectory of the play. After Act One, in which the women initially assume stereotypes or preconceived notions about each other based on stock character traits, Act Two presents the women as bonding together in their expressions of fear, anxiety, disappointment, and anger. Amongst them they have experienced collectively a variety of gendered social ills: self-mutilation, abortion, rape, sexual abuse, pre-marital and extramarital sex, homosexuality, homophobia, anorexia, bulimia, plastic surgery, liposuction, beauty anxiety, AIDS, and sexually transmitted disease. What emerges through their discussions is a model of consciousness raising. The five women share their experiences, support one another, and come to realize that there is more depth to each one of them than their respective surfaces reveal. By bonding around oppression and suffering, the women seem to break the boundaries of difference that separate them and open themselves to take on qualities of the others. They learn that they have been mistaking each other's exterior for an interior self. Just as the costume jewelry — used as a prop at the beginning of the play — can deceive and/or create pleasure for the unknowing eye, nothing is what it seems. Of course, Ball seems to suggest that such illusion is also a part of reality.

The play reveals this theme most directly through the staging and partnering of the characters. The entire play, in fact, revolves around the interior, domestic space of the childhood bedroom of the protagonist, Meredith. Not surprisingly, the setting of the play establishes the various thematic elements in tension with one another: the deep-seeded history and traditions of a southern turn-of-the-century mansion in an old-money neighborhood, the combination of architectural luxurious and ready-made décor, the juxtaposition of the family unit and the individual, the media technologies of the high-tech modern world, and the pop-culture visuals haphazardly attached to the walls. As Ball's stage directions suggest, "a prominent poster of Malcolm X on the wall" disrupts "the air of traditional privilege" of the environment (217). Iconic imagery is at play here. The five bridesmaids and one male guest move in and out of this bedroom, which functions as an enclave both removed from and caught within the larger structures and institutions of family, religion, and marriage.

Clearly, Ball manipulates expectations regarding public spectacle and private domestic spaces. A wedding ceremony is a ritual that displays familial, communal, and intimate relationships as well as social and/or religious rites in the form of public spectacle. This is the event that occurs outside the protagonist's second-floor bedroom; however, it is not separate from the bedroom because the family's home is the site of the reception. The house itself accommodates the overflow of guests, who move in and out of the first-floor rooms. As a pseudo sanctuary, the bedroom is somewhat porous: the large window, the bedroom door, and the intercom system function as the conduits between the interior private space and the exterior public affair. Moreover, each of these architectural elements serves as a site of disruption to the sanctuary of the bedroom. Whether or not the bedroom is a sanctuary, its position within the house and the social affair suggests that its inhabitants are never fully removed from the public, exterior event. As a part of the larger web, the bedroom and the women who move in and out of it are interconnected in the larger, overall space. Nonetheless, one by one each of the five bridesmaids find her way to this room as a perceived haven from the social dictates of the wedding; upon entering Meredith's bedroom each woman reveals a conflict between an interior and exterior self.

Act One opens with a trespasser. Frances, the token Bible-thumping

Christian cousin of the bride and stock virgin of the group, is the first to enter the room. She is a curious, naïve young woman who seeks knowledge but associates it with danger. Through her fascination of what she misperceives to be a glittering diamond bracelet (rather than the fake rhinestone that it is) belonging to Meredith, Frances introduces the theme of the play: nothing is what it seems. Frances is a woman of absolutes; she doesn't smoke or drink and embraces marriage as the penultimate marker of an operating and functional system of culture. Strict gender roles are not stereotypes but "natural" and essential components of that system. She believes that "God wants you to be married if you have a baby" and thinks that "the collapse of family values and all decent morality" are the results of failure to follow the "holy word of God" (260). It's not so much that Frances' beliefs will be tested or contested by the others, but that she herself begins the play by crossing boundaries and borders both ideological and physical. She is the tragic hero: her curiosity provides her with knowledge but leads to her fall from her supposed grace of conservative ideology.

In contrast to Frances, Meredith, the sister of the bride, is gruff and abrupt. Her outward, passive-aggressive behavior is a manifestation of her resentment and disappointment in the limitations of family roles and expectations. She is, however, superficially aggressive. Her declarations about the false pretenses of the wedding hide her own fears of isolation. Meredith is lonely because she lacks connections with others. Moreover, she doesn't know how to make such connections and has returned to live in her parents' home even though she feels alienated from it. She is verbally disrespectful to her mother and the values of her immediate surroundings, not to mention the event of the day: her sister's wedding. Upon entering her bedroom she rants on and on about the false pretenses and serious tone of the wedding ceremony, which she perceives as an illusion; the supposed blushing bride, according to Meredith, is anything but obedient. Just as her Malcolm X poster represents a vain attempt to differentiate herself from the WASP home environment of her childhood and claim solidarity with another community, her black leather motorcycle jacket, backpack and sunglasses — all worn over the peach taffeta dress, wide-brimmed hat, and matching dyed shoes she had donned for the marriage ceremony — reveal a character struggling to find herself. Meredith immediately removes these self-declared articles of identity and the "costume" of the bridesmaid dress and relaxes in her undergarments: male boxer shorts and a strapless brassiere. Her various garments combine elements in conflict; the layering, however, falsely establishes interior and exterior identification.

Following Meredith's entrance is Trisha's. A former high school and college friend of the bride, Trisha is the older, "experienced" woman: her sexual independence as a teenager that has continued into her adult life (symbolized by the strip of condoms in her purse) landed her the title of "little whore" by the mother-of-the-bride. Trisha is the bad girl who follows her passions and drives, from marijuana to alcohol to men; she is equally brash as Meredith, but in a more mature sense because she serves as the voice of reason throughout the play—the older sister, of sorts— who is wise and knowledgeable. Mastering the art of and manipulating gender and generational roles are Trisha's fortes. She is a strong, independent woman who is a consumer of people. For this reason, when she expresses a bashful interest in the groom's cousin, Tripp Davenport, she reveals a new side to herself that surprises Meredith and the other women. Trisha is not a woman to be shy; her history reveals quite the opposite.

Georgeanne, a married woman and mother of a young son, is the victim of male neglect: we learn that she and her husband no longer have sex; and her former boyfriend Tommy Valentine, who ten years ago abandoned Georgeanne when she needed to have an abortion—for a fling with the woman whose wedding they are all currently attending—is now at the wedding reception and ignoring Georgeanne (Tommy, it turns out, is the connection between all five bridesmaids). Furthermore, we learn that not too long before the present moment, Georgeanne ran into this ex-boyfriend at a bar and they "ended up doing it in the parking lot, on the concrete, right behind a Dempsey Dumpster" (236). Because that incident was the "best sex [she] ever had in [her] entire life," she purchased expensive lingerie to wear under her taffeta dress for the wedding in the hopes that she might continue the illicit affair with the ex-boyfriend; however, as we learn, those undergarments will remain covered (236). For the majority of the play Georgeanne is hideously drunk from a bottle of champagne and moves in and out of bouts of hysteria. These behaviors as well as those she manifests in private—including self-inflicted wounds—reveal Georgeanne's suffering as a traumatized woman who is struggling desperately to survive.

The final bridesmaid is Mindy, cousin of the groom and stock lesbian of the crowd. While Trisha is the one who declares that she "detests men" as well as "doubts most men," Mindy is a beautiful, non-threatening dyke who merely perceives she lacks the grace of the otherwise assumed heterosexual bridesmaids (238). Despite the fact that Mindy is the only bridesmaid who has grace, a trait admired by the others, she thinks her personality does not "fit" the gown because she constantly bumps into furniture and objects around the house. She confesses that she feels clumsy in her dress, which she loves, but fears her clumsiness "will ruin this wedding," an event that she — like Frances — admires (237). At the moment of her entrance in the play she is the lipstick lesbian, the femme who, for all exterior purposes, does not threaten the social structures of heterosexuality and family. Yet there is something about her — particularly her self-perceived clumsiness — that foreshadows her potential destructiveness.

Mindy's inner thoughts and outward appearances are in constant contradiction, and neither her interior nor exterior presentations of her self are consistent. This is not as much a complexity to Mindy's character as it is a fault in character development. For the other characters, Ball engages a bit of dramatic irony: each reveals a struggle between interior and exterior self where the interior represents a secret and the exterior is a projected social identity, and the audience is more privy to this than each woman. As the play progresses, Frances, Meredith, Trisha, and Georgeanne each evolve in such a way that their "revealing" of a secret enables them to accept the contradiction between their interior and exterior selves. Mindy's character, however, undergoes the stripping away of not just one but two inner layers — the first contradicts her exterior self and the second reinforces her outer self. Because the innermost core compliments the exterior self, Mindy's character elides rather than embraces her contradictions.

Re-Seeing Visibility

Making visible a prior invisible is a central device in Ball's play. Each woman, it turns out, is not so different from the others. They all share the complexity of having surface and depth to their respective identities and they learn that beneath their shells they all yearn for love, sympathy and connections with others. More importantly, they learn that their opposite character — the person with whom each least identifies — is, in fact, more similar than initially realized (one's exterior is the other's interior and vice versa). Yet in Act One, the women have yet to realize this connection. Instead, each feels threatened by her binary opposite because Ball sets the women against one another: Trisha and Frances, Georgeanne and an unnamed woman as well as the bride, and Meredith and Mindy are the pairs of characters. What Ball presents to his viewing audience are pairs of women who, in encountering the other, undergo processes of transformation. Their various before-and-after scenarios are based on stereotypical expectations of archetypical characters.

Trisha and Frances are at constant odds with one another. The good girl-bad girl; virgin-whore; inexperienced-experienced; naïve-wise; young-old scenarios all play out between these two. And marriage, sex, love, reproduction, God, and religion are the large topics that these scenarios engage. For example, Trisha and Frances' encounters ask such grand questions as, is sex as an act of lust or an act of God? As Trisha asserts, "You don't need a man to have a baby" and you certainly don't need "to cement yourself to him" if you do include a man and not just anonymous sperm in fertilization (260). Frances, who believes in "the holy word of God," cannot fathom a perspective such as Trisha's. These two women never resolve their differences, but it becomes apparent that both have strong feelings that are neither right nor wrong. This is best symbolized in and through the makeover that Trisha provides Frances: a "fresh and natural" with a touch of "a woman with a past" look (250).

Georgeanne's foils—an unnamed guest at the wedding who wears a blue dress, and the bride—function as her opposites even though they never actually appear in the play. Georgeanne, who resorts to drinking a bottle of champagne and hanging out in the bedroom — both as forms of escape — avoids opting for the two paths represented by these two women: embracing marriage or embarking on a public flirtation. Georgeanne refers to her first foil as "this total bitch in a navy blue linen dress with absolutely no back, I mean you could almost see her butt," yet she envies the woman who's getting the attention of her ex-boyfriend (233). The bride represents another form of public display, which for Georgeanne is the opposite of her own personal experiences, which have remained secret. The following is Georgeanne's imagined exchange with the bride:

> Tracy, I don't think I can be in your wedding, because you remember when I had that nervous breakdown my junior year of college? That was because your boyfriend knocked me up and I had to have an abortion all by myself while he was taking you to the Kappa Sig Luau, and things have been just a little, well, *strained* between you and me ever since [234].

The irony, of course, is that Georgeanne *is* in the wedding as one of the bridesmaids. Unlike Trisha and Frances, though, Georgeanne never gets the opportunity to speak to her foil directly. Instead, we see her possible path in and through these two women: chasing the one-night-stand or following the structure of marriage. In Georgeanne's world, women are either with or against one another.

Meredith and Mindy present the last pairing of characters. Meredith, who does not fit the archetypical female-daughter role (she is, after all, the one bridesmaid wearing men's boxer shorts under her taffeta dress as well as a motorcycle jacket over the dress), feels threatened by Mindy, who is an out lesbian. Meredith is willing to receive advice from everyone but Mindy, who is the one to call Meredith on her superficiality and hypocrisy. Moreover, when all the bridesmaids learn about the sexual abuse Meredith experienced as a young girl, Mindy exclaims that what happened to Meredith "was not harmless" but "was abuse" (274). Meredith refuses to accept assistance from Mindy, who offers several options for help. In response to Mindy leaving a card with some names on it, Meredith declares, "Look. Get this straight, Mindy. I am not interested in meeting any of your friends. I'm not ... What do you think, I'm an idiot, Mindy? I am not blind, I see the way you look at me. But I am not like you. I'm just *not*, okay? So it really wouldn't do much good for me to meet any of your friends" (275). Meredith's response is anything but rational. She perceives the gay-straight binary as rigid. Her homophobia clouds her judgment. Even more surprising, none of the other women counter Meredith's response.

The bridesmaids, as an ensemble cast, model for the viewing audience how one is to respond to the various characters and their experiences. In other words, as each bridesmaid reveals her inner and outer self, the viewing audience, like the bridesmaid audience, perceives the discrepancy between the two selves. They reinforce the binaries they present. For example, well into Act One, and much to the others' surprise, Mindy declares that she loves beauty pageants, a result of being forced to attend "Miss Amelia's Charm School" when she was in the sixth grade. She explains that the school held its own pageant as a graduation ceremony, and the following exchange ensues:

Trisha: You're kidding. You went to charm school?

Mindy: My mother *made* me go when I was in sixth grade, I think she was dimly aware of my dyke potential and was hoping Miss Amelia would nip it in the bud. ...

Meredith: That must have been so humiliating.

Mindy: Are you kidding? I loved it. I wore a nautical bathing suit with a little skirt attached, and high heels, and I played "Crimson and Clover" on my bassoon for the talent competition and I won.

Georgeanne: You did not.

Mindy: It was the high point of my life. I'm serious. It's been all downhill ever since.

Georgeanne: I would have thought you hated beauty pageants.

Mindy: Why? Because I'm a lesbian? Hell, no. I haven't missed a Miss America pageant in twenty years [263].

Mindy then explains that "those girls are better than drag queens" who perform ideal albeit hypocritical femininity by asserting their piety and then displaying themselves as sex objects (263). She mocks the beauty contestants: "'I'm just so thrilled to be poised on the brink of a fabulous career combining broadcast journalism and teaching handicapped children but most importantly being a good wife and mother and a good American ... Here's my tits, here's my butt, here's my tits again. Thank you!'" (263). Because the other four women are more shocked to learn that Mindy attended a charm school than to hear her statement regarding pageants, Ball implies that the above is the kind of statement one would, stereotypically, expect to hear from the gay woman in the crowd, the woman who defies the "normalacy" of heterosexuality or else consciously strips away the gendered expectations of society and reveals the contradictions therein.

If the characters establish the binary of gay versus straight — including strict rules of operation between them — then the most surprising act of the play is when Meredith takes on Mindy's comment as her own. Without a moment's pause, Meredith moves in front of the open window and exposes herself to a crowd of guests gathered at a wedding reception at her family's southern estate. As Ball describes in his stage directions, Meredith "Pulls down her bra and flashes her breasts, then waves insanely" and, in a moment of desperate defiance, exclaims "Hey everybody! Here's my tits!" (263). Despite her antagonism towards Mindy, Meredith's moment before the open window, however, evokes not a beauty pageant but rather images of the popular-culture videos *Girls Gone Wild*. In the eyes of her audience outside the window — the guests at the wedding reception — her act lacks any context. She appears merely as a hysterical woman exposing herself.

One might expect a more understanding audience within the bedroom because the context of the act is Mindy's comment as well as Meredith's dialogue in the moments prior to the one before the open window. To them, Meredith's act could be an expression of desperate frustration: she too feels as if she's in drag parading in a dress at a wedding that she perceives exhibits false pretenses about women and femininity. Or, they might perceive her as presenting visibly — albeit ironically — the antithesis of what her boxer shorts and Malcolm X poster portray. Yet the women inside the room are as equally shocked as those outside in the garden. The five bridesmaids, who like Meredith, escaped to the bedroom to find respite from the social dictates of the wedding, should understand why Meredith responded in such a manner. Instead they quickly move Meredith away from the window in a moment of intervention, and Meredith's resistance to cultural norms becomes a closeted notion.

Contrary to Ball's intention of the revealing of secrets as a means towards personal growth, this act of removing Meredith from the window implies that the space of the bedroom and the secrets told therein are not a part of the larger world beyond the scope of the house. That whatever growth may be experience during this time of bonding among the bridesmaids does not apply to their lives once the women leave the room. One must ask, then, what good is consciousness-raising if it is self-contained? Do the women accomplish anything if they remain censored to the society in which they operate on a day-to-day basis? Does the private sphere function separately from the public? How might the sharing of experiences and the evolving progression of female bonding among all the women, despite their supposed differences, be undermined by this act of removal?

Veiling Conservativism

Feminism has been invested in making the female, the feminine, women, and women's experiences visible, re-visible, and re-seen. For political movements of the latter half of the century, such investment was central, radical, and necessary. The Women's Movement, for example, evoked visibility in terms of public and political presence (from woman-specific spaces such as women's theatres to political-process organizations such as NOW). Feminist political discourse of the 1970s identified visibility as the literal presence of women in the public sphere. In addition to changing and affecting the public and political environment, feminism worked to increase the visibility of gendered, racial, ethnic, and sexual "others," and their appearance as presence, which incorporated changing the power of seeing and breaking down the hierarchies of who exercises the control of sight and vision. Visibility, in these terms, operated as a strategy of oppositionality to assert an individual or a group's visible presence in the public sphere as a means to increase awareness and affect political change.

Such an approach deployed visibility in its most basic and literal sense: the condition, state, or fact of being visible. Of course, visibility became caught up in notions of embodied identity and presence (one need only turn to any social movement's invocation of the term to perceive a tension and negotiation of positing the body as a site of authority and recognizing the multiple identifications that constitute and undermine that authority). This was underscored by the theorizing of feminist aestheticians that located the female body as the referent for a feminist project and as a site for political activism.[3] The emerging feminist artistic production in the late '60s and early '70s appropriated this circulating discourse of visibility and began the process of re-transforming it into a trope. By identifying women's bodily experiences as a central tactic to representing political concerns around issues of gender, the Feminist Art movement aligned, if not equated, visibility with the body and established consciousness-raising as political action.[4] Combining feminist activism with visual and verbal metaphors of women's experiences — merging if not collapsing the political with the personal — enabled feminist performance to employ visibility of the body as a mode of consciousness-raising.[5]

The notion of recovery — making visible a previously invisible — is at the core of much of political and artistic work, which Alan Ball's play inherits.[6] Ball is not alone. We can perceive this inheritance in many contemporary pieces. One need only turn to Eve Ensler's *The Vagina Monologues* (1996) to find such an example. In the opening narrative that frames *The Vagina Monologues* the speaker — who delivers all the monologues as well as the narrative interludes— exclaims, "I bet you're worried. *I* was worried. That's why I began this piece. I was worried about vaginas.... So I decided to talk to women about their vaginas, to do vagina interviews, which became vagina monologues" (3). The opening lines provide an overview of the structure of the play, which is a series of monologues separated by narrative interludes. Moreover, it establishes the political action component of the play by positing consciousness-raising as that which will transform the audience just as it transformed the speaker and the women whose experiences comprised the content of her monologues. The speaker *was* worried until she listened to women, collected the interviews, and translated them into the monologues. The audience *should* be worried, that is, until it has the opportunity "to hear" others' voices. Working from the premise that "everything [women] knew about ... vagina[s] was based on hearsay or invention.... It had never occurred to [women] to look at [vaginas]," the monologues are that which can transform members of the reading or viewing audience from passive, docile objects into active, assertive subjects (45).

While this is a very different performance text than *Five Women*, *The Vagina Monologues* emerged on the regional and national college stages around the same time period as Ball's play. *The Vagina Monologues* shares with *Five Women* a notion of stripping layers of signification that surround women's bodies so as to reveal a hidden interior truth. The speaker of Ensler's play is the individual who leads her reading or viewing audience through a series of woman-identified experiences (some stereotypical or overly generalized) including but not limited to masturbation, menses, heterosexual intercourse, sexual assault, and childbirth (employing essential notions of the body to represent and/or stand in for all women's experiences). As the monologues proceed, they establish a narrative of "woman" as a survivor who overcomes trauma or sexual ignorance and moves toward self-knowledge and the acquisition of visibility: to be a woman is to have little or no access to one's vagina (physically, emotionally, and epistemologically) until one survives and/or undergoes a personal and political awakening. This posits a specific kind of identity that is linked to the unconscious and the keeping of secrets; to have identity is to have possession of such secrets and to have the agency that results from deploying or uncovering such secrets. Similarly, the play is predicated on the pleasure and danger in discovering if not revealing and speaking those secrets, or rather, revealing and speaking the taboo that isn't (anymore) taboo: the vagina.

The *Vagina Monologues*, like *Five Women Wearing the Same Dress*, seeks to ground and verify the injuries and violations women suffer; however, it does so rather uncritically. Certainly, there is nothing wrong with the promotion of empowerment, fundraisers for women's shelters, or feminism's increased exposure on college campuses; however, I am concerned with the extent to which contemporary plays rearticulate an essential identity of Woman under the banner of radical performance politics and/or uphold consciousness-raising as an end. While these are merely two examples, there are a slew of plays—from Ntozake Shange's 1970 *for colored girls who have considered suicide/when the rainbow isn't enuf* to the more recent *Laramie Project* by Moisés Kaufman — that employ the trope of visibility as a major dramatic and theatrical device.[7] For earlier 1970s feminist cultural productions such as *for colored girls*, this approach was innovative. Moreover, such theatrical representation achieved its goal of employing visibility to increase women's presence on stages and in public discourse. As such, representation provided a first and necessary step toward radical politics.

But what does this mean for contemporary feminist, race, and sexuality politics? E. Ann Kaplan suggests, with regard to feminist film documentaries of the 1970s, there is an assumption that mimetic representations, in making women's experiences visible, might have an activist impact on women's oppressions. This stance assumes that realist representations might do more for women than representations of representations. While in the 1990s Kaplan critiques this position — she argues that deconstruction "taught us that realist texts betray how their own maker does not guarantee what a given text will show, let alone what it may 'do'" — it offers insight into the desire to locate one's politics both in the content and form of representation (85). Visibility has served as a crucial political strategy for feminist, black, and gay political organizations, the distribution of identity-specific information and knowledge, the development of a literary and artistic tradition, and the articulation of aesthetics among a variety of groups. What began in the mid-twentieth century as radical politics should continue to develop. After all, a generation of practicing and theorizing of aesthetics has enabled artists to challenge the evolving notion of what constitutes the relationship between politics and aesthetics. However, there are serious limitations to visual representation as a political end or goal in and of itself. While the visibility of identity should be, at most, a starting point for expressing artistic and feminist politics, we need to continue creating projects of redefinition. While there are several stakes in such projects— disrupting notions of the body as an original, authentic site of experience;

of the materiality of the body as a site of feminist politics; of a politics based on the legitimating narrative of consciousness-raising as self-liberating — the potential benefits outweigh the risks.

Notes

1. The avant-garde, as a series of historical movements, was marked by a similar aesthetic-political debate. The aesthetic camp, most identified with the theoretical work of Peter Burger, worked to disrupt, displace, and/or replace accepted formal devices of art. See Peter Burger. In contrast, Renato Poggioli suggests the avant-garde was a movement defined by the use of art in the service of ideological concerns to bring about social change. While Burger located politics at the level of art creation, altering form and structure as a way to affect social perceptions, Poggioli located politics at the level of the individual artist and his relationship to art and ideology. See Renato Poggioli.

2. Representatives Dana Rohrabacher and Robert Dornan are responsible for these quotes respectively. See "D.C. Council's 'Sanity' Questioned as Hill Learns of 'Dinner Party'" By Jonetta Rose Barras (*The Washington Times*, 19 July 1990: A1). Of the two quotes, Rohrabacher's is most frequently cited in articles covering the development of the Chicago donation story. Both comments were made during congressional sessions in July 1990 and are documented in the *Congressional Record* for that month. For an excellent critical study of the events in 1990 surrounding Chicago's donation, see Lucy Lippard's article "Uninvited Guests: How Washington Lost 'The Dinner Party'" *Art in America* 79 (Dec 1991) 41. In the 1970s, many viewed *The Dinner Party* as a representation of women's identities and experiences (many feminists, though, did criticize the work because it assumed a unified womanhood that levels women's diverse experiences). In 1990, when Chicago offered the artwork as a gift for the permanent collection at the University of the District of Columbia, to be a part of the Multicultural Art Center on the campus, the U.S. Congressional Committee seated to approve the $1.6 million for renovations of the center suggested it would reject funding if Chicago's work was to be housed there. Needless to say, Chicago withdrew her gift.

3. In these terms, the body as the site of women's power, creativity and production became that which could grant authority and authenticity to a text. This suggested that, on the one hand, the body stands in for what cannot be represented in a text. On the other, the body becomes that which returns as a site of X ("X" being that which could not be represented in the text). The body either lurks in the background, as a referent for or evidence of some experience one must access but never quite can, or else sits prominently in the foreground as the site of experience, truth, and knowledge.

4. As Moira Roth details in *The Amazing Decade* (1983), the Feminist Art movement founded by Judy Chicago and her cohorts in Fresno, California, institutionalized the engagement of women's experiences in the visual arts not only as a means of expressing one's politics but also as a literal declaration or act of those politics.

5. For example, Chicago's "Womanhouse" (1970) highlighted representations of the female body and women's bodily experiences to promote consciousness-raising and critique a misogynist patriarchal society. "Womanhouse" transformed a residential home into a performance art space for installations addressing women's issues in the domestic sphere. Each room became a gallery/performance space for representing a different woman's bodily experience: menstruation, childbearing, maternity, age, and sexual violence. Through imaginative interior decorating, painting, sculpture, or full-room installation, the three-dimensional art made an otherwise private sphere, the home, into a public one, a museum. "Womanhouse" expanded the scope of visibility to include and liberate the domestic space in relation to the female body. Such work would evolve into possibly even more shocking performance art: during Annie Sprinkle's "Public Cervix Announcement," a component of the 1990 performance of *Post-Porn Modern*, Sprinkle invites the audience to walk onto the stage and peer into her vagina with the aid of a speculum and flashlight. Here, the visible becomes that which literally can or cannot be seen. Sprinkle uses her body and others' sight to return visibility to its most base definition.

6. To a certain extent, one could claim that feminist theory as well as psychoanalysis could be rendered in terms of making something visible, since oppression is often cast in visual metaphors.

7. Ntozake Shange's *for colored girls who have considered suicide/when the rainbow isn't enuf* (1970) achieved huge commercial success on Broadway and emerged on the national scene during the period of increasing public discourse on women's visibility. Originating as a series of seven poems, *for colored girls* combines multiple personae to create a unified account of black women's interconnected experiences of racial, gender, and class oppression. Seven unnamed female characters, who have no identity other than the color of their dresses and the locale of their residences, present monologues through which they narrate and enact the stories of others. The ladies-in-colors are at once representative of any and all black women who exist within multiple identity positions: women who are in the margins of cultural, economic, social, and political imaginations. These women operate as both the vehicles and sites through which Shange makes the invisible visible. As seemingly blank slates, they serve as universal messengers; their bodies become that which transmit — through narration and enactment — the experiences of others. In *for colored girls*, the respective monologues address such topics as rape, abortion, abuse, love/hate relationships, mothering, death, and life-philosophies. As the monologues progress, the choreopoem moves from innocence to experience, youth to adulthood, ignorance to knowledge, and lack of self-awareness to self-awareness. There is a shift from experiences that are potentially self-destructive to those which provide self-confidence and opportunities to reassess self-esteem. Moreover, by representing various archetypal characters, each "lady" confronts different stereotypes associated with role-oriented representations of black women. At the performance's conclusion, the seven ladies join together in a ritual gathering and celebrate the spirituality that unites them all.

Works Cited

Ball, Alan. *Five Women Wearing the Same Dress. Leading Women: Plays for Actresses II.* Eds. Eric Lane and Nina Shengold. New York: Vintage, 2002. 216–298.

Burger, Peter. *Theory of the Avant-Garde.* Trans. Michael Shaw. Manchester, England: Manchester University Press; Minneapolis: University of Minnesota Press, 1984.

de Lauretis, Teresa. "Aesthetic and Feminist Theory: Rethinking Women's Cinema." *New German Critique* 34 (Winter 1985): 154–175.

Ensler, Eve. *The Vagina Monologues.* New York: Versa, 1998.

Hart, Lynda. *Between the Body and the Flesh: Performing Sadomasochism.* New York: Columbia University Press, 1998.

Kaplan, E. Ann. "Feminism(s)/Postmodernism(s): MTV and Alternate Women's Videos and Performance Art." *Analysing Performance: A Critical Reader.* Ed. Patrick Campbell. Manchester and New York: Manchester University Press, 1996. 82–103.

Kaufman, Moisés. *The Laramie Project.* New York: Vintage, 2001.

Poggioli, Renato. *The Theory of the Avant-Garde.* Trans. Gerald Fitzgerald. Cambridge: Harvard University Press, 1968.

Rich, Adrienne. *On Lies, Secrets, and Silence.* New York: Norton, 1979.

Roth, Moira. *The Amazing Decade: Women and Performance Art in America.* Los Angeles: Astro Artz, 1983.

Scherzer, Amy. "A Life of Feminism, Art, and Heartache." *The Tampa Tribune.* 1 Dec. 1996: Metro 5.

Shange, Ntozake. *for colored girls who considered suicide/when the rainbow isn't enuf: a choreopoem.* New York: Collier Books, 1989.

Sprinkle, Annie. *Post-Porn Modernist: My 25 Years as a Multimedia Whore.* San Francisco: Cleis P, 1998.

Always a Bridesmaid, Never a Bride: The American Dream in *Five Women Wearing the Same Dress*

Mardia Bishop

Five Women Wearing the Same Dress addresses one of the great American pastimes— the American Wedding. Like all rituals American, the wedding is intricately tied to the American Dream, its promises and its disappointments. Unlike the majority of American love stories though, in *Five Women* Ball interrogates the myth of the American Wedding and through the course of the play we discover that, like the American Dream, the American Wedding is empty, exclusive, and unhealthy, but extremely appealing, persistent, and at times fulfilling for certain people in certain situations. Ultimately, however, Ball's interrogation is problematic in that as he critiques the myth, he reinforces aspects of the myth that are detrimental to women.

In addition to serving as the foundation of American government, Thomas Jefferson's words from the Declaration of Independence "all Men are created equal, that they are endowed by their Creator with certain unalienable Rights, that among these are Life, Liberty and the Pursuit of Happiness" serve as the foundation of the American Dream. Over the years, the words and the concept of the American Dream have been interpreted and manifested in different ways, including the Horatio Alger stories of the nineteenth century, which centered on the theme that if one worked hard enough, one would achieve success. John Truslow Adams coined the term "American Dream" in the twentieth century and defined it as "a dream of social order in which each man and each woman shall be able to attain to the fullest stature of which they are innately capable, and be recognized by others for what they are, regardless of the fortuitous circumstances of birth or position" (Adams as quoted in Brock 1). By the late twentieth century and early twenty-first century, the American Dream has come to mean success, status, and, primarily, wealth (Warshauer 1). In addition, many would argue that the American Dream is exclusive, that it is not attainable by "each man and each woman"; but, it protects the status quo by discouraging "those at the bottom from developing a viable political and economic analysis of the American system, instead promoting a blame-the-victim mentality ... a belief that if only the individual worked harder, tried harder, he would 'make it'" (Sidel 22).

For women, one of those "bottom" groups, the American Dream has long been represented as the American Wedding — an event that brings not only the "happily ever after," but success, status, and wealth. In other words, the way for women to achieve the American Dream is to marry. Consistently, stories targeted at girls and women define a happy ending as one where the heroine marries and lives happily ever after with her rich, successful husband. As Rita Freedman points out, Cinderella mythology — narratives in which a beautiful woman is rescued from poverty by a rich, successful man — became popular in the nineteenth century as a counterpart to the Horatio Alger "self-made man" stories that were aimed at boys and men (63). Despite the passage of more than a century, voting rights for women, advances of women in male-dominated careers, the Cinderella myth is still alive today and is offered as the way for women to achieve success, status, and wealth. Disney's animated movies might feature strong heroines, such as Pocahontas or Mulan, but the movies still culminate in marriage (for Pocahontas in the sequel). The Cinderella myth is not targeted just at young girls either. Reality television shows such as *Who Wants to Marry a Millionaire?* feature women competing to be chosen for a marriage that brings with it large cash prizes.

Like the traditional perception of the American Dream, which posits that if one works hard enough, one will achieve, the American Wedding also smacks of Protestant work ethic morality. Good behavior will help one win in the end.[1] Today, many would argue, however, that in reality, the American Dream, and by association the American Wedding, is about getting rich as quickly as you can through any means. Consequently, the American Dream is empty and shallow (Warshauer 1). Like the American Dream, Alan Ball presents the American Wedding as something good, layered with honor, Christian morality, and ritual — white dresses, a holy exchange of vows, tears of joy, family unification — a symbol of a happily ever after. From all appearances, Tracy's wedding in *Five Women* is the American Wedding: Tracy wears a "beautiful" white dress (10), the bride and groom are a "perfect match" being "both smart, good-looking, rich" (11–12), and the groom "really loves" the bride (12). Bridesmaid Frances even declares that a "wedding is a sacred occasion" (10). Yet Ball provides numerous contradictions to these observations. We quickly learn that appearances are deceiving and that at this "sacred" event the bride and her mother are probably sedated, several bridesmaids are smoking a joint and/or getting drunk, the majority of the bridesmaids dislike the bride and view the groom as "a piece of wet toast," the solemnity of the exchange of vows is diminished because the congregation laughed at the words "Help Me" painted on the unknowing groom's shoes, and the bride "will never honor" and "cherish" the groom (53). Bridesmaid Meredith, Tracy's younger sister, comments that Tracy's wedding is "so goddamn fake it makes me sick" (26).

But it's not just Tracy's wedding that is fake or empty. Towards the end of the play, bridesmaid Trisha and groomsman Tripp have the following exchange:

Trisha: This is a very weird wedding.

Tripp: They always are.

Trisha: They always start out fine, but everybody has such high expectations, and then gradually they just disintegrate, and things get …

Tripp: Hallucinatory [58].

The exchange indicates that the American Wedding, like the American Dream, encourages high expectations and hopes; yet, it is merely a hallucination — it is empty.

Although the traditional perception of the American Dream holds that anyone can achieve it, many have argued that the American Dream cannot be achieved by all; that it can only be achieved by the privileged, primarily rich, white men.[2] As demonstrated in *Five Women*, the American Wedding is just as exclusive and is only for beautiful, rich, white women. Tracy, who is never seen, only talked about, is described by Georgeanne as "the perfect woman, the ultimate 'do' girl.[3] She's beautiful, she has a great body, she has a fancy career, and now she's got herself a rich husband who worships the ground she walks on" (29). The five women wearing the same dress are Tracy's bridesmaids and will probably always be bridesmaids, never the bride, because as Trisha puts it, "we're all the 'don't' girl" (28). As presented in the script, the American Wedding is not attainable for the 'don't' girls—the fat (Georgeanne), the promiscuous (Trisha), the lesbian (Mindy), the rebellious (Meredith), or the poor (Frances).[4] Despite these classifications of the characters as stereotypes, a tremendous strength of Ball's writing is that he presents the "don't" girls as real women with many, sometimes conflicting, dimensions. By showing us the women as they "really are" as opposed to the stereotypes they become as they pursue the American Wedding, Ball again highlights the superficial nature of the Dream/Wedding.

Georgeanne, the fat character, is currently married, although she may as well not be as she admits that she hasn't slept with her husband for two years and plans to divorce him very soon. Although Ball provides evidence that her husband isn't the best husband material (he's a "wet toast" and verbally abusive), one can't help but wonder if Georgeanne couldn't get a better husband because of her appearance and her eating habits. She relates the story of the last time she and her husband tried to have fun together in which they drank tequila all night. "I just barfed all over the place, and felt so bad, and instead of trying to make me feel better, he just looked at it and said, 'God, Georgeanne, I could reconstruct your entire meal. Don't you ever chew your food?'" (54). We find out that when she was growing up she was consistently reminded that she was fat and therefore unattractive. At one point in the script she mimics her mother's "Georgeanne just needs to lose about twenty pounds, she's a fat pig" (46), no doubt a refrain she's heard most of her life.

Trisha, the promiscuous character, has slept with probably 100 men, so many that as she "looked out at the congregation during the ceremony, it was like half the men I saw, I think I may have slept with" (9). She admits that she is "the reigning queen of the bad rep" and that Tracy's mother "used to habitually refer to me as 'that little whore'" (15). Although Mindy points out that nobody is still a virgin when they get married, Trisha's excessive sexual activity prevents her from being bride material. Instead she can only be seen as a whore. At the beginning of the play, Trisha recounts being hit on by a wedding guest who is willing to go to a cash machine to get $300 so that he can be reacquainted with her.

Mindy, the lesbian character who is also the groom's sister, is the character who is most excluded. Since the American Wedding is traditionally perceived as one between a man and a woman, Mindy will never be able to achieve it. Unlike the others' exclusion, Mindy's is concretely seen in that her partner of nine years was denied access to the wedding rehearsal dinner because Tracy "wanted to keep it just *family*" (53). Moreover, Mindy's entire life, not just Tracy's wedding, has been filled with exclusion and shame. Mindy comments that at the reception are "the same old relatives who have been embarrassed by me my entire life" (29) and that she's always concerned about ruining events in her brother's life. Her mother even tried to eradicate Mindy's sexuality by sending her to Miss Amelia's charm school when she was young (42). Although *Five Women* implies that Georgeanne may be able to find a better husband if she loses 10–20 pounds and Trisha may become marriage-worthy if she stops sleeping around, Mindy will never be included in the American Wedding.

Meredith is excluded from the American Wedding for several reasons, primarily because she's a rebel and refuses to take on her role as a feminine, obedient, socialite daughter. She is described as being unfeminine in looks. Meredith comments that the bridesmaid dress makes "me look like a linebacker" (8) and she recounts how her mother just criticized her for getting "too much sun on my shoulders and they're all freckled and just ruined. 'It's not ladylike,' she says, whispering to me like she was telling me I had B.O. Ladylike!" (36). Meredith is disobedient. Throughout the play she refuses to acquiesce to her mother's requests made via the telephone. Most often, she either doesn't answer the phone or hangs up on her mother. She is aggressive and angry, having language filled with harsh expletives, such as "bitch" and "fuck," and numerous declarations of what she hates.

Meredith's rebellion against socially prescribed gender roles can be seen symbolically in that she refuses to wear various components of her bridesmaid dress— the shoes, the hat — or she covers up the dress with various items— her motorcycle jacket, a beat-up backpack. At one point in the play she mentions that she has "to get out of this dress. It is completely unnatural. ... I am going to be comfortable for the first time today, damn it" (35). With the character of Meredith, we see what happens to women when they don't fit prescribed roles. Meredith comments that according to her mother [and society], "there are two types of women, debutantes and dykes, and guess which category I fall into" (36). When women act outside of prescribed notions of femininity, they are declared lesbians. Consequently, Meredith's inability and/or refusal to wear femininity excludes her from the American Wedding.

Frances is Tracy's poor cousin who comes from a small town and doesn't have the sophistication and worldliness that wealth and privilege bring. When Meredith mentions that Tracy's dress cost six, Frances assumes she means six hundred dollars, not six thousand (10). She thinks Meredith's inexpensive rhinestone bracelet is a diamond one. Although the American Wedding supposedly offers economically disadvantaged women their ticket to success/money, Frances is excluded from the American Wedding because in order to achieve it she would need money to meet the right people, buy the right clothes, and pay for the perfect wedding.

Of all the characters, Frances most believes in the American Wedding. She covets Tracy's life and wealth, commenting that when she was little she would sneak up to Tracy's room and "pretend it was mine. Of course, I just worshiped her." (7). Frances' character will be examined more closely later in this essay because her naiveté and strong belief allow her to seemingly find inclusion in the American Wedding.

Despite their inability to ever achieve the American Wedding, these characters will continue to pursue it because, like the American Dream, the American Wedding illusion is persistent, attractive, and at times successful. It promises success to all those who work hard enough to achieve it. This continual belief in the American Wedding leads to the most significant problem with having women's success tied to marriage in that it forces them to engage in unhealthy behaviors, primarily pursuing men and pursuing beauty. In order to achieve the American Wedding, women focus their energies and goals on pursuing men, usually rich, successful ones. Women's preoccupation with pursuing men and the ramifications of that pursuit are very evident in *Five Women*. First, four out of the five bridesmaids share the primary goal of connecting with a man at the wedding reception. Mindy is the only one who doesn't have that goal. Frances wants to find a good Christian man who is older and taller than she and who would be strong husband material. Trisha wants to connect with Tripp. Throughout the play she looks for him from Meredith's bedroom window, trying to find opportunities to meet with him. Georgeanne wants to have sex with Tommy Valentine. Meredith also wants to connect with Tommy Valentine, probably not for mere sex, though.

Second, as the following exchanges demonstrate, the play points out the materialistic dating criteria necessitated by the American Wedding. In these exchanges the bridesmaids discuss Frances' and Trisha's post-reception dates.

Trisha: What does he do?

Georgeanne: Trisha. He's a bartender.

Frances: No, he's in law school.

Georgeanne: Really?

Frances: He only bartends part time, thank goodness.

Trisha: Well, you tell him he makes a superior martini.

Georgeanne: Law school! Frances, you have scored [33].

Later, a similar conversation occurs focusing on Trisha's date.

Meredith: What does he do?

Trisha: I forgot to ask for his résumé.

Mindy: He works for a bank, telling other people where to put their money.

Georgeanne: Way to go, Trisha, that means he's probably rich.

[...]

Trisha: I don't believe this. I have a simple conversation with him and now I'm supposed to be picking out my china pattern? What century are you women living in? [40].

In these exchanges, the characters are congratulated for their success in or are deemed successful for finding appropriate husband material. Although Trish's response to her inquisition criticizes the women for being out of date, as evidenced in the script, the belief that women's success comes with marriage still exists.

Third, the play demonstrates that women are socialized from a young age to find their success in men and marriage. When the characters discuss the careers they dreamed about when they were younger, Georgeanne asserts, "I always wanted to be a teacher." Her desire doesn't stem from logical career-oriented reasons, however. "Well, I wanted to be Miss Crenshaw, because her fiancé would come pick her up in a blue

Chevy Malibu with a white vinyl top and he was so cute, he had a blond crew cut and his sideburns were darker than the rest" (57).

Finally, the play shows the many ramifications for pursuing men. The bridesmaids spend a tremendous amount of time and energy pursuing men; but the results of their pursuit are not that great. Ten years ago, Georgeanne was impregnated by Tommy Valentine and had an abortion, which she had to go through alone because he was on a date with Tracy. Years later, she has unprotected sex with him on the concrete next to a dumpster. Yet, she still wants to reconnect with him at Tracy's wedding. Meredith confesses that she had a relationship with Tommy Valentine when she was 12 or 13. The other characters identify the relationship as one of sexual abuse, but having been socialized to pursue men, she insists that the relationship was "not like it sounds, he was really nice, he really — he really liked me" and that she loved him and wanted him (51). Trisha has endured a bad reputation and a lack of self-respect because of her pursuit of men. But the most significant ramification for the characters and women is the belief that in order to catch a man one has to be attractive. The pursuit of men causes women to pursue beauty, which has its own set of repercussions.

In his research on body image, Thomas Cash finds "that females who endorse traditional gender attitudes in their relationships with males (1) are more invested in their appearance, (2) have internalized cultural standards of beauty more fully, and (3) hold more maladaptive assumptions about their looks" (42–43). The American Wedding encourages traditional gender attitudes — a rich, successful male who will take care of the beautiful bride who achieves her status/value through him. Consequently, women who buy into the American Wedding will demonstrate the three characteristics Cash articulates.

In *Five Women*, the characters who have the goal of connecting with a man at the wedding reception are extremely invested in their looks; and their appearance often takes precedence over more important issues. The characters' investment is depicted by their obsession with the mirrors in Meredith's room in Act One. Meredith is described several times in the stage directions (three times in ten pages) as observing herself critically in the mirror. Each time she is frustrated with what she sees. She "*frowns*," says, "Oh, lord. ... [the bridesmaid's dress] makes me look like a linebacker" (8), and "How do I look? Hideous" (18). Trisha looks at herself in the mirror and states "God, would you look at me? I look terrible" (10).

Georgeanne looks at herself in the mirror and states, "God. Look at me. I am totally pathetic" (22). Frances, too, is invested in her looks. After a serious argument with Trisha, in which Frances has vehemently defended her religion, Trisha tells Frances to leave. Frances immediately backs down. Not because she believes Trisha is correct, but because Trisha, who has been giving Frances a makeover, isn't finished. Frances looks in the mirror, panics, and says "But I can't go out there looking like *this*. I'm only half done! What would people think? I don't look right!" (42).

The characters in *Five Women* also demonstrate that they have internalized cultural standards of beauty. According to Nita McKinley, internalizing cultural standards of beauty means that a woman accepts cultural standards of beauty as the beauty norm. In addition, a woman experiences her desires to adhere to the norm "as coming from her own desires," not external pressures. Consequently, a woman compares herself to the standards and since "the standards are narrow and difficult to achieve," a woman will see herself as inadequate. Moreover, the internalization of cultural standards "predisposes women to connect achievement of these standards with their sense of self-worth" (57). The characters in *Five Women* have accepted cultural standards of beauty and identified Tracy as fitting the standards. She is the "ultimate 'do' girl"—she's beautiful, thin, has a great body, and appears feminine. They measure themselves against Tracy and see themselves as inadequate. They are the "don't girls." They also have self-worth issues, which can be seen by their maladaptive assumptions about their looks.

As shown by their comments when assessing themselves in the mirror, the women assume their appearance is inadequate. They describe their appearances as "hideous," "terrible," "pathetic," and "half-done." Georgeanne, who perhaps has the worst self image, calls herself "ugly" and when commenting on her future life, she says, "I ... will be as big as a house, I'll wear too much makeup, I won't have any hair left from a lifetime of bad perms, and I'll get skin cancer from going to the lake too much when I was in high school" (25).

In addition to a diminished self-worth, McKinley points out that the failure to meet the standards causes a multitude of other psychological and physical problems, such as shame, social anxiety, and eating disorders. By hiding out in Meredith's room, all the characters demonstrate social anxiety—the majority of them desiring not to be seen because of their appearance. Mindy and Georgeanne have eating disorders—overeating. They both also experience shame. Mindy is ashamed that she's ruined past events in Scott's life and is afraid she'll do so again. Georgeanne is ashamed of her body and her inability to control her eating and weight.

A final characteristic of women who internalize cultural standards of beauty is they believe they can control their appearance, which they do through various measures that are culturally accepted. The characters in *Five Women* try to control their appearance through dieting (Georgeanne lost 10 pounds for the wedding), through exercise (Meredith uses the treadmill in her room), through clothing (Georgeanne wears "over a hundred dollars worth of extremely uncomfortable lingerie from Victoria's Secret" [20]), and through makeup (all want makeovers from Trisha). Ultimately, the ways in which women try to control their appearance, and as such, fit the beauty standard, cost women economically, physically, and psychologically. It is this mandatory pursuit of beauty that makes the American Wedding so harmful to women. Equating women's value with their ability to snag a husband encourages the myth that women must be beautiful in order to attract a man. Naomi Wolf explains that the beauty myth is a story that claims:

> The quality called "beauty" objectively and universally exists. Women must embody it and men must want to possess women who embody it. This embodiment is an imperative for women ... because it is biological, sexual, and evolutionary: Strong men battle for beautiful women, and beautiful women are more reproductively successful. ... since this system is based on sexual selection, it is inevitable and changeless [12].

The myth, like most, is not true. Beauty is not universal, but is a culturally defined quality. As such, it is a reflection of and a political tool of the culture that defines it. By "assigning value to women in a vertical hierarchy according to a culturally imposed physical standard," women are forced to compete (Wolf 12). The end result is women are devalued and the competition leaves them economically, physically, and psychologically unhealthy. The American Wedding therefore, like the American Dream, protects the status quo by discouraging "those at the bottom [women] from developing a viable political and economic analysis of the American system, instead promoting a blame-the-victim mentality ... a belief that if only the individual worked harder [at being beautiful—exercised more, dieted more, bought and applied better makeup, suctioned fat, implanted breasts] ... [s]he would 'make it' [be beautiful]" (Sidel 22).[5]

In *Five Women*, Alan Ball portrays the American Wedding/Dream as empty, exclusive, and unhealthy. Yet at the end of the play, Frances symbolically achieves the American Wedding — she catches Tracy's bouquet (an American wedding ritual that means Frances will be the next to marry) and she poses as a bride in a group photograph that provides the play's final tableau. This final tableau can be read as a celebration that the American Wedding is attainable. However, by examining the character of Frances, her potential groom, and the ending "wedding" photograph, a different reading emerges.

Frances is the only bridesmaid that has a chance at achieving the American Wedding. Although she is poor, she is attractive (she even looks glamorous with makeup); she is a virgin; she is a heterosexual; and, she is feminine (she is innocent, obedient, and criticizes the others for their unladylike behavior). She heavily covets Tracy's life and wedding, which she sees as glamorous and perfect. She longs for the day when she can be married and have what Tracy has.

As mentioned earlier, Frances comes from a small town and is naïve and unsophisticated. The primary influence in Frances' mindset is not her small-town roots however, but her fundamentalist Christian upbringing, which transforms her naiveté into bigotry and self-righteous arrogance. She continually uses her version of Christianity to defend her behavior and judge others. She refuses to partake in marijuana, liquor, and cigarettes because "I am a Christian." When she learns that the flute players at the wedding ceremony are lesbians, she comments, "But — they looked just like *real* women. And them playing in church like that, isn't that kind of sacrilegious?" (12). When Trisha indicates that the Bible is just a book, Frances explodes: "Now, I will sit here and watch you all drink liquor and take drugs, every other word F this and GD that, honestly, you ought to be ashamed, you are *ladies*. But I will *not* tolerate you making fun of the Bible" (41). She continues by telling Trisha that she is not allowed to have an opinion if the opinion is "disrespectful to my religion" and that "This is America and I have a right to my beliefs" (41). Trisha's response emphasizes Frances' narrow mindedness: "Go someplace where people don't have ideas. Where everybody is willing to trade their God-given intelligence for any old blind set of rules just because they don't want the responsibility of making their own decisions" (41).

Frances' mock groom is fifteen years older than she, has been widowed for four years, works as a bartender while he attends law school, and is from a small town. Before he can sound like the perfect man for Frances though, Ball has the other bridesmaids roll their eyes when naïve Frances repeats the stereotypical pick-up lines he used on her. In addition, the bridesmaids jokingly call him a psycho killer and claim that he is a widower because he murdered his wife.

The "wedding" photo consists of Frances pretending to be a bride and the other women her bridesmaids. Frances wears Tracy's homecoming queen crown, the stereotypical, grotesque bridesmaid's dress, and a six-dollar bracelet made of rhinestones that Frances thinks are diamonds. The stage directions describe her as being "*beside herself*" and she says, "I feel so glamorous." The other bridesmaids don't treat the moment so reverently. Meredith wears her leather jacket, Trisha holds Tripp's shoes in lieu of her bouquet, Meredith and Mindy smoke cigarettes, and Mindy arranges the shoulders of her dress "daringly low." They all wear sunglasses. Although the bridesmaids are having fun being free from the constraints of the formality of Tracy's wedding and they are celebrating the closeness they achieved during the wedding reception, the contrast of their boisterous behavior next to Frances' radiant pose is telling.

Upon examination, an alternative reading of the tableau is that only the naïve and narrow-minded could possibly believe in the American Wedding. For them, the American Wedding is a glamorous dream, a fairytale filled with glittery jewelry and rich, handsome husbands. Anyone who has ideas or "God-given intelligence" or takes "the responsibility of making their own decisions" will recognize the American Wedding as an illusion. Even if they happen to achieve the American Wedding, what they will get is a mockery of their expectations where glittery jewelry is actually a six-dollar rhinestone bracelet and rich, handsome husbands are actually balding law students who carry around emotional baggage from previous relationships.

Ultimately, the play seems to suggest an end to the American Wedding — an end to marrying for wealth and status, an end to the idea that traditional marriage is the only way to find happiness. As the play concludes, Frances proposes a toast "To holy matrimony!" to which Trisha asks, "Can't we just drink to love?" (68). Surprisingly, Frances, who is the most conservative character and the one who most desires the American Wedding, agrees: "I'm sorry. To love" (68). Indeed, alternative, nontraditional relationships are offered as better unions of love in the play. Mindy and her partner have been together for nine years, and it seems that Trisha and Tripp, who are marriage-shy, are beginning a relationship based on mutual respect and love.

Despite Ball's condemnation of the American Wedding, which includes critiques of the Cinderella and beauty myths, *Five Women* reinforces both myths. Although the play suggests that alternative relationships to the traditional marriage may be better, the basic premise of women needing to be rescued is maintained. At the end of the play, Trisha and Tripp seem to be beginning a healthy relationship, yet based on the script it couldn't have happened without Tripp's rescue of Trisha from her own despair and feelings of worthlessness. Perceptive Tripp recognizes Trisha's pain and calls her on her casual attitude toward sex. When Trisha suggests they just go to a motel and have sex, he tells her, "I don't want you to be an easy fuck in a cheap motel. For me, that usually works best when it's with somebody I don't really care one way or the other about" (63). As the scene continues, he seems to give her the value she's longed for and rescues her from a future life of meaningless sex where she is nothing but a whore. Earlier in the play Georgeanne asks Trisha if she believes in love. Trisha responds, "I certainly believe in consideration. And respect. And I definitely believe in sex, because it's healthy and necessary. But love, what is that? I have had so many guys tell me they loved me, and not a single one of them has made any difference in my life" (22–23). Once Trisha is rescued by successful, respectful, considerate Tripp, she transforms and seems to now believe in love as she suggests toasting to it.

Furthermore, the play centers on the titular five bridesmaids who come to know each other, support each other, and try to fix each other's problems; yet, Ball includes a male character who fixes Trisha's problems. The play's final message then is that a woman might not need the American Wedding, but she does need a man.

Five Women also reinforces the beauty myth. On one hand, Ball excellently expresses the ramifications for women of having their value attached to beauty. Through Mindy, we hear how stupid and dangerous the pursuit of beauty is:

> I think it's high time women let themselves just be women for a change, and stopped trying to look like all these anorexic models that, face it, they look like men. ... these women who are willing to have their lips poofed up

and their tits inflated and their ribs removed? ... And that fat sucking thing? I'm sorry. There's something so desperately wrong with a culture which encourages people to go to such extremes. We think we are so civilized. But we're just as barbaric as those Aztec guys who played soccer with human heads [46–47].

The visual image given by the play's title —five women of differing shapes and sizes conforming to a dress of one style and color — is very apt, demonstrating that in the pursuit of beauty, women try to conform to contemporary beauty standards even if those standards don't fit. Moreover, Ball provides a realistic view of women and their contradictory relationship with beauty: the characters feel insecure about their appearance; they ponder various levels of adhering to beauty standards; and they pursue beauty despite knowing the pursuit is harmful (Mindy is having a makeover when she delivers the above speech).

On the other hand, the play reinforces beauty as women's primary success criterion. We learn much about the women, but we don't know what they do professionally or how much money they earn, which are the primary success criteria for men. We know Mindy is a real estate agent. We know Meredith just graduated with a degree in English, but she is currently unemployed. And that's all we know. Meanwhile, we know that Tripp is an investment banker and makes good money, and Frances' bartender date (who never even appears onstage) is in law school. Most problematic, however, is the final scene when the women pose for a photo. Through the course of the play, the women have bonded on several levels and have demonstrated numerous strengths and admirable qualities. Yet, as Tripp takes the photo, he comments, "This is some major babe action happening here" (70)—words that diminish their strengths and qualities, but words the "don't" girls long to hear. And in a way, there is major babe action here —first, the comment shows how little the photographer knows about the women — in this case, he's only looking at the surface of things, which is the major problem with the American Dream and the American Wedding. And for the audience who has seen these women and the difficulties they face trying to pursue the dream, as well as the contortions they must go through to meet it, we may be inspired to look at women differently, the American Wedding more complexly, and the American Dream as illusory, at times satisfying, but ultimately an inadequate pursuit of happiness.

Notes

1. The nineteenth-century perception of the American Dream contributed the notion that if one employed the Protestant work ethic, one would not only be successful, but would become closer to God.

2. Malcolm X referred to the American Dream as a nightmare. Martin Luther King Jr. in his "I Have a Dream" speech called for an American Dream that included "all of God's children-black men and white men, Jews and Gentiles, Catholics and Protestants" (as quoted in Brock).

3. This is a reference to *Glamour* magazine's "Do's and Don'ts" column regarding fashion, which features candid photographs of real women caught in their fashion successes and gaffes.

4. Ball even provides a wonderful visual emphasis of their exclusion by having the action take place in Meredith's bedroom where the bridesmaids are separated from the wedding reception and occasionally look in on the wedding activity through the window or a brief visit.

5. The majority of feminist theorists use Michel Foucault's theories on the body as a political tool in order to explain the beauty myth. They identify the female body as a locus of control in gendered power dynamics. As articulated by Susan Bordo, "The social manipulation of the female body emerges as an absolutely central strategy in the maintenance of power relations between the sexes over the last hundred years" (91). A primary way that the female body has been manipulated is through the assignation of beauty as a feminine characteristic. In Western societies, which operate on dualistic constructions, women have traditionally been associated with characteristics such as emotional and merciful, while men have been associated with characteristics such as intellectual and just. Since beauty has been associated with women, it becomes part of their identity; thus, they need to pursue it. Furthermore, "Western societies also define men's bodies as the standard against which women's bodies are judges, and women's bodies are constructed as deviant in comparison. ... The perceived deviance of the female body ... create[s] the context for women's body experience. This context encourages the construction of women and girls as objects to be watched and evaluated in terms of how their bodies fit cultural standards" (McKinley 56).

Works Cited

Ball, Alan. *Five Women Wearing the Same Dress*. New York: Dramatists Play Service, 1998.

Bordo, Susan. "Anorexia Nervosa: Psychopathology as the Crystallization of Culture." *Feminism and Foucault: Reflections on Resistance*. Eds. Irene Diamond and Lee Quinby. Boston: Northeastern University Press, 1988: 87–118.

Brock, Charles. "What Is the American Dream?" *The Institute on the American Dream*. http://www.pserie.psu.edu/academic/hss/amdream/dream/amerindx.htm.

Cash, Thomas F. "Cognitive-Behavioral Perspectives on Body Image." *Body Image: A Handbook of Theory, Research, and Clinical Practice*. Eds. Thomas F. Cash and Thomas Pruzinsky. New York: Guilford Press, 2004: 38–46.

Freedman, Rita. *Beauty Bound*. Lexington, MA: Heath, 1986.

McKinley, Nita Mary. "Feminist Perspectives and Objectified Body Consciousness." *Body Image: A Handbook of Theory, Research, and Clinical Practice*. Eds. Thomas F. Cash and Thomas Pruzinsky. New York: Guilford Press, 2004: 55–62.

Sidel, Ruth. *Women and Children Last: The Plight of Poor Women in Affluent America*. NY: Penguin Books, 1987.

Warshauer, Matthew. "Who Wants to Be a Millionaire: Changing Conceptions of the American Dream." *American Studies Today Online*. 2 February 2003. http://www.americanse.org.uk/Online/American_Dream.htm.

Wolf, Naomi. *The Beauty Myth: How Images of Beauty Are Used Against Women*. New York: Morrow, 1991.

Appendix: Works for Theater, Film and Television

Plays

The following plays were written and performed in the early 1980s for the General Nonsense Theater Company in Florida.

Cherokee County
Frostproof

The following plays were written and performed for Alarm Dog Repertory in New York (1986–1994).

The Two Mrs. Trumps (1986/1987)
Power Lunch (1989)
Your Mother's Butt (1990)
Bachelor Holiday (1991)
The M Word (1991)
Made For a Woman (1993)
Five Women Wearing the Same Dress (1993)
The Amazing Adventures of Tense Guy (1994)

The following play was recently workshopped in New York.

All That I Will Ever Be (2005)

Film

American Beauty
   Script: Alan Ball. Dir.: Sam Mendes. Dreamworks, 1999.

Television

Grace Under Fire (1994–1995)
Cybill (1995–1998)

Appendix

Oh Grow Up (1999)
Six Feet Under (2001–2005)

Season 1 (2001)

Episode 1 (1:1) "Pilot." Teleplay: Alan Ball. Dir.: Alan Ball. HBO. 3 June 2001.

Episode 2 (1:2) "The Will." Teleplay: Christian Williams. Dir.: Miguel Arteta. HBO. 10 June 2001.

Episode 3 (1:3) "The Foot." Teleplay: Bruce Eric Kaplan. Dir.: John Patterson. HBO. 17 June 2001.

Episode 4 (1:4) "Familia." Teleplay: Laurence Andries. Dir.: Lisa Cholodenko. HBO. 24 June 2001.

Episode 5 (1:5) "An Open Book." Teleplay: Alan Ball. Dir.: Kathy Bates. HBO. 1 July 2001.

Episode 6 (1:6) "The Room." Teleplay: Christian Taylor. Dir.: Rodrigo García. HBO. 8 July 2001.

Episode 7 (1:7) "Brotherhood." Teleplay: Christian Williams. Dir.: Jim McBride. HBO. 15 July 2001.

Episode 8 (1:8) "Crossroads." Teleplay: Laurence Andries. Dir.: Allen Coulter. HBO. 22 July 2001.

Episode 9 (1:9) "Life's Too Short." Teleplay: Christian Taylor. Dir.: Jeremy Podeswa. HBO. 29 July 2001.

Episode 10 (1:10) "The New Person." Teleplay: Bruce Eric Kaplan. Dir.: Kathy Bates. HBO. 5 August 2001.

Episode 11 (1:11) "The Trip." Teleplay: Rick Cleveland. Dir.: Michael Engler. HBO. 12 August 2001.

Episode 12 (1:12) "A Private Life." Teleplay: Kate Robin. Dir.: Rodrigo García. HBO. 19 August 2001.

Episode 13 (1:13) "Knock, Knock." Teleplay: Alan Ball. Dir.: Alan Ball. HBO. 19 August 2001.

Season 2 (2002)

Episode 14 (2:1) "In the Game." Teleplay: Alan Ball. Dir.: Rodrigo García. HBO. 3 March 2002.

Episode 15 (2:2) "Out, Out, Brief Candle." Teleplay: Laurence Andries. Dir.: Kathy Bates. HBO. 10 March 2002.

Episode 16 (2:3) "The Plan." Teleplay: Kate Robin. Dir.: Rose Troche. HBO. 17 March 2002.

Episode 17 (2:4) "Driving Mr. Mossback." Teleplay: Rick Cleveland. Dir.: Michael Cuesta. HBO. 24 March 2002.

Episode 18 (2:5) "The Invisible Woman." Teleplay: Bruce Eric Kaplan. Dir.: Jeremy Podeswa. HBO. 31 March 2002.

Episode 19 (2:6) "In Place of Anger." Teleplay: Christian Taylor. Dir.: Michael Engler. HBO. 7 April 2002.

Episode 20 (2:7) "Back to the Garden." Teleplay: Jill Soloway. Dir.: Daniel Attias. HBO. 14 April 2002.

Episode 21 (2:8) "It's the Most Wonderful Time of the Year." Teleplay: Scott Buck. Dir.: Alan Taylor. HBO. 21 April 2002.

Episode 22 (2:9) "Someone Else's Eyes." Teleplay: Alan Ball. Dir.: Michael Cuesta. HBO. 28 April 2002.

Episode 23 (2:10) "The Secret." Teleplay: Bruce Eric Kaplan. Dir.: Alan Poul. HBO. 5 May 2002.

Episode 24 (2:11) "The Liar and the Whore." Teleplay: Rick Cleveland. Dir.: Miguel Arteta. HBO. 12 May 2002.

Episode 25 (2:12) "I'll Take You." Teleplay: Jill Soloway. Dir.: Michael Engler. HBO. 19 May 2002.

Episode 26 (2:13) "The Last Time." Teleplay: Kate Robin. Dir.: Alan Ball. HBO. 2 June 2002.

Season 3 (2003)

Episode 27 (3:1) "Perfect Circles." Teleplay: Alan Ball. Dir.: Rodrigo García. HBO. 2 March 2003.

Episode 28 (3:2) "You Never Know." Teleplay: Scott Buck. Dir.: Michael Cuesta. HBO. 9 March 2003.

Episode 29 (3:3) "The Eye Inside." Teleplay: Kate Robin. Dir.: Michael Engler. HBO. 16 March 2003.

Episode 30 (3:4) "Nobody Sleeps." Teleplay: Rick Cleveland and Alan Ball. Dir.: Alan Poul. HBO. 23 March 2003.

Episode 31 (3:5) "The Trap." Teleplay: Bruce Eric Kaplan. Dir.: Jeremy Podeswa. HBO. 30 March 2003.

Episode 32 (3:6) "Making Love Work." Teleplay: Jill Soloway. Dir.: Kathy Bates. HBO. 6 April 2003.

Episode 33 (3:7) "Timing and Space." Teleplay: Craig Wright. Dir.: Nicole Holofcener. HBO. 13 April 2003.

Episode 34 (3:8) "Tears, Bones, and Desire." Teleplay: Nancy Oliver. Dir.: Daniel Attias. HBO. 20 April 2003.

Episode 35 (3:9) "The Opening." Teleplay: Kate Robin. Dir.: Karen Moncrieff. HBO. 27 April 2003.

Episode 36 (3:10) "Everyone Leaves." Teleplay: Scott Buck. Dir.: Daniel Minahan. HBO. 4 May 2003.

Episode 37 (3:11) "Death Works Overtime." Teleplay: Rick Cleveland. Dir.: Daniel Attias. HBO. 11 May 2003.

Episode 38 (3:12) "Twilight." Teleplay: Craig Wright. Dir.: Kathy Bates. HBO. 18 May 2003.

Episode 39 (3:13) "I'm Sorry, I'm Lost." Teleplay: Jill Soloway. Dir.: Alan Ball. HBO. 1 June 2003.

Appendix

Season 4 (2004)

Episode 40 (4:1) "Falling Into Place." Teleplay: Craig Wright. Dir.: Michael Cuesta. HBO. 13 June 2004.

Episode 41 (4:2) "In Case of Rapture." Teleplay: Rick Cleveland. Dir.: Daniel Attias. HBO. 20 June 2004.

Episode 42 (4:3) "Parallel Play." Teleplay: Jill Soloway. Dir.: Jeremy Podeswa. HBO. 27 June 2004.

Episode 43 (4:4) "Can I Come Up Now." Teleplay: Alan Ball. Dir.: Dan Minahan. HBO. 11 July 2004.

Episode 44 (4:5) "That's My Dog." Teleplay: Scott Buck. Dir.: Alan Poul. HBO. 18 July 2004.

Episode 45 (4:6) "Terror Starts at Home." Teleplay: Kate Robin. Dir.: Miguel Arteta. HBO. 25 July 2004.

Episode 46 (4:7) "The Dare." Teleplay: Bruce Eric Kaplan. Dir.: Peter Webber. HBO. 1 August 204.

Episode 47 (4:8) "Coming and Going." Teleplay: Nancy Oliver. Dir.: Daniel Attias. HBO. 8 August 2004.

Episode 48 (4:9) "Grinding the Corn." Teleplay: Rick Cleveland. Dir.: Alan Caso. HBO. 15 August 2004.

Episode 49 (4:10) "The Black Forest." Teleplay: Jill Soloway and Craig Wright. Dir.: Peter Care. HBO. 22 August 2004.

Episode 50 (4:11) "Bomb Shelter." Teleplay: Scott Buck. Dir.: Nicole Holofcener. HBO. 29 August 2004.

Episode 51 (4:12) "Untitled." Teleplay: Nancy Oliver. Dir.: Alan Ball. HBO.

Season 5 (2005)

Episode 52 (5:1) "A Coat of White Primer." Teleplay: Kate Robin. Dir.: Rodrigo García. HBO. 6 June 2005.

Episode 53 (5:2) "Dancing for Me." Teleplay: Scott Buck. Dir.: Dan Attias. HBO. 13 June 2005.

Episode 54 (5:3) "Hold My Hand." Teleplay: Nancy Oliver. Dir.: Jeremy Podeswa. HBO. 20 June 2005.

Episode 55 (5:4) "Time Flies." Teleplay: Craig Wright. Dir.: Alan Poul. HBO. 27 June 2005.

Episode 56 (5:5) "Eat a Peach." Teleplay: Rick Cleveland. Dir.: Daniel Minahan. HBO. 4 July 2005.

Episode 57 (5:6) "The Rainbow of Her Reasons." Teleplay: Jill Soloway. Dir.: Mary Harron. HBO. 10 July 2005.

Episode 58 (5:7) "The Silence." Teleplay: Bruce Eric Kaplan. Dir.: Joshua Marston. HBO. 17 July 2005.

Episode 59 (5:8) "Singing for Our Lives." Teleplay: Scott Buck. Dir.: Matt Shakman. HBO. 24 July 2005.

Episode 60 (5:9) "Ecotone." Teleplay: Nancy Oliver. Dir.: Daniel Minahan. HBO. 31 July 2005.

Episode 61 (5:10) "All Alone." Teleplay: Kate Robin. Dir.: Adam Davidson. HBO. 7 August 2005.

Episode 62 (5:11) "Static." Teleplay: Craig Wright. Dir.: Michael Cuesta. HBO. 14 August 2005.

Episode 63 (5:12) "Everyone's Waiting." Teleplay: Alan Ball. Dir.: Alan Ball. HBO. 21 August 2005.

About the Contributors

Thomas Fahy is an assistant professor of English and director of American Studies at Long Island University. He is the author of *Freak Shows and the Modern American Imagination: Constructing the Damaged Body from Willa Cather to Truman Capote* (2006), a monograph on Gabriel García Márquez, and two novels, *Night Visions* (2004) and *The Unspoken* (2007). He has also edited several collections, including *Considering Aaron Sorkin* (McFarland, 2005), *Captive Audience: Prison and Captivity in Contemporary Theater* (2003), and *Peering Behind the Curtain: Disability, Illness and the Extraordinary Body in Contemporary Theater* (2002).

Ann C. Hall is a professor of English at Ohio Dominican University. She has recently edited the convention journal for the Midwest Modern Language Association on Performance.

Susanna Lee is an assistant professor of French at Georgetown University. Her book, *A World Abandoned by God: Narrative and Secularism*, is published by Bucknell University Press. She is also co-editing a special issue of *Yale French Studies* entitled "Crime Fictions," with Andrea Goulet.

Susann Cokal is assistant professor of English at Virginia Commonwealth University and author of the novels *Mirabilis* and *Breath and Bones*. She has published articles on authors such as Jeanette Winterson, Marianne Wiggins, and Georges Bataille, and on pop culture subjects such as supermodels and Mary Poppins.

Kirstin Ringelberg is an assistant professor of art history at Elon University. She has an article in the forthcoming anthology *Representing Pain*, edited by James Elkins, and has published in *Prospects: An Annual of American Cultural Studies*. As a scholar, she is interested in gender and class in nineteenth-century American art, the dialogic relationship between Japanese and American art from the nineteenth century to the present, and television and film studies.

Robert F. Gross teaches theatre at Hobart and William Smith Colleges. He is the author of *Words Heard and Overheard* and *S. N. Behrman: A Research and Production Sourcebook,* the editor of *Christopher Hampton: A Casebook* and *Tennessee Williams: A Casebook,* as well as the author of numerous articles on modern dramatists, from Henrik Ibsen and Gerhart Hauptmann to John Guare, Edward Albee, and Wendy Wasserstein.

Lorena Russell is an assistant professor at the University of North Carolina Asheville where she teaches in the department of Literature and Language. Her most recent articles have appeared in *International Journal of Sexuality Studies, Horror Film: Creating and Marketing Film,* and *Gothic Studies.* Current projects include an article on queer intimacies and family violence in *The Deep End* and *In the Bedroom,* and a book project on Angela Carter, Jeanette Winterson and Fay Weldon.

Craig N. Owens earned his Ph.D. in English at Indiana University, Bloomington, and teaches drama, critical theory, and Irish studies at Drake University. His research interests lie mainly in late twentieth-century absurdism, though he has written on Bernard Shaw, Oscar Wilde, and William Butler Yeats as well as on Samuel Beckett, Harold Pinter, and Sarah Kane. His has directed and performed in numerous stage productions, writes the occasional play, and has begun writing about filmic representations in addition to staged ones.

Johanna Frank is assistant professor of English at the University of Windsor. A former Mellon Postdoctoral Fellow at Cornell University, she publishes on women and drama. She is working on a book titled *Performance as Embodiment: Presence and the Illusion of Corporeality.* She is a founding member of SteinSemble Performance Group, a collection of actors and scholars dedicated to performing avant-garde, modernist, and other generally un-staged texts of the twentieth century.

Mardia Bishop is an assistant professor of theatre and performance studies at Kennesaw State University in Georgia where she teaches theatre history, theory, and literature. Her research areas include cultural practices associated with the fabrication of the body, as well as directing approaches to Harold Pinter's plays. She lives in Alan Ball's hometown of Marietta, Georgia.

Index

Index

Index

Index